Combined and Uneven Apocalypse

Evan Calder Williams

Winchester, UK
Washington, USA

First published by Zero Books, 2011
Zero Books is an imprint of John Hunt Publishing Ltd., The Bothy, Deershot Lodge,
Park Lane, Ropley,
Hants, SO24 0BE, UK
office1@o-books.net
www.o-books.com

For distributor details and how to order please visit the 'Ordering' section on our website.

ISBN: 978 1 84694 468 0

Design: Stuart Davies

Printed in the UK by CPI Antony Rowe
Printed in the USA by Offset Paperback Mfrs, Inc

We operate a distinctive and ethical publishing philosophy in all
areas of our business, from our global network of authors to
production and worldwide distribution.

Combined and Uneven Apocalypse

CONTENTS

Acknowledgements

Many thanks to many people. First and foremost, Erik Bachman and Ben Noys, whose comments on an earlier draft were invaluable. Marsh Leicester, along with Erik Bachman and Katie Woolsey, with whom I've watched a lot of movies over the past few years and whose thinking impels, challenges, and shapes my own. Ongoing dialogue with Alberto Toscano, fellow catastrophile, and China Miéville, without whom salvagepunk is near unthinkable, has been crucial. My parents for decades of friendship and love. Olivia Egan-Rudolph for countless conversations and for making this past year infinitely better. Tariq Goddard and Mark Fisher for taking on and dealing with this behemoth, helping make something sharper of it. Laura Oldfield Ford for the cover image and for sharing the same love for things ruined and same hate for things that deserve to be.

Above all, thanks to my comrades in crisis out here in California. In these grey days, you're a hot torch, a joyous mob, and a promise to never go quiet into that bad night.

This book is dedicated to the anti-gentrification, abandoned zone-defending, yuppie-eating militant superwolves of Michael Wadleigh's *Wolfen*.

Introduction

In the dark times, will there also be singing?
Yes, there will be singing
About the dark times.

— *Bertolt Brecht, "Motto"*

Strange. I'm sure I had them this morning.

The crystal ball doesn't appear to be working. At the Economic Faculty's council of experts meeting in Roy Andersson's 2000 film, *Songs From the Second Floor*, nothing is clear. Or rather, things are too clear. The ball doesn't cloud and provides no shadows of what is to come. Worse, the chairman can't find his future perspectives in his briefcase, and he can't imagine where they've gone. The facilitator notes, "it appears that we shall have to skip the strategies and concentrate on tactics instead."

This book is an attempt to produce some of those shadows. It is a theory of the apocalyptic fantasies of late capitalism[1], manifested above all in the cinema and the wider cultural, political, and economic landscape from the end of the '60s to now. If these films and novels, political struggles and cultural obsessions are scattered tactical expressions that try to grasp the consequences of this world order coming to an end, the task of this book is to try and discern the obscure strategy lying behind them.

This book is written in the crux of, and is necessarily inflected by, a crisis that may very well turn out to be both a genuine end and an opening out. The "financial" crisis of the past two years now shows itself to be much more than the bursting of a few speculative bubbles, the massive injection of bailout money to jumpstart a temporarily flat-lining heart, and a few lean years of "recession" before things go back to normal. No, we stand at the front edge of something massive, a genuine tectonic shift in the organization and future sustainability of global capitalism. We have yet to see the real fallout of the height of financialization and other emergency mechanisms that propped up wealth creation in the long downturn of manufacturing profits. But what we certainly aren't seeing are green shoots of a shaken but healthy market pushing up through the rubble. Just a fierce doom and bloom.

Undergirding the analysis and tone of this book is a real and reasoned conviction that this crisis is terminal, that, from here out, there is no return to "normal" – both the shared image of capitalism as the natural, eternal state of affairs beyond which no horizon can be seen, and the system-wide profitability it takes to support that. . The fundamental fantasy of plenitude, regener- ation, and persistence lying behind our structures of accumu- lation grinds to a halt. And more drastically, with the end of endlessly available credit, a new void of the future itself. The late capitalist present was necessarily staked on the capacity to realize and replicate itself by borrowing against the guaranteed promise of the future as the site of *more of the same* and of the endlessness of reproduction without difference. A future contingent upon getting the loan (in the present) for the capital to produce the surplus-value without which the loan can't be paid back. Consequently, the legitimated condition of borrowing in the present is the temporal feedback loop of having already been given the money, an auto-verification now become auto-consumptive. In the wake of this, the permanence of the *here and now* comes unstuck, leaving the uncertain shell of the ensured future and the nervous repetition of the defaulted present to plow forward into nothing.

Yet this is not to devolve into the fantasy of the present's imminent self-destruction, of waking tomorrow to find ourselves free of the logic of profit and the neoliberal state. To retrofit a now infamous image from Walter Benjamin, that of the angel of history being blown backward into the future and watching the catastrophes of the present becoming the ruins of the past, we should make sure that in trying to put our feet down and take stock of where we stand, we aren't dragging our feet. That we aren't trailing along backwards on some froth of the present, that we don't mistake the small clouds of dust and bits of detritus stirred up by our attempts to read a history for a real deadness and brokenness of the era. In other words, even that which seems on its way out – a certain late capitalist mode of accumulation predicated on global growth, related state forms and foreclosed political horizons – isn't likely to disappear before our eyes overnight. On the contrary, the character of the years to come will likely be that of the not-ending, the outmoded but going nowhere. If we call these apocalyptic times, we do so because of what is revealed. Namely, the pervasive structures of capitalist apocalypse and the fantasies needed to approach and mediate them, not in the simple fact that an era is drawing to a close.

Why "apocalypse"? What is the value of a word at once over-dramatic and overloaded with historical, and particularly religious, baggage? The first reason is practical: the objects of my analysis consists largely of "end of the world" movies and other cultural imaginings of civilization's collapse or the total destruction of human life. These things get called "apocalyptic" in the broadest sense, designating scenarios concerned with *how* our world is destroyed – less frequently with *why* – and with *what* happens in the aftermath. Furthermore, there is a structure of feeling and a repetition of content wound through the cultural production of certain periods that is fundamentally apocalyptic: a deep-seated conviction that things are teetering on a precipice, that disaster is not just around the corner but that the corner has already been turned. Now is one of those times. The anxiety and urgency are palpable, and not just because movies about the dead returning to life and waging war on us all are making a killing at the box office. We stand on the nervous razor edge of bad years bound to go worse, if we don't intervene, and we can't help but feel this.

The second reason is more important, and also more theoretically thorny. It has to do with the particular relation of "revelation" and "end" that makes apocalypse distinct from other modes of collapse, decay, decline, or disaster. *Apocalypse* - specifically *capitalist apocalypse* – needs to be understood in distinction from *crisis* and *catastrophe*. A crisis is a cyclical, expected expression, not a permanent state of affairs. It will pass, and be passed through. It will pass, and be passed through, clearing out systemic dead wood along the way. And it is not an end in itself. A crisis might be read as threatening times of non-recovery to come, but those are the times when it can no longer be called a 'crisis'.

Catastrophe, on the other hand, is end without revelation, a historical void, an end of the road that cannot point beyond itself. Worse, if it does point elsewhere, it is to a post-world nostalgic and desperate to shore up the remnants of its outmoded status quo. Catastrophe, in the imaginary of our time, is more than just the fears and predictions of global warming, flu pandemic, or peak oil. There is a likelihood in which the general contraction and decline of late capitalism into its sickly frantic state now will, over the next decades, become statically catastrophic. At the emergent moments of what would come to be called neoliberalism, both its apologists and its antagonistic symptoms – punks – declared there was *no future*: just the eternal present of this world declaring itself to be the only show in town, even as it veered off the rails. The situation to come is a different *no future*, the slow entropic loss of energy and profit, coupled with the state's brutal refusal – and ways of demanding the same of its citizens and subjects – to acknowledge that the eternal present has become an eternal past.

What we need, then, is an apocalypse. An apocalypse is an end with revelation, a "lifting of the veil." However, we don't need an apocalypse in its early Christian usage, the chosen few shown things hidden from the rest of ignorant flock. The chaotic chorus of those "who know better" is already a muddy din. The sense we pursue, instead, is the end of a *totality*, here meaning not the sum of all things but the ordering of those things in a particular historical shape. This end, therefore, is the collapse of a system of "real abstractions" and their real effects, of the inter-sections and stresses between ideas about the world and how the world is shaped into accordance with those ideas. As we'll see in the films and cultural legacies examined here, this doesn't mean *total destruction* but rather a destruction of *totalizing* structures, of those universal notions that do not just describe "how things are" but serve to prescribe and insist that "this is how things must be." What is revealed is what has been hidden in plain sight all along, previously only caught askance from the corner of our eye: the sudden exposure of what was present but not visible, because it did not accord with those real structuring forces of a totality. Malcolm Bull's influential account is worth noting:

> apocalyptic is dialectical and revolutionary. It is not the oppositions dissolved in the period of undifferentiation that are re-established, but a new set. The undifferentiated returns, that which was included is reincluded, and a new order is created, less exclusive than that which previously existed.[2]

To unpack this a bit: "differentiation" here implies the process of making something visible, which requires it be categorized and set into opposition. To extend Bull's visual metaphor, we can't discern and make sense of shifting traces of indeterminate gray. We need a system of oppositions to make any order out of the mess of information, in order to see clearly. This doesn't only involve determining recognizable shapes or an opposition of what is "present" or "absent." It involves a universal ordering system, one according to which certain things are worth seeing or even can be seen. The "undifferentiated" is that which cannot be seen.

The specificity of this model appears in terms of how it is distinct from the Christian eschatological one. In that revelatory structure, the revelation is a clarification along the lines of *krisis* (separation/judgment), allowing you to know fully where good and evil stand. In the mode described here, apocalypse is a surging into the managed, ordered world of differentiation (which is to say, a world in which oppositions are fixed) of all that is not. As such, the point is that apocalypse is not the clarification itself but a wound of the present that exposes the unseen – but unhidden – from which after-work can begin to dig out all the failed starts, possible histories. The apocalyptic describes not just the spilling forth of the unseen, but also of the undifferentiated matter of the possible, of what could have been and was not, of what neither came to be nor went away.

John Carpenter's 1988 film *They Live* dwells wholly in the gap between these two modes. It is also one of the most literally apocalyptic films ever made, the story of suddenly seeing what "was there all along," even as it insistently works, against its own grain, to blow its own cover story. In brief, *They Live* tells the story of a drifter, Nada, who comes to realize with the help of special sunglasses that the bourgeoisie are actually aliens, the "they" of the title. We live in a world of illusions, we don't see their hideous faces, and all mass media boils down to the simplest of injunctions – *OBEY, CONSUME, SLEEP*. As such, this would seem to be the classical revelatory *krisis*: all is laid bare, and the dividing lines are incontrovertibly clear. With this knowledge, Nada becomes a lumpenproletariat avenging angel: he kills cops and bankers who we know to be one of "them" and eventually destroys the giant transmitter that beams the illusion to us. In the final moments of the film, we see them revealed, their blue skeletal faces amongst us. And, in a great last turn of the film, beneath and inside us: a topless woman on top of her partner looks up dreamily from sexual pleasure to the TV, with its unmasked newscasters, and down to the face of her alien lover, who seems unaware that the gig is up. He asks casually, "what's wrong, baby?" Cut to black.

That said, nothing is nearly as black and white as Nada would like it to be. The film is not really the allegory of the "alienated" injustice of capitalism it plays at being. It is the wish-image of an absent clarity, and it is the necessary frustration of such desire. For lingering behind the sense that, *can you imagine how awful it would be if the world was run by powerful aliens?*, is the real question: *wouldn't it be nice if it were run by powerful aliens, if we could find some inhuman driver at the wheel, if we knew who to blame all along?* Isn't that what we really want, to know once and for all that there is some conspiratorial reason and order behind the blind contingencies of the world order? Because, at the end of the day, the problem isn't how to defeat those who run it all. It's how to find and direct anger at an other kind of apocalyptic world. The film itself splits between two kind of apocalypse movies, two modes of apocalypse. There is its dominant arc, the end-of-the-world plot of final battles and dividing lines that let you be the ass-kicking agent of retribution you've waites to be all along. And then there is the ongoing, durational, and horizontal apocalyptic mode in which the film begins. The apocalypse is not the revelation of who's behind this mess: it's the fact, persistence, and resistance to thought of the mess itself. It's the impossible line of flight Nada's eyes trace between the shantytown and the skyscraper.

Like that diffuse backdrop of *They Live,* this book is interested in *capitalist apocalypse.* This does not mean just an end of capitalism or even an end that suddenly reveals things about it which we didn't know before. Rather, capitalist apocalypse is the possibility of grasping how the global economic order and its social relations depend upon the production and exploitation of the undifferentiated, of those things which cannot be included in the realm of the openly visible without rupturing the very oppositions that make the whole enterprise move forward. And by "undifferentiated things," we mean all that we know very well yet regard as exceptional nightmares or accidents to be corrected with better, greener, more ethical management: hellish zones of the world, whole populations destroyed in famine and sickness, "humanitarian" military interventions, the basic and unincorporable fact of class antagonism, closure of access to common resources, the rendering of mass culture more and more banal, shifting climate patterns and the "natural" disasters they bring about, the abandonment of working populations and those who cannot work in favor of policies determined only to starkly widen wealth gaps. Underlying all of this, the basic and fundamental undifferentiated is all that cannot be contained in the valuation of life according to the logic of surplus-value. In other words, everything that is worth a damn yet which does not produce value.

Out of an apocalypse comes the hard work of the post-apocalyptic. This is perhaps the main theme of this book: the pitched effort to prevent falling back into either the expected passing of crisis or the historical stalemate of catastrophe, to not let the crisis pass or the catastrophe bleed out. Because what "comes back" in the apocalypse isn't necessarily – or ever – a happy unity of broader inclusion. Apocalypse is the coming-apart of the rules of the game, and in the ruined wake of this, the task isn't one of rebuilding, of mourning, or of moving on. It can only be, to draw on the three central metaphors and tropes of the book (salvage, zombies, and cities), the ceaseless struggle to dismantle and repurpose, to witness the uncanny persistence of old modes of life, and to redraw the maps and battle lines of the sites we occupy. In other words, we do not become post-apocalyptic because the plague swells, the bomb drops, or the earth cools. We become post-apocalyptic when we accept the present as rubbish, as undead, and as under attack. And when we refuse this acceptance, to salvage the scraps of antagonistic history that we inherit, to articulate militant reason out of the obscene persistence of what refuses to die, and to make the apocalyptic not a temporal event but a spatial organization. To be post-apocalyptic is to make of a given condition a decision and a commitment.

This isn't to be bleak about it. If anything, apocalypse is comedic: what is it but the punch line of a good joke, that turn that's neither the radically new nor the simple continuation of the information already given? It is the groan of realization, when the punch line reveals a sub-current already present from the start, something dirtier, meaner, or more joyous. This book remains insistent on the comedic function of it all, the graveside smile and black laughter, taking pleasure and rejecting all that navel-gazing melancholy, dour "realism," and crippling sadness and sincerity. A crooked grin to break the dead air ...

We should also stay vigilant about the dangers of endless deferral, of waiting for the punch-line to come and assuming that we'll recognize it when we see it. Against this, my point is two-fold.

1. Capitalist apocalypse, and the consequent and recurrent openings it provides for the struggle for communist post-apocalypse, has already been coming, unevenly and across time. It is not something to be held out in front of us at the end of a teleology. The very bad joke of the global order is told out of sync but with a cursed order of necessity: it

cannot function other than this.

2. This impossibility of staring it in the face or striking it directly – for what is it to strike a totality? – means that our approach and analysis needs to pass through its *symptoms* in order to strive toward both its abstract and embedded sources.

Working on these symptoms can involve serious consideration of financial data, geographical and demographic patterns, political trajectories, changing legal codes, and so on. In the case of this book, the symptoms in question are, primarily, rather odd films, often horror or "art" films, many of which aren't watched widely. They aren't written of here because they are "expressions" of popular sentiment or thinking. They are instead dealt with as concrete expressions – tactics, if we wish – of the attempt to force a connection between the wider constellation of symptoms we see and the apocalyptic revelation that withholds. More particularly, they are apocalyptic *fantasies*, though not in the sense that they simply show what we perversely wish would happen. (That's not to say that we don't take a lot of pleasure in watching the edifices of society crumble while neo-primitives get sexily dirty, behead zombies, and lustily-grimly take a roll in the radioactive hay while it all goes to shit.) Rather, *fantasy* here is a structure of simultaneous approach and deferral, appearing to work through possibilities while also foreclosing them, keeping them at the arm's length of the impossible imaginary. But it is precisely for this reason that they remain uniquely capable of drawing out the indistinct shapes of the apocalyptic. They are symptoms that actively try to work through their absent cause, and they are the fantasies constructed around the difficulty of that working through.

What are the particular relations between imagined scenarios considered here and the potential of apocalyptic revelation? And what are the corollary forms taken by my writing and analysis in the three following chapters, each of which can be read independently of the others?

In my consideration of salvagepunk, a proposed cultural "movement" not yet fleshed out but present in scattered antecedents, the cataclysmic catastrophe (figured as a potential apocalypse whose revelations have been forgotten) has already happened. The work is to uncover the revelations that never showed themselves: they are buried in all the rubble. This chapter is essentially a manifesto, and like all manifestos, it tries, by the act of its writing, to create the subject it describes. It therefore attempts to stand as a singular example of the critical work of salvage as both a metaphor for a relationship to the catastrophic ruins (and all the waste generated by cycles of consumption) and as a particular way of dealing with buried use-values, alternative histories, and false starts.

The zombie film, and the contemporary mainstream obsession with all things corpse-like, cannibalistic, and shambling, forms the focus of the second chapter. In the shifting and long history of the undead in late capitalism, we receive a vision of terminal crisis that never ends or resolves: either you win or the zombies win, yet neither actually does. You don't cohabitate, or construct an dialectical overcoming in the wound and stress of apocalyptic knowledge. The One of the managed world splits in Two and reaches a bloody deadlock. The undifferentiated are doomed to never fully die, and they are understandably furious about this. Formally, this chapter is the closest I come to a cultural history. It organizes itself around that single trope and follows it out chronologically, to try and uncover a logic that, fittingly, keeps coming back for more.

The final chapter moves from the dream image of salvagepunk and the nightmare image of the zombie to think about the broader schematics of apocalyptic time and space (in the form of combined and uneven apocalypse), crystallized around the image of the post-apocalyptic city. It is here that I unpack explicitly what has been expressed throughout, the sense that the world is already apocalyptic and that there is no event to wait for, just the zones in which these revelations are forestalled and the sites where we can take a stand. This is both summation and gesture beyond, an effort to refuse either a sense of reconciliation with this world order or an illusion of the ease of bringing it down.

As a whole, this book is historically situated, fixed to the present moment even as it rummages through pasts, but it is decisively not a history. It is not particularly descriptive, it does not follow the model of a survey, and it certainly isn't a work of criticism. It is a project of *prescriptive theory* (posed against the prescriptive force of capital's real abstractions): while my argument is indeed one developed out of my watching and reading, ultimately it is shaped by the point that I want to make and by the optic onto this era that I try to offer. The films and other objects I consider are picked and worked on in accordance with the principle of salvage. At times they are part of our most shared cultural knowledge, but above all, they are considered because they open up other lines of thought and say more sharply what I cannot. Many of them are minor works of art or mass production, either considered inaccessible or cast out as bits of trash. This doesn't particularly concern me. What concerns me is what can be made of them now, this work of construction in the age of wreckage.

My theoretical lens and mode of writing are equally inconstant. You should expect a shifting tone, one that veers among the kind of lyrical melancholy I warn against, detailed descriptions of the texture of films, broader discussions of political economy, and borderline misanthropic, rhetorically militant rejections of what I perceive to as the blockages to critical thought and radical politics. Most of all, this is an unabashedly a work of communist theory. By this I do not mean "Communist": there is no alignment or interest with a party or with certain legacies that should indeed be finally put to rest. I mean a conviction that capitalism is a world system and social relation to be forcibly dismantled, that a war against it is to be fought on all fronts, from careful analysis to planed attack. A conviction that until we think of ourselves as the post-apocalyptic agents of this system's ongoing apocalypse, we cannot counter this bleak trendline toward catastrophe. And a conviction that the thought of something better and fairer, something that doesn't systematically hinge on the destruction and forestalled development of whole zones and populations, is something to be salvaged, brought back from its shallow grave, and made part not of our lost opportunities but of our daily life.

The historical shifts and cultural tendencies described in the book are not new. What was once striking – the financial tendencies and new imperialisms of neoliberalism, pastiche and the fractured cultural logics of postmodernity – are now a stale echo. The story of combined and uneven apocalypse is the story of a yawning duration, an accretion so slow and naturalized that we can no longer recognize it. The shifts described and mapped here have none of the blush and flash of novelty. They have become the most basic shapes of our moment, as they are the shards of past moments trampled underfoot, lost in the waste heap. No, what is new, never drawn from scratch but retrofitted and reawakened, is the apocalyptic end. And with it, the rough work drawing forth what has been there all along, ongoing, unrecognized, yet marked deep by the history of the present, scarred all the more by how it dreams what comes after. We don't believe that "another world is possible," because we know that things superseded still stick around and stink, unwelcome remainders with which we have to deal. Another world is necessary, but only built from the gutted hull of this one.

Salvagepunk

SHADES: No one's gonna repopulate the Big Apple now, not with the rat population what it is. Ya know, stuff's just going begging! It's salvage city, Max. You'd love it ...
MOSES: Don't call me Max.
– from Richard Stanley's Hardware

They are residues of a dream world. The realization of dream elements, in the course of waking up, is the paradigm of dialectical thinking. Thus, dialectical thinking is the organ of historical awakening. Every epoch, in fact, not only dreams the one to follow but, in dreaming, precipitates its awakening. It bears its end within itself and unfolds it - as Hegel noticed - by cunning.
– Walter Benjamin, "Exposé of 1935," Das Passagen-Werk

THREE MOMENTS

One

World War I lays out a scattered corpse-scape, a shattered night of the world and its waste. Europe freezes, looking at its own death mask, cast from scrap wool and oil, black mud and dropped casings, all beneath the weight of a rotting international order and surging industry. Further east, the Bolsheviks say *No* and carve a trench into the plane of history. And in Berlin, Kurt Schwitters draws forth *Merz* from *Commerz*, pulling the innate venom of fragmented things from the bad sheen of commercial life.

Two

The '60s go *kaputt*. Then the long '70s roar into view, in all their gritty urgency and Satanic deformations of hippie non-thought, with real militancy losing a pitched battle to the triumphs of counter-revolution. In Italy, the Red Brigades shoot Moro and leave him in the trunk of a Renault. In New Hampshire, the end of the Bretton Woods system undoes the filaments of currency as certainty and shape. In England, 1969, *The Bed Sitting Room* and Monty Python think the end of it all as little more than the relentless repurposing of the same old shit. Ten years later, Mad Max heads toward the Outback.

Three

Neoliberalism's febrile tremors, and finance overcompensates, hysterically. There are small cracks and shimmers in this surface, like an old reptilian brain catching the whiff of older possibilities, false starts never quite taken. Cyberpunk already came and went: how could it not, given that it coldly sang along with what it felt like on the ground? Steampunk, the wet dream of Obama-time, acts twee and old fashioned while it sails smugly over the oceans of dead labor that got us here and sweeps the messy reality of progress out of sight. Salvagepunk isn't here yet, except as the unsteady movement of hands and brains trying to learn new tricks that have been there all along. Of the trash heap, only its romance of frozen decay should be discarded. There is no new construction, just the occupation of other architectures.

DREAM IMAGES

To return to and clarify the epigraph from Walter Benjamin: we are not talking about dream residues of a world, the nostalgic fantasies and fashionings of what once was. Rather, these are residues of a *dream world* that form a historical border to the next era, not as blueprints or utopian plans, but as leftovers. Rather, they are the unwelcome remainder of what won't go away. For what matters is neither manifest nor latent dream content. It's always the *dream work*, the underground currents that actually expose the loops of repression and the labor of making something out of these remnants.

The cunning of an era – the way it works against itself towards its own demise – is the dreaming of its grave. Not of its murderers or gravediggers, of who's to blame or who tried to put it to rest, but of the after-effect. The dream image, then, is the quiet cemetery.[3] For in rejecting the immediate past and the hard work of the living to bring around a new world order, one is left instead with the long dead and a pale writing of the *now* in their language. The ambiguous image, in contrast, (the un-worked-through dream image, not settled or stuck) is the rustling skeletons. It's the vision of a necromancer's toolbox, with which we can refashion the dead into what we insist they could have been, and in doing so, clear a place for ourselves amongst the salvageable dead and the never quite gone.

STEAMPUNK
Yeah, it's kind of like that

In short ...

Steampunk. Well, something kind of like that, indeed, but ultimately not at all. Steampunk – an aesthetic that rewrites the outcome of late capitalism according to a different, kinder industrial trajectory – is the false dream image of these years. That falseness, however, doesn't lie in its being anterior (as the vision of a resolutely past era) or too dreamy, too fantastic. Its falseness lies in it being the wrong dream image, even while it's the proper dream image of the liberal escape plan for the global crisis and its envisioned fall-out.

To track out this lineage of the present, we need to start with cyberpunk. If we are witnessing the slow self-dismantling of what can broadly be called a neoliberal order (the twin forces of financial deregulation and imperialism under the guise of "globalization"), we are also witnessing the eclipse of cyberpunk, at least as we've recognized it so far. Cyberpunk, that self-declared bastard child of science fiction, swapped out the cosmos and alternate worlds for a cooler, nastier version of this one: famous examples range from Gibson's *Neuromancer* (1984) and Stephenson's *Snow Crash* (1992) to the total massification of cyberpunkish appearance in *The Matrix* trilogy. (Not to mention *Cyberpunk*, the 1993 Billy Idol album that nearly destroyed whatever remained of his career.) As a whole, it was a supposed "non-movement," imitated all the same, full of artificial intelligence and information technologies run amok, neo-mercenaries and the revenge of the nerds (getting to wear virtual reality goggles and tight-fitting body suits, hackers playing postmodern day samurai), and glimpses of instantaneous data transmission stitched through the run-down corridors of the material city. Cyberpunk was the dream image of the neoliberal world par excellence, albeit one that encoded within it enough short-circuits to wake itself again and again. In particular, it wrote the fantasies of a post-state corporate global order. However, it did so with a canny awareness of the gap between the illusions of free-market ideology and the real need for states to act as support systems for corporate extension into recolonized spaces, material or virtual. Hovering over all this, in a froth alternately gray or giddy, were the visions of deindustrialization, of immaterial labor, of new hybrid multitudes, of nomadic subjects. And above all, of deregulation: credit, unchained and without master, races faster toward its own bartered-away abyss.

Cyberpunk was both creation and consequence of a gap between the paranoia of the technological sublime and a creeping realization that perhaps this is no brave new world. Just a nanotechnology dressing up of the way things already were going, and for that reason, it stands among the sharpest of critical realisms.

And then the fall ... In cyberpunk, neoliberalism did not see its inheritor, the dream of another world to come. It saw a distorted mirror image of itself and what the "neoliberal" was supposed to mean, a super-ego in all its taunting, sadistic glory. In hastening to meet that image, it forgot the cunning of its unfolding and collapse. (For at the "end of history" in which we supposedly live, the old tricks of history are dead and gone, right?) The deepening signs of the drawn-out end of neoliberalism happening as I write are properly cyberpunk: not brought about by anyone in particular, there are no heroes or victors, no actors with discernible will or capacity for willful action. Just the system let loose upon itself, speculative bubbles hiding all those toiling bodies and unused factories. An endless set of rational actors making rational profit decisions irrationally hollow out the core of profit itself.

Now, the reigning and scrambling order promises new direction, though a direction which digs into its bag of scraps to join together, in one touted version, new green Keynesianism with a "weaning off" foreign oil. Throwback economics, getting back to basics, investing in material things but in a way that reverses the trajectory toward the gasoline-soaked Armageddon.

Hence steampunk, the non-dystopian dressing-up of cyberpunk concerns with the trappings of steam power. In the novels, films, and comics that give shape to this tendency/genre, a world is envisioned in which the affective and social structures of the cyberpunk world – albeit largely stripped of their dystopian coldness – are preserved, cast back into an alternate history, without the material configurations of economic/techno-logical development that produced those structures. As such, steampunk is a romanticized do-over, a setting of the clock back to a time of craftsmanship and real (fetishized) objects, remaking the world, not in the mode of the ceaseless slow sprawl of cheap oil but in the Victorian self-aware world-making spirit. And this is what underlies the fantasy of overcoming our moment, seeing a crisis to be managed instead of a catastrophe already present.

The promise beneath this? Keep the technology, keep consumption, but make it "thoughtful," make it respon-sible, make it "sustainable."[4] Gild your laptop, hammer some bronze, and muse over the slow dance of the new wind-turbines on the horizon. All in all, a participation in that great  pastime of the pseudo-Left, remembering the era that never was, back when life was simpler and labor was meaningful. Steampunk has this cake and eats it, too: the difference engine clacks and hammers out a dirigible and gear vision of intricacy without ease, of lightly soot-stained sky never truly polluted, of machines that never get out of hand, of taking the auto-pilot back into our own hands.

This is not the dream image of our times. Why not? Quite simply, because it is just the *manifest* content of our dreams. It lacks the ambiguity that really halts and concretizes history, freezing to show the impossible past and the non-future locked together. It just shows the present's wishes bared. It has all the dialectical ambiguity of a Hummel figurine in a Robby the Robot outfit.

In the place of steampunk, that weak handmaiden of Obama-era capitalism, is what will be called *salvagepunk*: the post-apoca-lyptic vision of a broken and dead world, strewn with both the dream residues and real junk of the world that was, and shot through with the hard work of salvaging, repurposing, détourning, and scrapping. Acts of salvagepunk strive against and away from the ruins on which they cannot help but be built and through which they rummage.[5] The definitive examples I have here, if not necessarily the critical thought of it than at least the nascent "look": the *Mad Max* trilogy, Marker's *La Jetée* (and Gilliam's *12 Monkeys* as well), the New Crobuzon novels of China Miéville, Richard Lester's *The Bed Sitting Room*, the Strugatskij's *Roadside Picnic*, Dada and Surrealist collage and photomontage, Neil Marshall's *Doomsday*, *Waterworld* (as utterly terrible as it is), Godspeed You Black Emperor! and other derivations of anarcho-punk music, Richard Stanley's *Hardware*, barricades constructed in the service of insurrection and the accounts written of them, Yamaguchi Hiroki's *Hellevator: The Bottled Fools (Gusher No Binds Me)*, hip-hop sampling and early DJ culture, Jean Vigo's *L'Atalante*, *Steptoe and Son Ride Again*, much of Monty Python, Jeunet's *City of Lost Children* and *Delicatessen*, certain portions of *Wall-E*. An incomplete and scattered history of cultural visions of a scattered world after the fact. These are all antecedent versions of this, for salvagepunk is a tendency still in the making. It is particular to this historical moment, and our work, in this chapter and beyond, is to elaborate something that has yet to fully exist. Our point is that shifts in the political, economic, and cultural landscape have resulted in a situation to which salvagepunk is a necessary response, both as a cultural form and a material practice. Most importantly, it is a certain turn of thought to cut against current trendlines of nostalgia, the melancholia of buried history, and static mourning for radical antagonistic pasts seemingly absent from contemporary resistance to capitalism.

To speak of salvagepunk is necessarily to deal with the *Mad Max* trilogy. I prefer to think of these films as a subgenre, perhaps "gasolinepunk" (or the post-apocalyptic strain of dieselpunk, but I prefer "gasolinepunk" as way of differentiating it from the *Sky Captain and the World of Tomorrow* sort of dieselpunk, with its

WWI aesthetic). More broadly, it is the reactionary wing of salvagepunk. However, the *Mad Max* films are also the most recognizable example of the "look" of a mass cultural approximation of salvagepunk.

What is this look that, for better or often worse, has been picked up and replicated, parodied and unintentionally adopted far and wide? Things are very grubby. (And probably smell awful, albeit rather rugged and masculine, or so goes the fantasy structure of Max's cut-rate outback version of the Man With No Name.) If one is in a city/encampment/settlement, that grubbiness involves wetness: mud, dirty water, siphoned gas, pig shit, or, as a signal of supposed hope, clear splashing streams. Everywhere else? Blowing sand and empty highways, harsh sun, and fine coating of dust that settles on everyone and everything.[6] Apparently, the main type of clothing capable of surviving the collapse of civilization is leather bondage wear, followed in a close second by breezy linen, animal pelts, and awkward configurations of armor and long underwear.[7] The various combination of these and your commitment to dressing properly like a fetishist allow you to be mapped on a moral scale. White linen and headband, innocent if ineffectual; dyed hair and leather pants, perverted scourge of the desert; metal-spike studded codpiece, completely evil. There are plenty of dreadlocks and Mohawks, along with flawlessly desert wind-swept and feathered hair. In general, there is a broad punkness to dressing and appearance, something that will wind through not just the salvagepunk apocalyptic impulse but other apocalyptic figures considered later, such as the zombie horde and the lumpen street gang. Yet as with those cases, the question remains: to what extent does that superficial codification of a recognizably punk aesthetic merely act as a buffer for the broader conservative condemnation of what the films convincingly show to be a lot of posturing and petty nihilism?

The crux of the *Mad Max* appearance and trope is the

landscape itself, littered with debris, gutted cars, abandoned cities, pavement marked with burnt rubber and blood, of shanty-towns cobbled together from scrapped materials, the whole thing marked with smoke, grease, and fire. For all the deep goofiness of the films, their world remains one of the striking configurations of our time: detached from its politics, it is the look of an era on the literal skids, with all the attendant savagery, hustling, backstabbing, and implausible moments of shared hope. Forget the liberal cry of "NO BLOOD FOR OIL." The *Mad Max* world posits a starker, meaner, truly realist inversion of this, written into its sun-baked – and often half-baked – vision: "NO OIL WITHOUT A WHOLE LOT OF BLOOD SPILLED."

Beyond the genre-shaping landscape and populace, the films, as the most widely disseminated example of this genre, also give shape to its dominant political tendency. That tendency begins in the sense of what went wrong, a rather amorphous tale of peak oil and scrambling misrule. The narrator's opening-voice over in *Mad Max 2/The Road Warrior* (1981) should be included at length:

To understand who he was, you have to go back to another time. When the world was powered by the black fuel. And the desert sprouted great cities of pipe and steel. Gone now, swept away. For reasons long forgotten, two mighty warrior tribes went to war and touched off a blaze which engulfed them all. Without fuel, they were nothing. They built a house of straw. The thundering machines sputtered and stopped. Their leaders talked and talked and talked. But nothing could stem the avalanche. Their world crumbled. The cities exploded. A whirlwind of looting, a firestorm of fear. Men began to feed on men. On the roads it was a white line nightmare. Only those mobile enough to scavenge, brutal enough to pillage would survive. The gangs took over the highways, ready to wage war for a tank of juice. And in this maelstrom of decay, ordinary men were battered and smashed.

The narrator goes on, in the tradition of so many post-apocalyptic narratives, to focus back on the personal and singular: the evolution of Max from ordinary man to Road Warrior, forged in this maelstrom. But beyond this fable, beyond its doom-and-gloom lyricism and persistent assumption that it takes only 20 years or so to abandon geopolitical analysis in favor of tribal fetishization, what of the images that accompany it? We begin in a swirling "fog of memory," a pastel-hued zoom in on relatively fresh faced Max at the conclusion of the first film. Yet from there on, we revert to black and white stock footage: a montage of pumping oil derricks, refineries in the desert, and, as things get worse, WWII soldiers storming the beach, UN assemblies, politicians pushing and shoving, and late '60s riots and student protest (at the moment of "men began to feed on men").

What's striking here neither the severity of the envisioned apocalypse nor its ideological inconsistencies, but the way that it *salvages* established narratives of the war against fascism and social progress and uses them otherwise. In this case, to inscribe an anti-modernization polemic in which all roads end in gasoline-obsessed hoodlums prowling the post-oil desert. So, in turns out, the slaughter on the Normandy beaches and the Maginot Line were about the panic of disappearing "black fuel." The barricades of May 68: what are they if not a "firestorm of fear," the frantic clawing of the masses in the "nothing" that follows the end of affordable oil? Furthermore, the films are not set in the future: the historical images are drawn from and lead up to the time in which the film was made. As such, they aren't a projection of the far future, but a reinscription of previous events so as to make the "real world" present genuinely apocalyptic and to enable a flight into another type of fantasy. For the montage approaches the moment of the film's coming-to-be, the end of the 70s, and indeed switches "back" to color, but it does so by tying off this narrative in the roar of the "white line nightmare." Thus, the decline of the West becomes the occasion for sanctioned adrenaline and the closure of thinking otherwise. Creatures of habit become creatures of salvage, but only insofar as that preserves a distorted parody of the status quo. And more than this, not just the obscene shell of a past normalcy but, across the arc of the films, a "rebuilding" that is nothing but the slow and inevitable march toward a recreation of contemporary capitalism.

In *Mad Max* (1979), we see, on the outskirts of the collapsing cities, anarchic dissolution into the Hobbesian state of nature. It's *homo homini lupus* – man is a wolf to man – if wolves were interested in revenge plots and supercharged cars. But in the wreckage of the city, life still continues somewhat normally, centered around Max's nuclear family. Police and legal systems exist. The collapse is not immediate, but rather feels of attrition, the slow grinding down of resources coupled with the sudden emergence of men who are good at violence finally getting to show just how good. If there is an "evental rupture," it is not on a mass scale, or at least not visible in the film. The localizable point of no return is the murder of Max's wife and son, a metonymic stand-in for, and conceivable trauma of, the "unthinkable," for what remains genuinely beyond the reach of our intellect. Namely, apocalypse that has not *happened* but has been *happening*.

A train wreck in slow motion, a secret narrative: it has been about oil from the start. That uncomfortable intersection of montage and narration which begins *Mad Max 2* is one of the great truly apocalyptic instances of late capitalist cinema. It is a revelation not of hidden events (a prophecy of foreseen actions coming to be) but of hidden sense (a retroactive prophecy stitching together the scattered remains into a trendline). A mode of analysis that has eluded us becomes uncannily clear. And unpleasantly so, in that the moment of revelation is a revelation of complicity, in "not knowing" what had been known all along.

Mad Max 2 nails this issue of the choice that underpins the illusion of necessity. It is patently false that only "those mobile enough to scavenge, brutal enough to pillage would survive." Out there on the road, racing around, perhaps. But a possibility remains which is only approached at the very end of the third film: if they weren't so busy searching for, hoarding, or defending gasoline, one could easily "start anew," particularly in the ghost town ruins of the city. It isn't that they "have" to live this way, but rather that they quite enjoy it, the same over-the-top joy we approximate when watching a film about the end of the world devote the majority of its energy to large explosions and well-choreographed chase scenes.

Of course, we do get initial attempts to "start anew," and the second film is primarily structured around this collision between two orders: the "settlers" who attempt to form permanent communities versus the nomadic hordes who stick to the previous mode. (A previous mode that *did not exist previously*: what is the historical memory of the gas-scavenging swarms other than a misconstrued memory of the far past, here not mobilized to imagine a utopian way of being but as part of an attempt to be properly barbarian . . . To be the baddest of the bad, it becomes necessary to don the mantle of savagery from long ago and far away.)

Mad Max: Beyond Thunderdome (1985) continues this trajectory of retracing the steps toward emergent capitalism. We move from the battle between nomad and settler to the creation of a market, new "city" formation, non-warlord legal code managed life (bolstered by the autocratic force of Tina Turner). All this still stands as an outpost amongst the "wild," in which the willfully primitive tribes are those who remain committed to the visions of the past: that is, to the advanced state of late capitalism. The standstill of post-history crudely draws on cave walls the pre-historic vision of the glories of the global economy.[8] At the end of the film and the end of the cycle as a whole, Max and his band of primitivist Lost Boys and Girls go back to Sydney, the "Tomorrow-Morrow Land" of legend, its empty skyscrapers now lit by scattered fires and inane storytelling that folds Max and the reverse exodus into the tribalist narrative of starting over. And while the reclamation of dead spaces for other uses is a genuine articulation of what salvagepunk can be, we can't help but feel that something misfires here. As if going *beyond* is just going *back*: the new settlement that sees itself as a restoration. What we end with is just a grimier, leather-and-feathers, post-history equiv-alent of steampunk's anti-materialism. Here, the "fundamentals" may be different, but the illusion is still one of getting back to basics, basics that were never possible in the first place.

And all this bound to the absurd self-consumptive core: one needs gasoline in order to drive around and kill others to steal their gasoline, but in doing so, one consumes the gasoline that one had, and so one needs gasoline in order to ...

CONSTRUCTION IN THE AGE OF WRECKAGE

Whatever calls itself a break in the trendline necessarily calls out for a ground clearing. It demands that the piles of accreted junk be shoved into the gutter so as to gain visibility out of the clutter and to clear a space from which to move otherwise.

Or this is how it supposedly goes. And this has been the rallying and outpacing cry of prescriptive communist and radical cultural movements, from the manifestos of Dada and the Situationist International, Constructivist design and Brutalist slabs, dialectical film and anarcho-punk.

This mode of emptying the graveyard to make room for new dead is nothing new. It is the dominant minor logic of the 20th century, a blood-and-noise conviction running alongside its modern twin and enemy: the promise of global liberal democracy making capitalism itself a "basic human right." And there is little worth in our mourning and periodizing as lost: we just end up dwelling in the basement of the museum of avant-gardes, canonizing those things aimed to destroy all canons, fingering our collectible remnants of when times were different and when people believed in farther horizons.

So, like the very movements in question, we wind up backs to the wall of that non-choice: either we mark and mock, tell ourselves that it was always just aesthetic play from the start, postmodern equivalences from the get-go, and that real politics always lay elsewhere; or else we maintain a conviction in the thought of the avant-garde and unmoor even from our radical past in order to break the baleful spell of melancholic inaction, thereby discounting both the struggle that is our very history and the historical forces at work.

There are distinct corollaries here with the kind of schematic Alain Badiou (and others, albeit with different terminologies) have been proposing in recent years, that of the different inflections of a "passion for the Real." ("Real" here doesn't carry a strictly Lacanian meaning, as that which exceeds/escapes the symbolic. Rather, it is an insistence on a practice formed on the ground of what the world could be. This is neither utopian nor hemmed in by the reigning symbolic order. It is based on a sense of what lies below, of the bedrock of potential social relations and thought-forms to be rediscovered by revolutionary theory and action.) Without delving into the specificity of that project, we can still draw out two things: 1) its direct relation to political-aesthetic projects and 2) the symptomatic blindspot of the model, what it remains structurally incapable of perceiving.

The 20th century, as it tracks the supposed heroic arc of avant-garde art and vanguard political thought, is indeed marked by the relation between the ghosts and goals of unity and division, synthesis and contradiction, coalition and antagonism. And as such, the basic question is needed: are we to locate our way out of this mess via the unification of the opposed Two – bourgeois vs. proletariat, capitalism vs. communism, democracy vs. "totali-tarianism," religion vs. secular thought – into a new One, or do we need to keep ceaselessly negating, dividing, resplitting, to shove a wedge into the false unity of the globe and show who's on what side, plainly, harshly? The reformist and/or apologist overtones of the "unifier" position are unmistakable, and I find force and hope, with Badiou, in the latter, in the bringing-to-crisis of the Two. Yet with this position, he recognizes the possibility that was in fact the manifested historical tendency: our well-known annihilative, purgative, and partisan conviction that just might destroy the world – or at least the possibility of having a coherent position in relation to it – in trying to burn it clean. Yet the work of revolutionary consciousness, political or cultural, cannot be the antithesis to the world that annihilative passion poses itself as (the destructive embodiment of the antagonism itself), but something else. It needs to be a horizon toward a third way that escapes either the unary phantasm of the One or the terroristic deadlock of the Two.

Against this, as a third of sorts, Badiou offers

the subtractive path: to exhibit as a real point, not the destruction of reality, but minimal difference. To purify reality, not in order to annihilate it in its surface, but to subtract it from its apparent unity so as to detect within it the minuscule difference, the vanishing term which constitutes it. What barely takes place differs from the place wherein it takes place. It is in the 'barely' that all the affect rests, in this immanent exception.[9]

Concretized as cultural strategy, what does this look like?

Essentially, it is minimalism, that particular (historical) form of abstraction drawing forth the most "barely" of minor difference. Robert Ryman, Carl Andre, Agnes Martin. Morton Feldman, Mies, Mondrian, Malevich at his starkest best. Late Beckett, minus the scatological humor. (Which is to say, minus a lot.) Warhol's films, but not his paintings. Late conceptual names and their antecedents, all.[10]

To return to the schematic Badiou offers, 3 modes:

1. Annihilative passion for the Real: burn it all down, very militant, very destructive.

2. Subtractive passion for the Real: minimal difference revealing the vanishing term around which the order is supports it, very subtle, very formal.

3. Two unite into One: coalition building, synthesis and papering over difference, very liberal.

But there is a blindspot in all this, and not the productive blindspot of anamorphic vision, where you shift position and get what you've been missing. This approach to thinking radical political culture/culturally radical politics is accurate, particularly for a certain predominant moment in capitalist aesthetics. Yet something is left behind, a lack unacceptable for our conjuncture. We know a lingering dissatisfaction that there need be something else, and a sense that these modes – petty nihilism, self-subtracting unwillingness to play the game, and compromised unity – are modes of apologetic participation. More simply, we might say that each of these have historically been more potent than that. But they are no longer.

Here we have to track out the other possibility not elaborated: the passion for the Real should not be allowed to count only when the dialectical model is that of One divides into Two. For simply making as Two is not dialectics, at least not the dialectics of our project, from the rust knowledge of salvagepunk to the uncanny existence of our world with its co-present apocalyptic collapse. Capitalism is the bringing into existence of a world of the non-dialectical Two (there is only that which is capital and that which might become capital, and this itself rests on the irresolvable antagonism of workers and capitalists). All this under the shifting veil that insists that the world is global now, that it's a tremendous heterogeneous One. Our thought must be dialectical exactly because capitalism itself is not.

And as such, we need not just the division that creates the Two. We need also the insistence to not rest in this division, either as annihilation or subtraction. Specifically, we need a model of *construction*, that other possibility anathema to contemporary dialectical thought so resolute in following the vitally important line of "negative dialectics" that it considers anything other than annihilation or subtraction to be the silly promise of unification, compromise, synthesis, and near-magical joining together.

What it can't think is the work of salvage and montage, of the work of construction in the age of wreckage.

In other words, to divide up the One neither for the sake of purgative annihilation nor for the subtractive insertion of a void.

Rather, to see what's worth saving in the One that was never visible. We begin indeed with the ratcheting up and cracking apart of the pseudo-totality of late capitalism. And then starts the harder task of knowing when to call it a wreck and to start to dig through that wreckage.

This is the inheritance of that avant-garde move which we can't afford to leave behind. But here, it is doubled. To clear away the waste - the wreckage at once *material* (the produced crap and scraps of our production processes) and *theoretical* (past gestures, manifesto fragments and strategies for repurposing) - to make a space for what can be made from it. Then the making and the remaking, not the smoothing of compromised synthesis, but welding, stitching, rewiring. All with the chances that were there from the start, too polished to see, too immense to grasp, too broken to have ever been whole.

PUTTING THE PUNK BACK INTO SALVAGE (WHERE IT WASN'T TO BEGIN WITH)

If salvagepunk is a genre to come, a radical principle of recuperation and construction, a certain relation to how we think those dregs of history we inherit against our will, a return of the repressed idiosyncrasy of outmoded things - if it is all this, it is also, rather obviously, defined against the longer lineage of salvage to which it is bound. Taking the initial linguistic form of *word + punk suffix* (cyberpunk, steampunk, etc) that started this investigation, salvagepunk is not – or should not be – salvage plus a rakish air, a self-declared *fuck the world* perspective, and a carefully located sexy grease smudge on the cheek. That aesthetic needs no work to be brought forth. It already exists, woven into in the machine-frayed hem of every fake vintage shirt sold at the mall.

Rather, to put the punk into salvage is *to occupy it too well*, not to stand outside the logic of the game, but to track it to its far horizons. There we see the frayed hems of a mode of thought. For example, and to reiterate the central point of our earlier discussion, the *punk* specificity of cyberpunk had nothing to do with noirish spike-haired heroes and digital samurai, not drugs or dub. (Of course, the massification of it, from *Hackers* to *The Matrix*, had very much to do with that.) It had to do with the intersection of a close attachment to its historical present with the fact that it no longer believed in a future – the present is already the hollowed-out promise of that future. In other words, it is not speculative fiction: it is just a dead stare portrait of what the neoliberal order wanted itself to be if it had the total hegemony to do it. Not neoliberals themselves, who always cared too much about shoring up nations and "wars of civilization." No, it was the asubjective shape of the thought, the toneless growl of capital turning back against on the remaining petrified forms of its makers' world. The dystopia of cyberpunk was this thought's acid bath, stripping down to the bones. No fussing around with supposed humanitarian concerns and spreading democracy, just financialization, total penetration of markets, and the frenzy of the invisible, as circulation zipped through shady back alley deals and the high architecture of finance with equal greased ease.

Cyberpunk hence was not the sneer at a barren speculative future. It was the hidden sneer of that present itself.

The end of that present – the end of speculation – is the site on which salvagepunk - not salvage - is emerging. Like all things apocalyptic, it reveals itself as that which was hidden, in the wrecked afterlife of the world dreamed by cyberpunk and lived, unevenly, by all of us for the last 20 years. It paces in the fallout and debris, the burst bubbles and factories that won't de-rust and start humming again.

And yet, salvage itself is a mechanism, both in practice and in thought, procedure and ideology, deeply ingrained in the circuits of late capitalism. And much further back than that.

From the total inanity of green "upcycled" goods (to borrow the term from the website of one company that makes bags out of truck tires, "i.e. recycled/reclaimed into something special," because "Ethical is Beautiful" and they insist on "only using laptops") to the recession horror of wrenching fillings from your teeth to sell to "Cash For Gold U.S.A" (no oral hoarding in these lean times!). From the total staggering obscenity of price mark-ups at trendy vintage clothing shops to children rummaging through the stinking mountains of trash. These are apocalyptic times generally, but in economic and material terms, the figure and action of salvage looms perhaps largest.

The whole totality is shot through with that scrap and hustle, whittle and swindle instinct. Hip hop's "made something from nothing" ethos. Pepsi bottles "purified" municipal tap water and labels it *Bottled at the source*. Advertising trawls the shitpool of consumer anxieties and petty fears, hauling up and polishing out new needs and ownership dreams.

More than all this is the fact that capitalism's great work of salvage is the salvage of *time*: making something out of every last bit. In earlier formations, the worker kept time to inhuman rhythms of the integrated factory, and Fordism streamlined movements to the single repetitive task. On from there: the colonization of our free time, never being able to punch out, free time only a self-subtracting countdown back to the time of value.

The work of "creative" capital, when being aware of "what's going on" culturally and socially is our supposed protection against the precarity of labor. No longer blocks of time or long cycles, just pseudo-cycles that never start or stop yet which don't advance. The factory never sleeps anymore.[11]

Even in the periods of profligate boom years (i.e. over the past 30 years, the consolidation of class power with the total explosion of consumer credit and the further "planned obsolescence" of commodities, while profitability on the whole declined), the system cannot fully let waste remain as such. The discarded objects are spatially displaced to South Asia, to give an example, where we find fields of dead motherboards ("e-waste," as if it were just another set of ones and zeroes waiting to be deleted from a server) left to be stripped for usable bits, and the silent hulls of oil tankers are scrapped, scrubbed, and broken down.

This "gutting of the boat" is a fitting contemporary world extension and transformation of the etymology of salvage. For the broader common sense of "recycling waste material" is a recent shift, to which we will return. The original use of it, from 1645, designated the *payment* one received for saving a ship which was sinking or about to be captured. Even the action of the *saving* itself did not come into usage until the late 19th century with the "salvage corps," those private companies who either did the job municipal firefighters couldn't in an era of rampant fire, or came in after the burn to dig through the ash for what was still usable. And so salvage is shot through with the sense of getting paid, or the transfer of exchange value, more broadly. Not for the work of sifting through the junk heap but for preventing the ship (and its sailors) from joining that realm of dead objects. Not even plundering cargo from the sinking ship or grabbing whatever you can as it goes down, but saving the day and keeping things as they were.

Our moment, when *salvage* primarily means "waste sorting and value recuperation," has also seen perhaps the largest and most desperate resurrection of this older mode. For what was that $700 billion U.S. bank bailout (not to mention the untold sums added before and after, now estimated to be somewhere in the long run range of $23.7 trillion) if not the fantasy of saving the ship of the entire capitalist financial enterprise and of getting some "salvage" in return, in the form of money flowing back through all the charred channels? The incessant pops of speculative bubbles may as well be the sound of this very fantasy imploding: you can't save a sinking monetary empire with more government sanctioned and directed money and expect to gain something in the process. And when an economic order refuses to allow for the total decline of industries which would result in "fire sales" of production materials, leveraged debt, and new competitor access to markets, we don't even get the kind of creative destruction ground clearing that allows for building and accumulation to start anew.

Fittingly and horrifically, the more common sense of salvage, that of trying to find some value in waste, emerged in 1918, in the naming of the "British Army Salvage Corps," who combed the battlefields for materials (tank parts, clothing of dead soldiers) to be redirected into the continuing war effort. The anecdote below gives a sense of the tenor of this (from the British newsmagazine 'The War Budget', January 3rd, 1918):

Unrolling my [gas] mask to read the directions for its use and to try it on, I noticed that the gray fabric had a strangely familiar look and that one corner of the "skirt" of the queer contrivance was pieced out from a rounded seam.

"What's this stuff they use in the gas masks?" I asked of Captain R., who reclined at my elbow. "I'm sure I've seen something like it before."

"Grayback," was the laconic reply. "I should hate to say anything to spoil your appetite, but if you must know, the flap of that mask you just had on was made from the tail of a Tommy's shirt picked up on the battlefield. Possibly he thought he could chase Boches faster if he threw it away; possibly it was cut off him when a comrade applied first aid; possibly — — — —"

"That will do," I cut in, hastily rolling up the mask and returning it to its case. "Here's hoping no asphyxiating shells sail over to-day to force us to the dread alternative!"

It is here, in both the unfathomable brute fact of the slaughter fields of WWI themselves and in the mordant and furious culture that emerged out of it, that our lineage of salvagepunk starts, although just barely. (With the possible earlier antecedent of revolutionary barricades in all their body-stacking, city-remapping montage.) That is to say, where the *punk* in salvagepunk begins. Not accidentally, in a European-wide catastrophic moment, when the savagery directed outwards by the Continent turned back on itself. The World War as the severed inheritance of the previous world.

Salvagepunk is the drawing out of the logic of salvage itself (in its WWI sense), past the point of its own consistency. It takes the basic ground of salvage (there is value here somewhere, if we sift through the ashes, or keep the ship from going under, or strip these bodies) on its own terms, and, in doing so, wrecks it. Salvagepunk wrecks salvage with the simple recognition that the world is now irrevocably structured as apocalyptic wasteland. The very notion of recuperation means that the former world is no more, but that we are left with its persistent remainders and after-effects.

Hence salvagepunk says: *it's already been burnt, already lost at sea.* We came to the rescue too late. There is no reward, and definitely no one there to pay it. And we can only begin again from here if we finish wrecking - in thought - what we know to be wreckage yet which refuses to call itself such.

Yet this alone would not constitute salvagepunk, at least insofar as it can escape simply meaning an aesthetic of rusty hulls and bleached bones. The key turn, the raising of salvagepunk to a capture of this historical conjuncture (the drawn-out catastrophe of late capitalism) and a rejection of where that will go, if untrammeled, is the work of construction of and from wreckage.

In this way, the "look" of salvagepunk should be less about how it appears, from cobbled together caravans to junk-world robots, and more about a kind of look *onto* that world. The look is two-fold, and German artist Kurt Schwitters, working in the aftermath of the first World War, gives the way in.

Schwitters is a pivotal figure in this history for several reasons: his association with Dada and Surrealism, his collages of selected refuse and trash, and his naming of his art practice as *Merz* by decoupling it from *Commerz*. In English, think stealing "merce" away from "commerce" to cut away the "with" ["com"] that describes the social relations of economic life so as to leave behind the isolated objects themselves, in an inversion of how reification happens.

"Merz," Schwitters wrote, "is the graveside smile and the solemn gaze at comic events." In a broken world of broken things, this graveside smile is a necessary response and one-half of the look of salvagepunk, how it looks out and what we would see on its face. Not the sneer of cyberpunk – that of the wanna-be automated world itself – but the expression of those born into this world, who refuse to either look away or submit to the hypnosis of cynical resentment. The work of construction only starts with breaking the baleful spell of decay and mourning, and nothing can do this without the obscene laughter at what we are supposed to be very serious and dour about. (And in reverse, Schwitters' other directive, that solemn gaze at what we are told is frivolous and light and gentle, tearing that open to find the utter nastiness of expected laughter.)

The look, then, is a dual mode: both the graveside smile and the perspective of looking for what can be reassembled "wrongly" and how. It is for this reason that the traditions of montage (Sergei Eisenstein, Dziga Vertov, Jean-Luc Godard, Chris Marker) and collage (Hannah Höch, Schwitters, John Heartfield, Terry Gilliam), détournement (Duchamp, Debord and the Situationist International, hip-hop, some of Italian *arte povera*) and farce (Monty Python, Richard Lester, Marco Ferreri) are so crucial here: all are forms of idiosyncratic uses of "given" materials.

It is worth staying with Schwitters' particular thoughts about construction and objects for a moment because, to reiterate, salvagepunk – not in its Mad Max appearance but in what it *could be* – is fundamentally about such questions, of how we relate construction to the inherited remains of historical encounters. Reading him on this requires a fair amount of unpacking. After all, he is the man who wanted both to use "household refuse to scream with" and to "remove the innate venom of things."

Oddly, though, Schwitters' art is never much of a screaming project, with far more of a mordant smirk than any sort of expressionistic yawp. His is a labor of devaluing and revaluing, of how to pull objects from their situated position within circuits of production, consumption, and discarding, and to locate them anew in the position of the artwork. Hence his statement that "the work of art is produced by the artistic devaluation of its elements." The problem that impels such devaluation is the "innate venom" of things, the eccentric, idiosyncratic aspect of objects which must be defanged in order to join the new combinatory logic of the collage. It is here that salvagepunk is radically opposed to Schwitters' work, otherwise its sharpest ancestor. For it is precisely that "innate venom" with which salvage is concerned: our task is to remove the veil of abstraction – the designation of an object in terms of its exchange value – in order to find that venom, the particularity of its use value which cannot be entirely subsumed.

So when Schwitters declares that "what is essential is the process of forming" when working with junk and trash, we can detect an early vision of salvagepunk's work of wreckage/montage. However, the gap widens on the question of where value comes from. He writes,

> I set Merz against a refined form of Dada and arrived at the conclusion that while Dadaism only points to opposites, Merz resolves them by giving them values within a work of art. Pure Merz is art, pure Dada is non-art - each consciously so.[12]

Leaving aside the question of whether or not Dada is truly "non-art," the central difference between salvagepunk and Merz is that the former, even as an "artistic practice," provides the occasion for the already-present singular values of things (now visible in the very moment of their ruin, of their monetary and often functional devaluation) to come to the fore. More precisely, perhaps salvagepunk can stand obstinately between these points: a production of "values" (the task of construction and assemblage as producing a second life to the already broken) which does not subtract that innate venom but mobilizes it.

It is this belief in "innate venom" or the "idiosyncrasy" of objects that gives salvagepunk a stranger, unsettled, and prescriptive relationship to its historical moment: it manifests a needed kickback against the still dominant logic of postmodernism. We might debate the degree to which the terms of postmodernism theorized by Fredric Jameson and others in the '80s still apply to our moment – they surely describe nothing "new" – when subsequent developments in media technologies and massive shifts in the global order produce a perhaps uncrossable rift between then and now. Regardless, we can say that the notion of salvagepunk we construct, including both its existent cultural examples and the possible manifestations of its conceptual moves, indicates a lost promise of modernism swept under the rug.

For if one strand of modernism (including those practitioners of montage, collage, détournement, and farce) was born of a contentious tarrying with the orders of capitalist imperialism and its consequences, as well as an exploration of a wider set of possible relations between workers and the realm of mass-made things, it has always been about salvage, mapping another current alongside the work of capitalist salvage itself. This modernist tendency made its task to find value in the scrap heap, although it maintained a specific sense of a whole that must be cracked and made into said scrap heap before salvage-construction can start. But above all, there remains, against Schwitters' own words, a sense of both the eccentric value of things and that not all images are equivalent. In the work of junk-montage and the recreation/recombination of the most banal sub-regions of the cultural realm, we get glimpses of a different kind of sneer back towards us: the tough, unwanted, and venomous insistence of the objects of mechanical production, from plastics that will don't decay to unsettling singular properties of mass-produced things.

The "postmodern turn," despite its emphasis on pastiche, mash-up, and hybrid forms, closes off the punk aspect of what salvage could be, precisely because of that emphasis. At stake is the inherent flatness and equivalency of postmodern cultural production, in which the disappearing sense of a lived history of the world opens the cache of cultural options to endless reuses, all unmoored from the original situation of the images, sounds, genre conventions, and so on. To be sure, the number of excep-tions to this trendline indicate that this may never have really been the case. However, like all real abstractions whose description of a situation feed back into and dictate the terms of that situation, the postmodern turn has believed its own lines. Whether or not this has been the experience of living through the past couple decades, the cultural sphere has been necessarily marked by its degrees of deviation from, or adherence to, the hollow frisson of postmodern ahistorical sampling.

Most simply, salvagepunk is not postmodern. It is a modernist project never fully started. Fundamentally opposed to pastiche, salvagepunk realizes the eccentricity of discarded, outmoded, and forgotten things still marked by the peculiar imprint of their time of production and the store of labor and energy frozen in their form. A form from which all value has supposedly been lost. Above all, it is that work of construction, not simply gutting to see what can be sold back to the industrial suppliers, but a production of "valueless times" to see what values might emerge outside of the loops of circulation and accumulation.

Particularly when combined with other aspects of waste. We don't want to hold up single objects as treasures, like so many vintage lamps or kitschy artifacts of a political world gone by. Instead, starting with a world after the fact of its collapse, an endless series of world collapses. (The catastrophe across time, on which we have to work in order to reveal anything.) Constructing anew from leftovers of what was once very new. And then inhabiting the old worlds, pushing a moment to the point of its stress and crack, taking up those parts of it already belonging to another time, waste zones of history one and all.

ANTI-CAPITALIST REIFICATION

To pull back for a moment, we should ask: but isn't this whole salvagepunk enterprise bound to mirror other forms of object worship, from crass consumerism to the financial crisis call to "get back to real things"? The primitivist urge to rediscover a natural life of pure use-values? The fantasy of the most radical tendencies emerging in the most desperate configurations of global slum dwellers, and a lyrical drool before the postindustrial loveliness of all falling apart? Both the fetishization of the tool's rough-and-ready possibilities of world fixing, and the fetishist's excited glance at what cannot be fixed?

In short, is this not just more reification, totally unable to escape the hypnotic fixation on objects, however innately venomous or thrown from the cycles of capitalism, as symptom and solution?

To which we answer: *yes, indeed.*

This is a position and line of thought intentionally taken in order to do that same dialectical work of "punk" described, of tracking out to the point of collapse. Fittingly, to see what should be scrapped and what should be saved.

What must be scrapped is clearly this elevation of the object world of late capitalism, antagonistic as it may be to the world that created it. We end up back where we departed and with less clarity, over our heads in contemplation, holding up scraps to be recombined, thinking that if we just unlock the potential of all this crap, we'll have the weapons we need.

But, paradoxically, what must be saved is precisely that reification. Salvagepunk must draw out a mode of relating to the cursed inheritances of history through that very elevation of objects to the status of social relations.

What needs to be salvaged are social relations, broken forms of lived communist thought, discarded by our moment as the outmoded waste of a century.[13] These are lost utopian moments, to be sure, but they are also the massive weight of sometimes catastrophic attempts to live differently. Not just the spectral traces of theories and dreams, but the social and historical ruins of concrete attempts to move beyond capitalism. When we talk of occupying trash sites and of building tools from the junkyard, this is what we mean. Not that we should valorize either the waste dweller forced to live in abjection or the cluttered objects themselves, but rather that our relation to our radical history must take the form of salvage. The thought of salvage is the thought of all that is thrown out by the totality of late capitalism, the traditions and horizons of collectivity, solidarity, and true antagonism.

As such, we need this *anti-capitalist reification* of thinking human relations as things and things as embodiments of human relation , even as those things made "for our use" remain darkly independent of us. We need this in order to grasp – apocalyptically, with a sense of both the immanence and imminent returns of these relations – how to relate to what has been ruined, yet persists. The constitutive excess (those material relations of suffering and domination addressed by thoughts of the communist reorganization of life, and the thoughts themselves) cannot ever quietly shuffle off the stage, because it is always created anew, ceaselessly, in every moment of the reproduction and circulation of capital. Like the objects of this outmoding world of planned obsolescence, they are made anew and tossed aside, not broken but declared broken and devoid of value.

Along with being a kind of cultural object that hasn't fully come into its own, salvagepunk is the attempt to use the shards of antagonism and solidarity in the same way that we might sort, sever, detangle, and grasp objects of insistent value from the wasteland. This requires a keen eye toward what needs to be left to rot and a keener eye for how the world order has shifted since the time the things joined the realm of the unwanted. (The exclusion of possibilities and other failed histories itself changes the shape and terrain of the present to be inherited. Our moment is not just defined by what "happened" but equally by what was prevented from happening.) And from there, the grim smile that recognizes past struggle in its momentary successes and its resonant failures. A hacking apart of those past moments, saving something and tossing away more, particularly those traditions in which we've invested too much to see them for the lumbering hindrance they've become. And the montage and assemblage of our moments of real shock and slow resistance, constructs of waste to face off against this hurtling crash of a system predicated on the construction of waste.

KEEPING OURSELVES BUSY AFTER THE END OF THE WORLD

"Oh, we'll just have to keep going?"
"What for?"
"Because we're British."
"British! What a lot of use that is."
- The Bed Sitting Room

The trajectory from relations of waste objects with their venomous use-values to radical social relations lost to our historical moment involves, in the case of this book, a particular privileging of the "cultural" object. Mine is an account neither of the real material practices of sifting through trash nor of the people who have been forced into such labor. Our treatment of them is metaphorical or, more precisely, refracted through the films, books, and general discourse in which those practices and peoples make their figurative appearance. On top of that, these cultural examples are overwhelmingly from the part of the world (the "developed" nations and capitalist powers) who bear far less of the burden of cleaning up their mess. These are not the ideological and political representations of material salvage-work and its consequences.

Rather, they are documents of how the dominant architecture of the late capitalist system thinks itself, however symptomatically and against its better judgment. And more, they are documents of relations: of the world at large, of the labor that produces such a world, of its discarded artifacts, and of its discarded possibilities of other modes of life. Only in taking these relations as a whole, with an eye toward the last, does the work of analytical digging and searching for necessary antecedents result in a longer history of a constant apocalypse (here in its salvagepunk version) and its not very silver linings.

And so...

If there stands, tottering and joyful, a single cultural object of salvage-thought at its best, it is Richard Lester's 1969 film *The Bed Sitting Room*. Not salvage as the undercurrent and inconstant mechanism of capitalist recuperation (squeezing value out of every last scrap). And perhaps not salvagepunk per se, coming before the long downturn and the new world anxieties of cyberpunk. Rather, some kind of dark precursor, funnier and crueler, sloppy and razor-sharp, an under-watched and unmatched template that deserves its due forty years on. Therein lies its weird temporality: in this refuse (just another largely forgotten film), we find what will come to be but hasn't yet. From this dusty history, it casts a different light onto a different end of the '60s, a shaky birth of the long '70s, and the hastening toward the long slow fallout of late capitalist apocalypse.

As such, this is both a drawing forth of some aspects of what salvagepunk might be from the film that does it best and, more simply, an appreciation for a film not watched nearly enough. As such, what follows is a lot of summary and an initial gesture toward situating this amazing thing dropped from the tail of the '60s into our lap. It is very dark, it is very uncomfortable, it is very funny, and it is very, very British.

As one critic put it, it is "like Samuel Beckett, but with better jokes," which should be slightly modified: it's like Samuel Beckett with more obvious jokes. Nominally based on the 1963 Spike Milligan and John Antrobus play, Lester's cinematic version is a staggering vision of waste and remnant, of frozen, necrotic social relations, and of what we keep doing to keep ourselves busy after the end of the world.

What we do, at least at first, is gaze onto the stillness of a world abandoned. The film starts, backed by the soft opening horns of its score, with images of fuzzy flux: staring into the sun, the movement of lava. This gentleness all adds up to the quiet of a world reclaimed by nature, a new pastoralism without shepherds.

However, the reels of unspooled history (not my metaphor: a literal image recurrent throughout the film) start to pile up onto this unspoiled tableau.

With this glimpse of the bomb-hollowed dome of a partially submerged St. Paul's Cathedral (thereby marking the wasteland as London), the sense of a nuclear fallout emerges immediately. Here, in the center of the British empire, is an unavoidable echo of the Hiroshima Atom Bomb Dome.

This resonance acts as an ominous designator of "what happened," but more importantly, as an early sign of the tensions behind the distinct look of the film and its spaces. For the lyrical solitude of the single stump in the rippling water and the minimalist elegance of the sunken dome meet their negation in the unfathomable amounts of waste filling this world, in the oceans of trash, slabs of concrete, rusting infrastructure, all the hallmarks of a catastrophe that left its mess to be cleaned up by the survivors.

In short, the unresolved aesthetic of the film – and its corollary political messiness – is staked on the gap between the empty and the overfull, between a depopulated, vacant world that cannot be filled and a world where repopulation can't start until the rubble is cleared away. There may be only 20 or so survivors, but the ground is never clear. Any starting over anew is still life in the ruins, and not just in a theoretical sense of the end of history.

Yet this is a film which does not beg such a theoretical reading: it insists on it, shoves it on the surface, transforms it into a gag, and repeats it until it is no longer a joke. The film is shot through with a surprisingly subtle dialectic of event and process, which here takes the unsteady form of both the Event (the Bomb, the catastrophic rupture that literally cannot be spoken, resulting in odd gesticulations, much hemming and hawing and making bomb sounds with your mouth) and static process (after the Bomb, the interminable durations and banal rhythms of everyday life, keeping up appearances as long as even one witness remains, going on because we cannot not go on otherwise). In other words, the film takes place between what is done (and over with) and what is done (over and over again). The call of what is to be done, Leninist or otherwise, to jumpstart this halted progression is the stillborn question that hangs over the whole film. One shares the unspoken feeling that *the problem with the apocalypse was that it wasn't apocalyptic enough*: it did not clear away the dead weight of the previous world configuration.[14] It was nearly an anti-apocalypse, a catastrophe in overdrive, in that it seemingly did not reveal the hidden but made hidden what was already visible, what *was* to be done.

This is, of course, the false angle, for isn't really about mourning for the absent New. Rather, it is a real struggle to find the Old worth salvaging. It is a struggle to become post-apocalyptic, a task which requires both remembering the past (speaking the Bomb, preserving old forms of social relation) and forgetting the past (letting it become History, throwing away the inherited relations of domination). You aren't post-apocalyptic because the apocalypse happened, the film stresses. You become post-apocalyptic when you learn to do something better, or at least more morbidly fun, with the apocalyptic remains of the day.

However, the brutal black comedic edge of the film lies in the characters' obstinate non-recognition of this need to do something different, even as they unwittingly forge new relations by play-acting, messing up, and overdoing the old ones. (Inhabiting a world in which one might mutate into God knows what helps encourage this atmosphere of trying to keep a straight face while all that was solid melts into fields of broken crockery.) Theatricality and British stoicism rule the day, but only in name. For despite all these gestures toward the mortified freezing of the stiff upper-lip, the film is so gleefully messy that what rises to the surface is the real creativity of the survivors, scrappy and shabby bastards all. Including, of course, those who adapt to become shaggy dogs and roasted parrots, used dressers and cheap rent bed sitting rooms.

In this way, even the great degree of normalcy becomes merely a junkyard to be raided, primarily for pleasure. A distinctly perverse pleasure that, by getting to be a kinky *Lady Chatterley's Lover*-quoting priest or interrupting your monologue to the dead Queen by dropping your pants and taking a phone call from a lover, doesn't come from poking fun at "boring" social norms but by misplacing them. Continuing to act like we always have in a setting drastically changed can work to excavate the pleasures of acting the part and of faking it.

One of the first characters we meet, the last remaining BBC broadcaster (Frank Thornton), does just this sort of work. Because the BBC ceased to exist when the bomb fell and hence ceased to produce new news, our half-tuxedoed anchor can only repeat, endlessly and in person through the frame of an empty TV set, the "last news" reported before the full nuclear holocaust set in.

In his pitch-perfect newsman baritone, even stopping for the "viewer" to smack the empty TV box to fake-fix the signal, he

gives the last news. The last news, as it turns out, was a summary of the "nuclear misunderstanding that led to the Third World War," a summary occasioned by it being the "third, or is it the fourth" anniversary of the "misunderstanding."[15] And then, the "last recorded statement of the prime minister," in which he boasts of this being the shortest war in recorded history (2 minutes, 28 seconds, including the signing of the peace treaty) and of the speed with which Britain's 40 million dead were buried. Later in the broadcast, as the PM and Mao Tse-Tung enter negotiations to draw up a lease for the rent in "yen-dollars" of an apartment ("this lease means peace in our time"), the real Bomb falls, the one that reduces Britain to the 20 or so survivors.

Striking, here, is the sense of an already post-apocalyptic world driven back into apocalypse: the work of peace and burying has already begun, the new order of the earth in its early solidification (new hybrid currency combinations, a turn from war to battling out conditions of everyday life), and then the Bomb, in all its anonymous fury, unable to be tracked back like the British bomb returned to sender for insufficient postage (more "Chinese dollars" required) later in the film.

This in-folded apocalyptic structure gives the film – and the mode of apocalyptic thought we might draw from it – its peculiar texture of double trauma, of constant work with no end in sight and no capacity to remember historically. Yet the survivors consummately remember the affective textures of life beforehand: those form the source material for both the goofing-off and the weary awareness of having done this all so many times before.

And as mentioned before, this "problem of history" is one made explicit in the film, nowhere more so than in the Prime Minister's speech, which ends with the question, "have we forgotten the Bomb?" and answers itself in the real return of the repressed Bomb. His rhetoric, the official discourse in the film about what's wrong with what's going on, establishes the idea that we need to remember the Bomb better in order to really bury the dead, insofar as the worry is less the stink of corpses and more the psychic and political burden that prevents the refashioning of global economic flows. (A forward echo first to Britain entering the European Economic Committee in 1973 and then the deregulation and financialization of the Thatcher years ...)

Initially, this seems dead-on, a capitalist inversion of Marx's call to cast off the dead weight of the past to write the poetry of the future. But this is arguably the central blindspot – and target – of the film, the false truth that it drags through the filth and mocks, ultimately pointing out that it leads only to new regimes which will drive us straight back to hell. Remembering better may restart the wheels of history, but the question remains: which wheels and which trajectory?

Because what *The Bed Sitting Room* really wants to do, what it is about, and what it ultimately shows the extreme difficulty of, is the full emergence of a salvage mode of life, rather than one of starvation, poverty, and the bellicosity of a post-catastrophic survival of the fittest. Rather, this salvage mode would be one of new networks built on the reclaimed paths of the old, in which forms of care, utility, invention, and mutual aid overwhelm the strictures of class and power by treating them as the obscene jokes they've been from the start.

For example, the PM states in his speech: "We know this great country of ours often sticks in the mud of the past and searches out and holds up to the light the mistakes of past times." In a film at least in part about frivolity in a time and place literally mired in the mud and filth of the past, these words indeed get us halfway to productive salvage thinking. But against this dourness and urge to hold up the mistakes so as to throw them back into the filth and start anew, the lumpen wanderers, hoarders, scammers, and comedians of the film provide an alternative both more pleasurable – for why should the post-apocalyptic world be the dreadful oscillation between boredom and terror? – and more radical in its capacity to reshape the rubbish of their time. And what this looks like, at least initially, is keeping the reels of the past and, etched onto Harry Secombe's remarkable near-orgasm face, taking some serious *the horror, oh the horror* pleasure, like a sweaty teen fingering old and faded 8 mm smut prints.

Clearly, the salvagepunk stance we are advocating does not hit its terminal point in the fallout bunker masturbation of the man who refuses to come out, dwelling with his nasty bits of history. (What he is looking at is documentary footage 'showing' the use of chemical weapons.) But it comes closer in his later role in the film, when an unexpected visitor impels him to leave the bunker, no longer waiting out the dark days, but entering them, with the particularly aim of sharing what he knows. Unspooled reels in hand, he wanders, looking for someone to look at what he loves. In doing so, he comes closer to the notion that what will really break the post-catastrophic spell of "not being able to do better" isn't remembering the Bomb more clearly; after all, the constant memory of it is what allows the sadistic police to keep everyone on the move. Rather, the possibility of a break lies in patching together pleasure and knowledge from what the atomized post-atomic stragglers have.

For what we really want, like our furtive bunker man, is a collective pleasure to be taken in collective work on this. If we stand in a wasteland, the best hope would be to enjoy each other's company, to trade expertise, and to forge collective modes of being together out of the best failed efforts of the past. To repurpose an older formulation, post-apocalyptic survivors have hitherto only remembered the world; the point is to salvage it.

KEEP MOVING!

If this horizon of collectivity persists through the film as a possibility, the real question is: how do people treat one another? The answer falls somewhere between extraordinarily badly, insofar as those people in question are the remaining vestiges of pre-Bomb authority, and with surprising tenderness and care, even if that care takes the form of taking the piss, insofar as those people are everyone else. It's a film whose population might be divided into three as follows:

1. Those who purport to care for your interests are sadistic twits (and we don't mean sadism as a moral judgment but rather as a certain pathological structure of enjoyment, although *twit* remains a moral judgment) whose fidelity to the old structures of power take on new, insidious forms.
2. Those who want something from you are relatively harmless but imbecilic, the guardians of the post-apocalyptic status quo of non-progress.
3. Those who don't have much reason to care whatsoever turn out to be your comrades in making something of the world.

(The notable, and only, exceptions here are the mother, her daughter Penelope, and Penelope's boyfriend Alan, all of whom stand as last vestiges of fidelity to loved ones, and, in this way, often come off a bit sappy, albeit sympathetic.)

To the sadists, then ...

As hinted, the apocalyptic sadist – to be clearly distinguished from the utopian pervert of the trash-heap – is the one whose sadism is not the reason for, but rather a symptomatic consequence of, a kind of vicious new behavior that masquerades as the responsible protection of the few remaining shards of the world before the apocalypse.[16] They are the guardians of bureaucracy and administration: not the aristocratic Lord Fortnam in his eccentric doddering and disconnection from the production of value, but the arch representative of the middle class (the subway family patriarch) and the apparatuses of the state management of life (the police and the National Health Service). While they incessantly invoke family values, convention, keeping up appearances, and maintaining the systematic ordering of society, their speech is merely a blind for the cruelty of their actions. They try to bring forth from the ashes of civilization a new, nastier, more efficient world. They are those for whom the apocalypse was a happy accident.

The father (just called "Father" through the film) most embodies this sense of capitalizing on the Bomb to shore up his authority, allowing him the primal fantasy of hunting for his tribe, even if what he hunts are candy bars left in the subway loop's vending machines. If anything, the tough repetitive work of keeping up appearances shoots holes in his fantasies, although he guards it as an option for whenever he needs to assert his position as anchor to the lost past. Rather, when he returns from the "hunt," and his wife responds politely, "ah, you're home early tonight, Father," one gets the sense that what he really wants is to be treated like the brute caveman he'd like to be. In lieu of that, at least he can take satisfaction in knowing that he has secured his position as the only one who brings home the bacon, or chocolate, no matter what the sexual revolution and the broad social shifts of the '60s may have said.

Eventually, the limited resource economy of an abandoned subway loop – both chocolate and suitors for Penelope of whom Father would approve – runs out, and the family, boyfriend Alan in tow, enter the world above, dumped unceremoniously into the light by an escalator to nowhere.

The world they enter is a world of ceaseless movement, of never being able to stop and rest. The electricity to power the train (and the "nation" as a whole) is just one man on a stationary bicycle, who, fittingly, pedals constantly and goes nowhere. In the first minutes of the film, he is seen slumped over his bars and is woken, with the encouragement to "liven him up with your truncheon, Constable" from the film's arch-sadists: the inspector (Peter Cook) and his sergeant (Dudley Moore, who will end the film transformed into a sheepdog), who circle the wasteland in a rusted out car held aloft by a hot air balloon and tugged about by the constable, a sort of mobile scrap-metal panopticon.

Later, in a much more direct show of coercion, Britain's pedaling power source is interrupted while brushing his teeth by the one remaining instrument of state violence, the bulldozer with its wrecking ball. Unsurprisingly, he finds the energy to pedal madly and smile to the circling Inspector.

But while the coercive injunctions to the cyclist at least have a degree of utility (his movement produces energy to power the train, although the need for the train to keep moving is deeply questionable), the general and incessant command to the rest of those below lacks this entirely. To take one such example of this urging from above (which primarily takes the truncated form of the bullhorn-distorted injunction, "Keep moving ... Keep moving!"):

> "We don't want to stay in one place long enough for the enemy to have another chance at us, do we, sir? Not until our preemptive strike is launched, do we, sir? Do we, sir?"

Behind the absurdity of this (given the fact that clearly no member of this ragged and hungry bunch is in any condition to launch a strike, pre-emptive or not) lies a more serious sense of the fallout of the Bomb. For what the film makes clear is just how unclear everyone remains about who the enemy is and, moreover, to what degree the enemies were themselves reduced to a group of chocolate scavengers, aimless roamers, and, eventually, animals and inanimate objects. In other words, *post-apocalyptic* here does not mean that we have witnessed the destruction of our society or nation. It means that we don't know who our enemies are anymore. The very category of enemy is rendered diffuse, reduced to the bad smell of fear stinking up the place.

The crisis this provokes, consequently, is one of not knowing who we are anymore. Following the thinking of German political and juridical theorist Carl Schmitt, we might draw out the basic point that it is only the conception of the enemy – of what constitutes not just an existential threat to us but a political-cultural threat to the primacy of "our way of life" – that produces a conception of the "friend," (in this case, Brits and their allies). The concept of the political is this very opposition, for Schmitt: it is the structuring principle on which the whole architecture of citizenship and national allegiance turns. In other words, this messy collection of different class positions, occupations, histories, and all the rest only become a nation, or a politically bounded entity, when they hate in unison. All together now ...

Two things come of this, about what the "post-apocalyptic" does and could mean, in this film and beyond.

First, if an apocalyptic Event is the revelation of the hidden, the post-apocalyptic stance and position is that of managing that new old knowledge: what's been there all along, what we should have known. In the Christian eschatological vision, the apocalypse is the making-clear that makes possible knowing who the real enemies are. No more masked devils or cunning unbelievers, no more faceless violence of the system. Rather, the good versus the bad and the ugly.

However, *The Bed Sitting Room* and the salvagepunk aesthetic more generally grasps that we've been living after the apocalypse for a while now, and that *the problem is too much of the hidden has been revealed*. Too much uncovered data, too many telling images, too many public secrets. It's piling up everywhere and making it impossible to find the correct enemies, the right cracks to widen, the right ways to attack and build better. In this sense, salvagepunk post-apocalypticism is concerned with being more apocalyptic than the apocalypse: clearing away the clutter to reveal the true hidden-in-plain-view, namely, the deep, permanent antagonisms on which capitalism runs and the untenability of that system's capacity to still run.

Second, the "end of enemies" is more than the dissolution of what "we" are. It is the end of politics itself, not here defined as the friend/enemy opposition itself but closer to what Badiou has offered: "collective action, organized by certain principles, that aims to unfold the consequences of a new possibility which is currently repressed by the dominant order."[17] As such, it is the end of the kind of "we" that we could become. Without the real sense of the enemy (both the abstraction of the dominant order itself and the human agents of its perpetuation), we cannot unfold, into the ruins of history, any thoughts of consequence.

However, this "end of politics," in which *The Bed Sitting Room* may be situated, does not mean that the old structures of power go away, resulting in disorder and non-antagonistically defined possibilities. To the contrary: it is this end of politics that allows for a monstrous work of holding onto power, guarding its previously defined positions while changing its shape and directions. More concretely, it lets you use the inertia of social structures as a cover-story while you go about constructing domination all the nastier for your claims to be the rational administration of care and resources.

And there certainly is plenty of social structure inertia here, a tenacious holding onto old roles, at least in their trappings. You may get to "tell off your betters" now that the established social hierarchy isn't there to condemn it, but the positions don't really change. All that is known is what we were, or so we tell ourselves. Meanwhile we all just become a bit shabbier and a lot better at surviving and innovating.

The particular set of stock roles we have in the film produce this effect, a sort of cross-section portrait of British society. As such, we have a mailman, a doctor, a broadcaster, a lord, policemen, a middle-class patriarch, a health service bureaucrat, industrial labor, royalty, the solid and stoic mother, and the young hip generation. (Plus a wandering Chinese Red Army solider.) We have the promise, although frozen, of the reproduction of the population. We have both the labor of running – and running around – the country and the diversions that make it enjoyable, including casual sex, dancing on broken plates, domestic fetish scenarios, throwing rocks, and, mostly, a constant stream of puns.

It is worth drawing out the historical particularity of the film, shot in 1968, and held back from release by its deeply unimpressed backers before its release in early 1970. The end of the British '60s lacked that sense of imminent change, of real social unrest and the possibility of systemic collapse, that marked France in 1968 and Italy in 1969, or the height of the American civil rights movement and the increased visibility of mass "counterculture" in the same period. Britain's 68-69 came in 73-74, one might say, the years of mass strikes, bloody IRA violence, economic turmoil, and the return of Harold Wilson and the Labour government.

Compared to that other great film of wreckage and the collapse of a Fordist model of capitalism, Jean-Luc Godard's *Weekend* (1967), which is shot through with the slow-motion bloody violence of the apocalyptic crash itself, *The Bed Sitting Room* remains a quieter film, brutal in its own ways. This is ultimately a consequence of the fact that it is a post-apocalyptic, rather than an apocalyptic, film. But not simply because the apocalyptic content of violence and destruction has already happened, and we're stuck in the aftermath. Rather, *The Bed Sitting Room*, against the grain of its salvagepunk aesthetic, depicts the formation of a new mode of governance and life, namely, the neoliberalism born out of the crises of the early '70s. More simply, the film isn't about the end of the '60s. It's more about the start of the long neoliberal nightmare – the one crystal- lized in cyberpunk – from which we are just beginning to wake, perhaps to something worse. (Hence the deep resonance of the film for our times, in which we again witness that regime of accumulation in an unstable, uncertain state, albeit from the other end of its historical arc.)

In the film's extended moment of uncertainty, it is those hollow shells of absent governance and administration which are most preserved. One goes on working in one's capacity, even after the old form of compulsion is gone. You keep acting like a policeman even when there is no more police. And you make damn sure that everyone is doing his or her part to maintain that fragile edifice of the past.

The real horror that emerges, out of the sadistic fun of getting to be the kind of yelling, floating cop you've always wanted to be, is the emergence of "biopolitical" administration. Or more precisely, a death-centered ordering of life under the rationalized veil of keeping everything in line.

This broad concept of biopolitics, which has numerous itera-tions not worth going into here, can be broadly thought as the kind of governance concerned not with a society of individuals but with a population of bodies. Politics becomes the "management" of that population, working on it through all the channels of health services, disease prevention, welfare, housing, spatial distribution, and so on. Politics becomes the attempt to dictate the terms of mortality, with a particular emphasis on the "death" end of the life cycle.

In *The Bed Sitting Room*, this becomes even more necropolitical in its orientation, given that the nightmare-haunting, pure-sadist remainder of the National Health Service (Marty Feldman in all his cockeyed creepy glory) spends his time passing out death certificates to those still alive, as well as delivering, or perhaps aborting, dead babies in his inflatable operating room. The occasion of the death certificate, handed not to the living "dead" (the mother of the family) but to her husband, produces the chilling core of the film, of death in the record books that no one keeps as the harbinger and guarantee of real death to come: "What I have here, sir, is your wife's death certificate."

This phantom reach of bureaucracy and administered death into the realm of the living works as a perfect example of the logic of the real abstraction, the basic thought-unit of capitalism itself. It is both description (that which is already past, the whole nation already dead and the few survivors on their way, an echo of her recollection that before the Bomb, she wished it would come and kill the whole world) and prescription (the certificate, like a speech act, makes it so, condemns her to her descent into the underworld, literalized here in her entering the subterranean bunker). Real conditions on the ground must be forced to comply with the records of the world: the ultimate sleight of hand that declares how things are as a way to bring about that state of affairs. (Think here of oil futures: speculating on the future value of oil, a "calculated" guess as to what economic conditions and factors will be, itself changes the conditions described and pushes the price toward the estimate. Or, if we prefer, like the third pre-cog seer in Phillip K. Dick's "Minority Report," whose prediction of the future is based on the effects of previous predictions being known, which thereby affects the future actions described.)

Most unsettling is the lack of resistance to a declaration which clearly has no force behind it. There is no government, only the historical residue of names and procedures from the past administrations. Her own resignation to it ("I thought I was alive, but here it is in black and white . . .") is the consequence of the younger generation silently accepting the fact, cowed in the face of Father urging her to accept the fact of her death. In the most vicious recourse to a false sense of what being British means in terms of respecting order, he urges this acceptance so as to complete their scrapbook of official records, from birth certificates to the marriage license. As Feldman's NHS man puts it, "it's your wife being alive that seems to be all the trouble," and we get the impression that Father might well agree with this.

This is indeed a death-world in which being alive is all the trouble and perhaps not especially worth the trouble. For all the jokes and joy taken in playing around in the junk heaps, weariness and fatigue hang heavy on every scene and in the faces of the newly nomadic, threatened that if they stop moving, those prescriptive death certificates may be made murderous fact. Just the slow entropy and sadness of the remnants of the nation, unable to reproduce and prevented, by their own complicity with the last gasps of police order, from settling down to form a community.

That is, of course, until a new option appears on the scene. And one does appear here, just in the nick of time: not finding a space to settle and start over, but becoming that space yourself. (In the mother's case, not finding a hiding place but becoming one herself.) Not occupying temporary buildings, but becoming, radiation-cursed, a real building for temporary occupation. The resistance to biopolitical horror and forced transience may lie in the transformation into something that escapes the realm of the administration of human bodies and that cannot keep moving, a sticking point of inertia on the strewn plains. At least until the bulldozers come.

KNOCKED DOWN WITHOUT THE OPTION

This possibility of becoming an object or an animal, and thereby escaping the shittiness of being human in this post-apocalyptic world, becomes desirable in response to two conditions.

First, the end of the sexual reproduction, the No Future birth crisis resulting from both radioactive sterility/mutation and, more importantly, the refusal of the prospective mother, Penelope, to bring her baby into this "wicked world." She carries "little Rupert" around in her for 17 months rather than birth him to this world, and he is still-born – or murdered – at the hands of the National Health Service. This issue of post-apocalyptic birth crisis is a major one, both here (of the three women we see alive, two are post-menopausal, and the third isn't sure she wants to even be a mother) and throughout the scattered examples of the genre.[18] That said, it is arguably the least interesting aspect of *The Bed Sitting Room*'s apocalyptic imaginings, insofar as it functions as a sort of non-option magically restored at the end.

The second condition, the one around which our investigation has been circling, is the constancy of movement and the inability to resettle. These are neither the hardy survivors clinging tooth and nail to a last outpost nor hardscrabble settlers starting anew in a Mad Max outback. Scattered across the space of ex-London with as much care as the rest of the refuse and broken things, those who were situated leave those spaces (the train car, the bunker) to join the rest of the permanently itinerant.

It is only when Lord Fortnam becomes a bed sitting room that this changes.

It is not incidental that this transformation gives the film its title, for the bed sitting room itself is at once the center of its arc, the site of hope, and the casualty of the ruling order's destruction of that hope. If salvagepunk represents an attempt to think lost social relations via relations to discarded objects, in this instance, we witness this process in a very particular reversal: the social parasite – the aristocratic Lord Fortnam who slept blissfully through the Bomb – becomes a site of ultimate use-value, shelter from the nuclear storm. In becoming object, he becomes the direct negation of his social role (the one who stands above, and indirectly profits from, the poor and their need for temporary housing) in the material form of a site for collective social relations, for (in a bad and literal pun) post-nuclear families to take shape.

Not that he is happy about this in the least. We meet him far before his long march, when he visits the doctor to complain that he is worried of what he suspects is his imminent transformation. (In this he differs very much from the mother, who seems relieved to become a cabinet, insofar as it lets her rest for a minute, as well as becoming a sexually desirable "thing" again: the great "get your hands out of my drawers, I'm a mother" joke as well as the later sounds of surprised pleasure as the long-suffering doctor steps inside of her.) Lord Fortnam, on the other hand, is rather frightened and quite pissed off by the prospect, as in the following exchange with the doctor on what he can take to remedy his condition of becoming a place of lodging.

"What can I take for it?"
"Three guineas."
"Three guineas."
"Three guineas ... for your rent."
"Rent! I ... I don't want rent! I want to be cured!"

Even after his transformation, he remains a bristly curmudgeon, reluctant to accept not only the fact that he is a lodging for the poor but that he now stands in what would have been the Paddington borough ("That's pretty bad news, I'm afraid. Paddington."), a zone not up to his aristocratic standards. In response, he demands: "Put a card in the window. No coloreds. No children. And definitely no colored children."

Yet in spite of these protestations, these lingering poisons of the old social hierarchy, the bed sitting room is a constitutive break in the logic of this self-repeating, self-consuming world of the nearly dead. While the characters speculate that Lord Fortnam's disappearance might be the result of the "first act of post-war murder," what we see is the first act of *settling*. Echoing the Mao and PM treaty to fix the rent of the apartment, this is co-habitation beyond money, a dismantling of the structures of *rentier* capital that freeze wealth into a site for the constant bleeding of wages from the already destitute. The doctor's response to finding the lord as bed sitting room - "I'd recognize you anywhere, my lord. I must say it suits you" - is at once a jab at the idiotic pride of the lord and the mark of a genuine move forward: what suits the lord now is the total unmaking of what he would have meant, not via an act of purgative destruction but by an act of construction. Nuclear or magical it may be, but it is nevertheless an immobile outpost for life above ground, a solid point of resistance in the wind-swept open expanse, opposed to the pocket underworlds of bunkers and subways we've seen so far.

In other words, a new topology in its barest, shoddiest incarnation, a fixed node that can't "keep moving" and around which a community could crystallize. Or, at the very least, around which something like a community could even start to be thought once more. The New, here, is far from utopian, at least in its form of positing an other world. It is simply taking the world – and "taking the room" – as it is, settling for and settling down.

However, while this approximates a crucial sense of the salvagepunk aesthetic (taking the dead world as it is), it also cuts back against it, in a willful betrayal of this possibility that comes to fruition in the deep dystopian core of the "happy ending" that is anything but. For what we see in the bed sitting room itself is a tendency caught between two positions:

1. the idea of making do with what cannot be undone, colonizing better, and settling down
2. the fantasy of creation out of nothing, starting from fertile scratch, a birth of life and light, the transformation of the species, the new in all its messianic eschatology of the world (and its occupants) becoming unlike itself

The deep intelligence of the film lies in recognizing not just the tough work of salvage but the extreme difficulty of holding out one's right to the ruins of the old world against a political order quick to snatch up any advances, any new models, any new knowledge produced from below. It requires not just the innovations of those barely scraping by but also the destruction of those innovations, their energy and kernels of new thought blasted apart and swallowed into the rhetoric and administration of the ruling class. Concretely, in *The Bed Sitting Room*, you wait for the wandering poor to learn how to settle down before destroying their settlement. And you wait for them to remember the Bomb for you before you become the embodiment and inheritor of what the Bomb means.

At the end of the film, it takes the form of following through on the doctor's warning to the lord/bed sitting room: "try not to look conspicuous, or you'll be knocked down without the option." In a rather hectic sequence, an itinerant declares, "that's why He dropped the bomb!" Immediately following the vocalization of "the bomb," those two unspeakable syllables, we get a flurry of quickly cut shots, in which each character, tenuously or with a rising joy, repeats: *the bomb?*

At this very moment, the wrecking ball of the police bulldozer smashes through the wall of the bed sitting room. Panic ensues, as the Bomb (the memory of the total, anonymous destruction of the nation) becomes the willful Bomb (the material fact of conscious destruction of what was built without the sanction of those who claim to rule). And then this exchange, starting with the booming voice of Lord Fortnam, cutting through the melee.

LORD FORTNAM: "Stop. Stop. Stop in the name of the Lord."

POSTMAN: "It's God. He's come back on us. Good, good old mate. For he's a jolly good fellow. He's a socialist, you know."

LORD FORTNAM: "Quiet, Labour scum."

POSTMAN: "Ah! He's ... he's a bleeding conservative!"

DOCTOR: "Now hold on a minute, you don't sound like God, you sound like Lord Fortnam!"

LORD FORTNAM: "I also, I uh, I also do impressions"

This is followed by various pleas for God to save them from "the dreadful radiation," to give back Penelope's dead child, and to be saved generally, backed by the promise of giving up atheism. Then the "real" voice of God steps in: the floating police inspector, to whose first words the doctor responds, "That's God. I recognize the voice." (Of interest here, among other things, is that if anyone is to step in to the role of the new God, it will not be the icon of the old social order, Lord Fortnam. It can only be the lead voice of the post-apocalyptic sadists we have heard from the start, waiting for the rest to remember so he, and the emergent biopolitical regime, can claim to be what everyone was waiting for all along.)

The speech he gives, arguably the high point of the film's already razor-edged writing, needs to be included here in full.

The full brunt and cut of British late '60s satire – *Monty Python's Flying Circus, Steptoe and Son,* and *O Lucky Man!,* among others – deploys here.

> *I expect you may be wondering why I've invited you all here this afternoon. I've just come from an audience with Her Majesty, Mrs. Ethel Shroake, and I'm empowered by her to tell you that, in the future, clouds of poisonous nuclear fog will no longer be necessary. Mutations will cease sine die and, furthermore, I'm the bringer of glad tidings. A team of surgeons at the Woolwich hospital have just accomplished the world's first successful complete body transplant. The donor was the entire population of South Wales, and the new body is functioning normally. I, myself, saw it sit up in bed, wink, and ask for a glass of beer.*
>
> *All in all, I think we're in for a time of peace, prosperity and stability, when the earth will burgeon forth anew, the lion will lie down with the lamb, and the goat will give suck to the tiny bee.*
>
> *At times of great national emergency, you'll often find that a new leader tends to emerge. Here I am - so watch it.*
>
> *Keep moving, everybody, that's the spirit! Keep moving!*

There is more here than can be digested without somehow capturing just how it feels to hear these words at the end of watching the film, a combination of triumph, disgust, bile, and laughter. We can, nevertheless, draw out a couple of points to situate this within, and largely against, the salvagepunk strain of post-apocalyptic thought. This speech itself is an apocalypse, the third one of the film (the first and second being the nuclear war and the Bomb, respectively), for it is the revelation of the hidden, the laying bare of the not-so-covert violence of coercion with a more vicious sense of what had been out of view, namely, that this was managed from the start. It shows us that the post-apocalyptic crisis was willfully created to do two things: first, to wear down the resistance of the last remnants of the old (via the injunctions to keep moving), and second, to give the excuse to smash up the first remnants of a emergent new order (now visible in the gaping hole of the bed sitting room). The management of the "necessary," the declaration of a "national emergency," even when there is nothing of the nation left beyond that very emergency: is there no better vision of this state of exception, of claiming extrajuridical power, than this defense of the nation against the already evident fact of the nation's total destruction?

On top of that, biopolitics removes its facade and show itself, the full horror of calculating the value of lives. Echoing Jonathan Swift's "A Modest Proposal," here we find an entire population recombined into a single body, a fact calculated both to represent the moving forward of the world from here (if not birth, then Frankensteinean undead life out of the assemblage of corpses) and to make clear what kind of world it's going to be: if too conspicuous, you'll be knocked down, if not conspicuous enough to matter in the global order, you'll be hacked up to make one new post-apocalyptic citizen.

On top of that, there is a hyperfecundity to the new order, the cross-species "laying down with each other" forming the backdrop for the sudden birth of a new child for Penelope and Alan. To foreshadow the nightmare image of zombies, this is a world both of the possibilities of overpopulation (the teeming spheres of the babies "out of nothing," in zones that cannot support them) and of the false necessity of total decimation. The film remains, in part, a darkly cynical tale of what we lose when we agree to let ourselves be told what the apocalypse means. The threads of salvagepunk which remain at the end are hence a resistance to, and deep suspicion, of this morbid world. Salvagepunk is a kicking back against these visions of the rational management of life and death, of the industrial subcurrents hidden behind state care and humanitarian interventions. It is a different cartography of the already dead not even buried, surfaces we forget only if we stay below ground.

Cruelest of all: "Keep moving, everybody, that's the spirit! Keep moving!" Walking off toward the sunset means walking away from the only real hope for life. This is repetition compulsion not of the pathological individual but of History itself, the obscene brutality of doing it over and over: "Great Britain is a first-class nuclear power again." And so, like the *Mad Max* trilogy and like so much of salvagepunk, the deep, wracking sadness of knowing what will be forgotten and who will die, a feedback loop of rotting waste piling high toward the sky, too often overwhelms the adversarial role of salvage we have been advocating, the productive, innate-venom-releasing work of organizing minds, bodies, and needs better through sharper relations to the past's present ruins.

It is a problem, ultimately, of what mode of "the negative" we use. Salvagepunk is fundamentally a negative operation, even at its moment of construction, because it deals with non-wholes. The goal is never the restoration of a positive entity, but rather an assemblage of negatives: cast out by the system or, in the longer task of montage, cut out to be put together otherwise. To celebrate the given and the inherited by doing necessary violence to it.

It is always haunted, to be sure, by the prospect of a bad negativity of grey sadness, just staring blankly at the piles of refuse yet never refusing. Yet that is a risk to be run, given that the affirmation of the positive is decisively on the side of the enemy, the often asubjective structures giving shape to regimes and their historical moment. The positive, as we see it in *The Bed Sitting Room* and in the ruling ideologies of late capitalism, is at once a rejection of the New in favor of preserving (and restoring) an old social order seemingly lost in the rubble, and a defense of the New (as the ongoing process of making new whole beings out of nothing) as the thing to be restored. In other words:

the New as restoration itself (what is new is the "new leader" emerging, the police inspector's face as the guarantee of going back to how things used to be)

and the restoration of the New (the orders of domination are restored by a biopolitical and messianic language and practice of newness, from the earth burgeoning forth anew and babies created out of the air, to the era of new peace and new nuclear power status)

"Progress" means making one whole positive body out of the severed corpses of an entire population, burying the work of negation under the fantasy of the "transplant," of the metamorphosis of the undifferentiated into a single positive entity. The body politic made singular and manageable.

Even the sublime gag of Mrs. Ethel Shroake, the closest relative to the queen, awkwardly astride a horse beneath an *arc de triomphe* of debilitated washing machines, cannot fully mitigate this sense of defeat. Our graveside smile is one thing, the prospect of halting the ceaseless graveyard march another. Salvagepunk knows damn well that the issue is not to stop repeating and to fall into the logic of the enemy, the logic of the New restoration. The question is, has been, and will be how to repeat differently, how to make from the broken same the livelier constructs of something other.

A GRAMMAR OF RUST AND BOLTS AND THOUGHT

To conclude this initial attempt at salvage-thought, we ask: how do we repeat differently, then? Yamaguchi Hiroki's *Hellevator: The Bottled Fools* (2004) points in another direction, toward a literally underground possibility. In *Hellevator* (a rather remarkable J-horror/sci-fi that combines, at least for its powerful first forty minutes, the always-moving-standing-still of late

Beckett with a filthier, obscene version of Terry Gilliam's *Brazil*), we occupy a subterranean city traversed by elevators which travel up and down the monolithic slab of the underground society. It is haunted throughout by the implicit awareness of an unspecified and unspoken disaster that has forced dwellers below, under the fist of a totalitarian transit authority and their total surveillance, resulting in a mole-life of grime and rules, of sararimen and salvage-men. The ascendant proletariat move vertically past the floors of their lumpenproletariat black market associates.

All has the feel of salvage work, of an end to the digital age, returning to dials and gears and steam and pistons (nearly steampunk, even). There is none of the sleek sterilization of most sci-fi. We are given to think that this is the space of those who have taken refuge. When the protagonist is banned for psychotic murders and sent up to the surface, one waits for a nuclear wasteland populated with the likely mutated outcasts. Instead, in the film's final frame, we see her emerge to stand before the Eiffel Tower, illuminated in the night sky. Schizoid hallucination aside, the final turn undoes the implicit extra-narrative framework and shows us that this way of life is a choice, the choice of those who see their subterranean life as privilege, the seclusion from the cunning and contingency of the world above.

Perhaps, then, the salvagepunk world should be seen, like *Hellevator*, primarily as the dreamwork of choice and construction. Against the reactionary trendlines of *Mad Max*'s doomed-to-repeat trajectory, it is a world of stealing from the ruins, robbing the graves, and making do. Yet also against *Hellevator*, it is a refusal to secede from that world. And to do so not in stuck pockets but in a settling that remains mobile.

Raised to the figure of the city itself, we're moving from the "impossible" utopian visions of Ron Herron's Walking City ...

... to the clunking hull of *Howl's Moving Castle*, magical engine aside. Not constructed to remake the world one mobile city at a

time, but a principle of montage, of bits and pieces, rags and bones. Not the dwelling places and movements of a fluid multitude but our resistant will and resistant, willful things.

Salvage will bloom everywhere, but we're not there yet, not walking and clanking tall. As a first step, and moving in reverse back from cinema to its lived consequences, where better to start crossing wires and firing up repurposed old engines, than here, the *Waterworld* attraction at the Universal Studios theme park, built from scratch to look like it's built from waste . We might take the objects designed to approximate the end of the world and see what actually can be done with them, what can be barricaded and bridged. Sharpen fake oil drums and the worn grooves of culture and money into tools of dismantling and world-making, the gravedigger's spade and salvagepunk's grammar of rust and bolts and thought.

Plague in the gears

. . . it is evident that there is something uncanny about this reality. Its disproportion to the powerless subject, which makes it incommensurable with experience, renders reality unreal with a vengeance. The surplus of reality amounts to its collapse; by striking the subject dead, reality itself becomes deathly.
(Theodor Adorno, *Aesthetic Theory*)

BART: "Dad! You killed the zombie Flanders!"
HOMER: "He was a zombie?"
(*The Simpsons*, "Treehouse of Horror III")

BAD SURVIVORS

In these dark, anxious years, the undead are having their day in the sun. None more so than zombies: the contemporary vision of the walking dead horde has, without doubt, become the nightmare image of the day, a necrotic counterpart to salvagepunk's dream work. But "nightmare image" should be taken in a doubled sense. First, the image as vehicle for the explicit content of the reigning cultural bad dream – zombies! cannibals! graves! – and hence what is repeated ceaselessly until the trope generates no further profit. Second, the image as manifestation of that most contemporary nightmare, an eternal present of the world not coming to an end. It is the sign of a closure, a terminus of the chance of something being different, a rejoinder to salvagepunk. A morbid suspicion that no amount of repurposing can break the banal spell of the present without getting stuck in the stalemate of brain-eating nihilism.

In our transition from salvagepunk's grave robbing to zombie graves that rob themselves, we also pass from a cultural and political form to be cultivated to one that needs to be put to rest.

To adopt the language of the genre itself, we need to kill the undead so as to locate what may have been worth saving. This is a necessary excavation of something still very thriving, even as it becomes more and more hollow, its idiotic self-knowing smirk bleeding out from every conceivable outlet.

For it is a frenzy indeed.

If it wasn't already apparent, recent years have made it incontrovertible: the media flurry around Seth Grahame-Smith's lamentable mash-up novel *Pride and Prejudice and Zombies* (2009), LOLzombies (and "moar brainz"), zombie flash mobs, endless videogame versions (from new iterations of the *Resident Evil* series to *Left 4 Dead* where you get to be the zombie mob), zombie-themed knitting patterns, neo-grindhouse productions like *Zombie Strippers* (2008), bad kitsch zombie musicals (*Z! A Zombie Musical* [2007]), fake how-to survival guides and "reports" from the zombie holocaust (*World War Z* [2006]), our general discourse of the return of unwanted labor in the collapsing era of financialization, the desperate attempts to cash in again on the older George Romero legacy, the Danny Boyle *28 Days Later* (2002) version of contagion zombies, and *Shaun of the Dead*'s (2004) romantic comedy zombie gags. Hell, even *The Economist* can't leave it alone: a cover from February 2009 illustrates the "return of economic nationalism" with a necrotic, clutching hand bursting from its grave.

Our point isn't to be dour, or to fall into the trap of claiming master knowledge, a walking dead version of the cult music fan: *I've been watching these from back before they were cool, and now I feel betrayed by zombies selling out.* Rather, the story to be told is how the zombie film, now arguably *the* dominant vision of apocalypse in the latest stages of "late" capitalism, has produced distinct captures of a certain thought about totality and of how real abstractions affect real bodies. In the self-perpetuation of the genre, however, that thought has transformed, a consequence of shifting political landscapes, attempts to make "political films"

73

(for example, the not-very-veiled critiques of consumerism), and the internal pressures of the horror genre (out of which the attempts to repeat with fidelity and minor difference produce long-term mutations of what zombies do and what we do about them).

So if salvagepunk is the dream image vision of rust-and-bolts restructuring of the ruined built world, the lurch and rot of zombie hordes is its seeming negation. The obscene persistence of the human animal shows itself, and not as built or builder. Salvagepunk's *homo faber* (Man the Maker) meets its *homo superstes* (Man the Survivor), defined not by how it refashions the apocalyptic world but by the bare fact of its survival (beyond its own personal world-ending event, its death), a survival that nevertheless signals the end of the collective world as we know it.

In other words, in the zombie scenario, the problem is not the immensity of what is to be done by the too few survivors, the problem confronted and fetishized in so many visions of the ruined, vacant world. Nor is it how to make a world so as to avoid its trendlines toward systemic failure while still salvaging and repurposing the ruined tools of the "before." The problem, faced with zombies, is that there are too many survivors.[19]

Yet it is always the wrong kind of survivor. In an echo of surging anxieties about overpopulation, the "planet of the slums," contaminated commodities from afar, and the ongoing degradation of the global south, the passion for all things zombie has the quality of a perverse, almost subversive joke. Rather than the production of corpses that results from capitalism's management (supported coups, ignored genocides, blocking of access to food and medication, destruction of ecosystems, poorly constructed infrastructure) of its unwanted poor, the production of corpses in the zombie scenario becomes the assembly of *more* mouths to feed. World hunger at its most naked, the sick repetition of want let loose on a global scale. Yet we need to bear in mind the specificity of the recent period of zombie-fixated culture and its fixation with contagion. For in this wave, exemplified by Boyle's *28 Days Later* films, the focus is less on the insatiable hunger of the zombie and more on the danger of the bite and the transfer of the virus. To be sure, we might read in this persistence of fears about pandemics, AIDS, and other "literal" figures of contagion and transfer via the bodily act. But this would miss the crucial aspect at hand, namely, why the undead aren't even undead anymore – and why they perhaps never have been.

To give our investigation of the buried politics of the undead an appropriately "wrong" starting point, we might begin with this poster from the Situationist International. It was produced right around the years in which Romero made *Night of the Living Dead* (1968) and when the trajectory toward our zombie-present commenced openly. We start here with the bloodied, one-eyed glare of the accusing, raised up to get beaten down again, the endless cycle of not being allowed to die and being blamed for that fact. Not the campy schlock of the mass moaning "brains ..." but the quiet rage and planning of the group in formation. *Bourgeois, you have understood nothing,* and we have some things to teach you. The collective pedagogy of those beyond the pale.

FUNNY, IT'S NOT USUALLY THIS HARD TO KILL THE POOR ...

Romero's *Night of the Living Dead,* the real launching point of zombies into mass culture, is one of those odd "foundational" films. It has its antecedents, to be sure, in three major strands. First, the voodoo-inflected zombies of, for example, Victor Halperin's *White Zombie* (1932), Jacques Tourneurs's *I Walked with a Zombie* (1943), and the shoddy knock-offs of both (i.e. the remarkable/awful *Zombies on Broadway* from 1945). Second, a more direct inspiration for what Romero was "trying to do," Richard Matheson's 1954 novel *I Am Legend.* This would also include Ubaldo Ragona's 1964 film adaptation, *The Last Man on Earth*, in which we watch a survivor defend a house against hordes of the invading undead, perhaps the most common image found across zombie movies. Third, a tangled mess of aesthetic and formal influences that give the film its distinct look: film noir lighting, *Psycho*-era Hitchcock camera angles, newsreel footage, art-house discontinuous cutting and spatial disorientation, and the basic fact of doing the whole thing for very, very little money. All that said, *Night of the Living Dead* fires a shot in the dark: excepting the third strand of all the aesthetic/formal elements cobbled together, it is a singular film, largely in just how far it goes in leaving behind those antecedents.

But like other horror films that seemingly start a genre-defining image (*Nosferatu* [1922], *Frankenstein* [1931], etc), *Night of the Living Dead* is already weirder and more sharply knowing about its absent source material than it "should" be: it seem to play with, and off of, an established template that cannot be found.[20] Romero's film establishes the rules of the genre to follow in its wake, from the "look" of the film to the kinds of stock characters and settings, from the broad tones and set moves to the effects it aims to have on the audience. Yet at the same time, *Night of the Living Dead* is already screwing around with those very rules: it defines a genre by the way that it "misreads" source material that was never there, at least not in any immediately accessible direct lineage.

In other words, like other films that inaugurate endless series of imitators, spin-offs, reloads, mash-ups, and sequels, *Night of the Living Dead* – the "original" – is original largely because it nails something about "what we've seen before" and know very well. It articulates the new via the inherited tropes and moves of the old: the inherited language of film conventions eases us in and makes even that which we've never seen before seem familiar, well-worn, and expected. Conversely, what seems recognizable immediately, the "ah, yes, here we go again," is precisely the point of departure into the uncertain, where it turns and goes the wrong way. Fittingly for the film that starts "the zombie film" per se, the uncanny and unsettling happens because something goes through the motions wrongly, just like the zombie's obscene parody of the movements and habits of everyday life. The zombie film, both in its generic content and in how it relates to other genres, is situated in a gap between the inertia of a genre or historical moment's norms and a yearning pull toward other, weirder directions that entirely leave behind the expected and everyday. And more particularly, it elaborates and widens that gap as the crack through which the unwanted pour in.

Think here of the beginning of *Night of the Living Dead*, where the first zombie we see – the first recognizable zombie of late capitalism – looks like nothing so much as a homeless drifter of sorts, a gaunt raggedy man. Tellingly, Barbara and Johnny, her soon-to-be-zombified brother, hardly give him a second glance: at worst, he'll ask them to spare some change. He is not marked as undead, at least not in the technical sense. Just as unwanted. Therein lies the explosion out of and against the accepted codes of who we recognize and who we don't: the zombie's furious attack, which here has nothing to do with trying to eat them, is the feral assertion of the right to be noticed. Even to the end of the encounter, we can practically read on Johnny's face the bourgeois frustration: *funny, it's not usually this hard to kill the poor...*

GNASHING AT THE AIR

It is now a commonplace for theorists and critics to elevate zombie films, along with other splatter and dismemberment oriented film, by arguing that they tell us something new about the "real." (Or, when those of us who read psychoanalysis get our hands on them, the "Real.") As in the following:

– The primal "real" of deep reptilian urges that get to return in all their anti-Rousseau fury, tearing away at living bodies like very ignoble savages.

– The thought of zombies as a kind of meta-return of the repressed, the "Real" of contemporary life that cannot be included in the dominant symbolic order: a loopy perverted death drive whose cannibalism parodies the drives to excess consumption.

– What's "really" going on, the zombies as embodied manifestations of racial, class, and gender conflict, as well as registrations of anxieties and resistances to contemporary events.

– The forbidden, visceral, abject real of the body, where we get to see all the bloody bits brought to the surface, the abstract spirit of the mind rendered into just one more pile of succulent warm nutrition. Spirit is not a bone, but it is the juicy bits encased within bone.

Fair enough. None of this is wrong per se, and many of the films themselves court these interpretations. Nevertheless, these readings about the "real" content of zombies are limited because they aren't really readings: they just describe what happens in the films. To say that the ending of *Night of the Living Dead*, with the "accidental" murder of an African-American man by the white redneck zombie hunting mob, is largely about race relations is just to say that you've watched the movie all the way through. To say that *Dawn of the Dead* (1978), with its hordes of blank-eyed shopping mall zombies, is a critique of consumerism is just to describe the surface texture of the film. As with other films and cultural objects that upfront their political/social critique, that very critique often becomes an obstacle to better critical thinking: *Well, we know very well that it's against racism, sexism, crass consumerism, corruption* ... Simply because a film seems to point out problems of social inequality does not mean that it is a radical film, or even one that is therefore "smarter" and more aware than those films hell-bent on entertainment, social critique be damned.

Of real concern is the symptomatic content: the effects and sets of meanings whose sources cannot be found in the film "trying to say something" about social issues. Instead, that rat's nest of historical anxieties, concrete organizations and administrations of the world, and affective relations which cannot but inflect the final product. In a more Marxist language: the film is a capture not just of how the structuring effects of the "base" (the organization of productive capacity and the modes of labor there employed to produce value) are registered by the "superstructure" (the social relations that both support and are produced by modes of production, the realms of culture and "politics," the whole ideological project of a period and its tangle of contradictory impulses and rules). It is not the issue of cultural output reflecting or expressing the economic order, as in the parodic version of Marxism in which everything is unidirectionally "about" the economy in a banal and dogmatic way. ("What is this slapstick hockey comedy about?" "Class relations. Obviously.")

Rather, the capture is of the messy passages *between* base and superstructure. From the perspectival dizziness of the tracking back and forth (between the forms imposed on a world and the uncomfortable, uncertain fit of that world into those forms), the sharper edge starts to develop. This sharpness is not the result of criticism. It is honed both in our clumsy grasps at understanding objects and in how those objects themselves are constituted by attempts to understand the pressures and determinations of their historical moment. Under the diffuse weight of these pressures, this subjectless drive to knowing must be mediated, translated, fragmented, and shoved underground, emerging only in brief instances where we can tell that something doesn't feel quite right.

To apply this to zombies: the zombie film, we claim, had a distinctly sharp capacity to think these passages in both their sloppiness and painful accuracy. And this indeed takes the form of the "real." At their best, funniest, and meanest, they are the thought of *how real abstractions work on real bodies.* What this means is that they hold out a way to model and map what happens when seemingly spectral shifts in the global architecture of a totality (capitalism), which cannot be traced to any one cause or agent, touch earth and produce real consequences. Or, in this case, touch beneath the earth, stirring the dead. Of course, it takes the form of the fantastic and the impossible: *the dead walk!* Yet the point is that this operation – the mutations and developments in the impersonal global logic of value affecting every speck of the "real" it infects – happens all the time. It is precisely what capitalism does and what defines it. (This does not mitigate, however, the sense of this operation as fantastic, uncanny, and never quite fully comprehensible.) Capitalism doesn't just abstract, in the more direct way of seeing objects as "just" commodities, "just" material instantiations of a certain exchange value. It also deploys these abstractions to dictate the conditions of objects themselves, to force their flows and determine their right to existence.[21] Echoing the death certificate in *The Bed Sitting Room*, this takes its most directly sadistic form when the objects in question are human bodies.

This is the particularity of what the figure of the zombie does and its position in the mass culture of capitalism. It thinks how real abstractions work on real bodies, of the nastiest intersections of the law of value and the law of inevitable decay.

And more specifically, it thinks this via two central concerns:

reanimation (transmission)
consumption (hunger)

In each pairing, the latter term is not the underlying cause, contrary to appearances. Romero zombies are not reanimated because of infectious transmission of a "zombie disease" from the bite of a zombie, at least not until we get to the recent *28 Days Later* model. They are reanimated because the world has changed in a way we can't fully determine. (How did the dead get the message to rise up? Why weren't we informed? Worse, if it indeed is related to the radiation of the "exploded Venus probe," what the hell is that radiation doing to those of us who are still alive?[22]) And they do not eat because of hunger, in any physiological way[23]: think here of the moment in *Day of the Dead* (1985) where Dr. Logan has removed all the vital organs of the vivisected zombie to watch it still strain to tear the flesh from his hands, its gnashing teeth clamping down again and again on the air ...

Rather, the latter term is the asubjective truth of the activity: it is the obscure center of a thought that exceeds what a zombie does or does not do, not verified by the reason why an individual subject, albeit necrotic and "without reason," acts a certain way. Hunger decoupled from the act of sating hunger, and transmission that we cannot trace: each is the absent cause produced by the activity. Precisely because it is not the reason for these things happening (the dead rising and the dead eating the living), it is raised in relief, the strange shadow undergirding and blackly illuminating the deeper workings of a totality. It is the point of the whole enterprise, from yawning graves to gnawing meat, precisely because it is missing from it. For what is hunger at its barest and most obscene if not a consumption that cannot end, for the very fact that it was never caused by hunger in the first place?

But before tracking this out, we should mark the recurrent images of zombie apocalypse that first get full treatment in *Night of the Living Dead*. In other words, the construction of the tropes and clichés that show us what it looks like for the world to end at the hands and mouths of the stumbling dead.

Inside/outside: order/orgy

First and foremost is a spatial opposition that visually orients the zombie genre as a whole, between the domestic interior – or interiors that become sites of cobbled-together domestic living – and the wilds of the outside, always trying to break through the doors and windows. This produces, almost inevitably, the great money shot of the zombie film: the horror and ecstasy of a survivor getting dragged across the threshold, screaming as he or she is welcomed into the waiting horde. Hence we get one of our era's greatest fantasmatic images, of just giving up on the entire domestic sphere of responsibility and family values, pulled "against my will" into the orgy of irrationality and swarm collectivity. But no, in these films, a man's house – or any house secure enough to hole up in – is indeed a castle, and a castle exists for protection and siege, for shoring up the splintered remnants of the distinction between private and public spaces, between zones for family bickering and zones for all-out war.

The enemy within

Unfortunately, things aren't much safer inside. The consistent question across Romero's films seems to be: what divides us from them, the rational humans trying to survive from the zombie hordes? The answer: well, at least zombies won't stab you in the back or constantly pull guns on you during an argument.

In the later films, *Land of the Dead* in particular, zombies do learn indeed how to pull guns, but there it is in the service of a developing solidarity the petty and hysterical living can only envy.[24] The humans prove to be your real enemies. Unpredictable, stressed, and cowardly, they get everyone killed in trying to save their own skin, over and over again. Romero's films, like those of fellow "social critic" horror director John Carpenter, have been from the start about the clusterfuck that is group dynamics, joined to a deep, lingering awareness of the damage we remain uniquely capable of inflicting on one another. It may be the zombies who we are supposed to shoot in the head, but that won't be nearly so satisfying as blowing away the jerks who make surviving the apocalypse so unpleasant and dangerous.

Bad faith

Here we find the darkest, and simultaneously most joyous, heart of the zombie film: the consummate bad faith of the savagery you've wanted to inflict all along. It is bad faith because it veils the real desire under the sign of necessity: *I had to kill her, she was going to "turn."* It is the misanthropy of everyday life, the common urge to just stop talking things through, to stop biting your tongue, to unload on your friends, neighbors, siblings, and parents. And even more, on the stranger, on the human body we don't know. This is analogous to the response to the Columbine high school shootings and other supposedly random public massacres: so much of the horror and shock was due to the eruption in "real life" of what was supposed to remain a secret communal fantasy of nastiness toward our fellow human. The point here is not that there are certain pathological individuals who are the bearers of this wrong urge. The pathology is structural, shared by all social beings, or by all those who have successfully become good citizens and people, all who have learned that conflict and urges are mediated by and disseminated throughout all language and discourse, that massive horizontal net of rules and conventions. In this way, the zombie film lets us bare our open secret and celebrate in it, watch an endless sequence of strangers get shot in the head, the audience cheering at particularly "good" kills.

However, it keeps this bloodlust on a tight leash via that blind of necessity. It thereby replicates all the more the structures of what is and is not allowed. In a line repeated across the genre with minor variation, "that was before ... nothing is the same anymore." This is marshaled most often before or after killing a neighbor/mother/friend who has been bit and may "turn" into a zombie. The question it raises, obliquely, is how long you've been waiting to do this, before you got the excuse.

And "apocalypse" should be stressed here in its proper sense, as the revelation of the hidden. Namely, what is apocalyptic about the walking dead is what they reveal about the conditions of the *living*, all those deep, rutted grooves of antagonism and violence seething beneath daily life. The open secrets of an economic totality, at once the violence of abstraction (the brutal consequences of shifting patterns of valuation) and the abstraction of violence (this is just business, folks, nothing personal).

However, the zombie apocalyptic fantasy is that of a world in which just such abstraction is destroyed, producing all the utopian possibilities and ideological pitfalls of a world beyond value. In a desperate echo of salvagepunk, the world of zombie hordes is a radical contraction of what is desirable to possess: if it can't kill, heal, feed, help escape, burn, or barricade, then it only slows you down. Exchange-value rots even faster than the bodies, leaving behind objects in their naked utility and hardness.

Yet the vision of the zombie apocalypse is never a *post-apocalyptic* vision, not a single event and revelation out of which we regroup and attempt to rebuild.[25] Rather, they are the mapping and figuration of apocalyptic duration, the crisis that will not quit and the ceaseless work of slaughter, partition, burial, and moving on. So too the content of the revelation, the hidden re-revealed endlessly, from the deep inheritances of racial and class prejudice to lingering models of erotic possession and familial structure, from the cathartic pleasures of corporal savagery to the sinking realization that it was never the zombies who made this world unlivable. They just give the subjectless catastrophe of this century a necrotic, yearning form.

In the fundamental non-progression of this apocalypse, stuck and skipping like a record, a full recognition and mobilization of the revealed remains impossible. A full recognition and mobilization of the revealed remains impossible. This is both on the level of the diegetic content of the films (i.e. what's going on in their worlds) and the films themselves: in neither case can anyone get past the personal. The trauma is of the species itself, but the survivors, and the supposed critique internal to the films, cut themselves off at the knees by their resolute inability to think anything close to totality. To hearken back to the "missing question" of transmission, they lack the capacity – or, more frequently, refuse the consequences of such a capacity – to fathom how the global transmits to the local. As such, one faces two options. You can abandon whatever community to which you temporarily belong and get the hell out of town, preferably to the wilds of Canada (as happens at the deeply reactionary end of *Land of the Dead*) or a Caribbean island (the oddly unconvincing conclusion of *Day of the Dead*). Or you refuse to keep moving and establish your stronghold, whether it be mall, house, bunker, farm, prison, or factory.[26] Which essentially means, given the less-than-rosy view of what we do to each other, to stay in one place long enough for the worst tendencies of the human animal, post-capitalism, to come out. Hence the deep nihilism (at least concerning behavior toward each other) of the genre: stay with a group of other survivors, and soon you won't be a survivor, falling victim to what inevitably happens when you're trapped together in one house with too many guns and an entire social order worth of loathing.

Above all, the films institute a cycle of passages between these visions of fixity and flight. Their texture and tempo is precisely this gap: one gets to rest, but only uncertainly, with the awareness that the idyll is a calm before a storm that never stops. And just as these passages are stunted, thrown off course and kilter, rendered hectic and abortive, the passages of thought from base to superstructure are themselves messy, precise only in their failure. It is because we *don't* get a proper realism or cognitive mapping that zombie films better capture the logic of the times, that opaque "almost-thought" which always escapes the closure of facile critique. The work of sharper critique and under-standing, of making sense of what is revealed and what is hidden, is forced into this position of the itinerant, the unwelcome guest forever pulling up stakes at gunpoint. But the gun, here, is the inertia of the past, the savage insistence of the old roles and rules. A constant refusal to admit that things have changed: *no, the government will come, there must be a rational explanation for this, we aren't the kind of people who do this.* Coupled with this, the permanent flight, both in thought and action. *We need to keep moving.* All those forms of resistance that foreclose the possibility of real resistance, all the mental and social immobility that ends where it starts, back in the arms of the dead.

SURPLUS-LIFE

This isn't to disavow the critique – of race, class, nation, gender, etc – embedded in much of the genre, and in Romero first and foremost. Indeed, the vague, and often misleading, leftism of its perspective constitutes the texture and tone perhaps as much as the relations between interior/exterior, fixity/flight, and care/brutality. And it remains, from its incipient moments on, capable of real moments of vitriol and shock: the sinking stomach feeling becomes a freefall in the total horror of Ben's death, for instance. But, as raised earlier, the on-the-surface social critique is the least interesting part of the films, *particularly* from a political perspective. If there is a sharper turn of critique and thought, one not caught in the abortive passage bound to the personal trauma, it can only lie in the zombies themselves, the real protagonists of the films. For not since Eisenstein's films have we witnessed such a startling construction of the mass subject: the slow pained birth of the new group from the wreckage of the everyday. Not so much class consciousness, but the wracking formation of something that, like all revolutionary movements, starts from the universal and lurches, however ineptly, toward its negation.[27] Stumbling and swarming, single-minded and mindless, they are the unhalting drive toward the destruction of the world that exists and all it stands for.[28]

That said, they might be rather surprised to learn of their role as eschaton made flesh. In the Romero films, they are surprised to *learn*, period. And so before considering what it means for the "irrational" to develop a sense of what they have been doing all along as well as the advanced tactics of how to do it better, we return to that dual core of what they do without "meaning to": they consume, and they do not die.

What do they consume? Despite the endless LOL-zombie level jokes, it wasn't always about "Brains …". That particular iteration, with all its monotonous staying power, comes from

Dan O'Bannon's *Return of the Living Dead* (1985), to which we will return at length. No, for Romero and the meat glee of his SFX man Tom Savini, it is flesh, ripped from the bone, and it is entrails, the wet horror of the unraveling guts.

But even aside from the fact that consumption does not answer hunger, the very eating and hunting practices were never about filling bellies or persistently butchering the living to get every last bit of protein from them. Instead, they absent-mindedly snack. More crucially, they are distracted by the fresher living, the not-yet-touched by zombies. Pragmatically, they should stick with the kill they've already made, not waste energy chasing new prey that will likely turn out to kill the hunter. Of course, none of this matters or applies here, because of that odd doubling: they don't need to eat, yet it is what they do above all else. And not yet to turn the living to their side, not just a quick bite to convert the uninitiated and add to the ranks. (It can't be good for the effectiveness of your zombie horde to have a significant number of them missing large chunks of muscle and connective tissue.) They are consumers, so it seems, and the unaware manifestation of consumption compulsion hits its joking stride in the mall wandering slack-jaws of *Dawn of the Dead*.

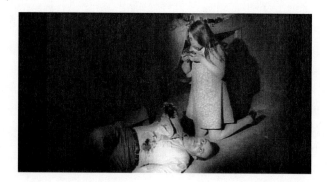

No moment so captures this bare anti-hunger and shameless consumption as that when, in *Night*, the basement door opens to reveal "zombified" Karen – a young girl holed-up in the farmhouse – munching away on her father. The shot is remarkable, an entire case-study of familial tension and libidinal investment in a single frame: her mother opens the door, a crack of light reveals Karen, and she freezes, mouth full of Daddy. Not in knowing shame at the act, but with, at most, the minor embarrassment and sudden stillness of one caught midnight snacking in the harsh glow of the open refrigerator. (To appropriate a Freudian moment, this is something approximate to, *Mother, can't you see I'm eating?*) The absence of her shame is more than compensated for by our revulsion, our knowing laughter and shudder. However, we should insist, our laughter/horror is not a response to the "body horror" (the tasteful black-and-white gore details are restrained, even for Romero), but at her fundamental misrecognition.

This is not the misrecognition of eating your father by accident, not even of being unaware of how awkward the situation appears to one who stumbles into it. It is the fundamental misrecognition of zombies and of our attachment to them. This is the misrecognition of one who has risen without reason, compelled to rise for no purpose beyond the mere repetition, consumption, and imitation of life. For the basic fact of the true zombie gesture is not the animation of the dead body *but the over-animation of the living body.*

To make this less cryptic, we might ask: how do the dead rise/walk in these films? And *which* dead?

As explained, these are not movies about transmission, at least in the explicit sense. You don't become a zombie by coming into contact with one. Being bitten may hasten the process (an unbrushed, rank, rotten-meat-reeking mouth plus a jagged bite will likely lead to a nasty infection), but it isn't the cause.[29] The cause is an irrevocable change, something that descends upon the living and the dead alike.

Indeed, we should stress the *living* aspect of this. In the graphic novel *The Walking Dead* (2003-present), which consciously expands the moves, tropes, and themes of a Romero film into a long, unfolding narrative, the central character Rick realizes, upon discovering that the "roamers" include those who happened to die without being bitten, that if "they revived without a bite – that means we're all infected. Or could be. That means we're just waiting to die before we come back as one of those things." Later in the series, as the death toll mounts and the survivors turn more and more ferociously against each other, he delivers the titular line, pointing out that "We ARE the walking dead": it isn't us the living against the animated dead, but the remapping of the entire world into the fields and enclosures of the already dead, the apparently living just biding their time before becoming the unavoidable.

In other words, it's not dying that makes you a zombie. It is *not-dying* that does, already present in you as you fight off the hordes you will one day join. It is the fact that you don't, can't or won't – in the varied inflections of will and non-agency of each option – stay down. All that is known, the one certainty after the tectonic shift of the "world revolution" that can't be repaired, is that the dead will rise because they never really die. Hence while the effects are personal (the pathos of the family consuming itself, the existential angst at the certainty of becoming a zombie), the cause is not.

Romero's own comments about this, and the relation of his film to Matheson's *I Am Legend*, are instructive:

I thought *I Am Legend* was about revolution. I said if you're going to do something about revolution, you should start at the beginning. I mean, Richard starts his book with one man left; everybody in the world has become a vampire. I said we got to start at the beginning and tweak it up a little bit. I couldn't use vampires because he did, so I wanted something that would be an earth-shaking change. Something that was forever, something that was really at the heart of it. I said, so what if the dead stop staying dead? ... And the stories are about how people respond or fail to respond to this. That's really all [the zombies] ever represented to me. In Richard's book, in the original *I Am Legend*, that's what I thought that book was about. There's this global change and there's one guy holding out saying, wait a minute, I'm still a human. He's wrong. Go ahead. Join them. You'll live forever! In a certain sense he's wrong but on the other hand, you've got to respect him for taking that position.[30]

One could say much about how Romero articulates the origins and trajectory of his project here, but for the moment, three comments.

First, the sense that it was never really about the zombies: they are representations – more precisely, the external embodiment – of how people respond to a global shift. In a strange doubling back, they are nothing but the registration of the response to them, an echo chamber with a hollow void at its center (you are just our response to what you are). Second, there is the slippery question of at what point *you* are still human. The Matheson schematic of obstinacy and refusal to adapt, for which we all do have some respect indeed, is centered less on the level of his unwillingness to become something other and more the problem of one who doesn't realize he is already a consequence and product of that change. Or, we should insist, at least the Romero reload of Matheson achieves this: if the zombies are a projection of how we respond to "earth-shaking change," such a projection is needed because we lack the ability – or willingness – to read ourselves for the signs of such changes and to grasp what has befallen us all. Third, and most crucially, is just that sense of tectonic shift, of that "global change," which provides the injunction to start from the beginning. However, to show the "beginning" of this revolution is not to locate a false origin or precise cause. The radiation loosed from the exploded probe may be "to blame," but what is never explained, through any of the series, is *how* it is to blame. There is a gathering storm of overdetermination, a blur of intersecting influences and pressures. All that we can witness is the point of no return.

And indeed it is a *point* of no return. For what is the world condition that occurs? It is clearly not that all the dead who ever died arise. It is not even just those dead with enough connective tissue and meat remaining on their bones to stand and shamble. The condition is the rising of those who died *after* the new set of rules came to be, after the radiation has spread.

In this way, zombie films are not about the living dead, at least not in any direct way. They are about the undying living. They are about *surplus-life*, the new logic of excessive existence: something has given us all too-much-life, an inability to properly die in a system that no longer knows how or when to quit. If there is an infection or viral model here, it is of a systemic change that infects all and demands of us that we not die. Instead, the continuation and modification of the human animal in its furious and unnatural perseverance. The instinct to survive turned against itself in parody, the conatus gone haywire.

And more than that, the end of the sovereignty not just of the subject but also of the working body, now given a task that it can't finish and a job from which it doesn't get to punch out. In this way, both on the local scale of each body and mind compelled to stop minding and just keep going, and on the global scale, the zombie apocalypse is not the end of the world. It's the "end of the end," the world never ending. The films may be obsessed with things that rot and fall apart, but they are visions of *frozen decay*, a halted approximation of the process of disappearance that serves only to insist on stasis. They are always decaying, but never decayed. That is what's so horrifying. Not the possibility of it ending this way, in plague and rot and terror, but instead, in the drawn out sigh of the thought, *My god, what if it never ends ...* And worse, the possibility that this may be so central to the dominant logic of our age that it no longer is capable of horrifying, the soft whimper of protest drowned out in the roar of the self-same.

WHEN HELL IS FULL, THE DEAD WILL BE MOCKED FOR THEIR CONSUMERIST TENDENCIES

Who, then, are the zombies? What are the ideological and political echoes of those unwilling survivors doomed not to die?

On a superficial (and perhaps more resonant level), they are "us," the everyman and woman, regular Johns, Janes, and all between. The genre takes deep and recurrent pleasure in raising the zombie types, so that the viewers get the game of spotting the shambling incarnation of "what they were before": zombie clowns, zombie hare krishnas, zombie cheerleaders, zombie bike messengers, and so on and on ...[31] One effect of this, beyond the mild chuckle, is indeed a sense of the zombies as the underbelly of the everyday. Not merely the manifestation of how we react to global shifts but also the detritus that persists through any of those shifts. If the apocalyptic New has yet to be fully revealed, it is in part because the old not only refuses to rot away, it also keeps doing anew, with an uncanny sense of fidelity, what it used to do.

Including, go to the mall and hang out, wandering aimlessly without really buying anything.

In Romero's *Dawn of the Dead*, arguably one of the century's greatest, cruelest, and darkly funniest films, that's just what they do, thereby inaugurating the endlessly recycled line of embedded critique: in the society of the spectacle (here in its vaguest sense), we already live like zombies. The zombies are us, in all our cowed ignorance, shambling through the motions of an impoverished existence. They are "unaware," stupid, and easily tricked, barely able to navigate an escalator, reeling in the perma-shock of the always new and the glossed bounty of commodities displayed.

Yet of course, they are also threat, a "monstrous otherness" made uncanny by its proximity to normal textures of everyday life. Their specificity and threat is to be found in the particular fantasy position they occupy: as a figure, they stand as an impossible triangulation between 1) concrete mechanisms of dominance and exploitation in capitalism, 2) capitalism's abstract form of valuation and antagonism, and 3) all those who populate this system, the full range from those too abject to register to those who reap its profit.

Any materialist account – or any account capable of thinking beyond internal genre shifts – must be conceived roughly along these lines, passing back and forth from *what* and *how* zombies threaten to *who* they are (rather than just who they *were*), all mapped onto the specificity of the envisioned world. And it goes without saying that this envisioned world is, with notable and powerful exceptions, the emergent late capitalist world: shopping malls and suburbs, postcolonial islands and teeming metropoles barricaded and eaten away from within.

What (or *who*) and *how* do zombies threaten? One influential account, best known in the version advanced by Robin Wood, is that the zombies threaten all that is not compatible with advanced capitalism: their cannibalism is consumerism in literalized reification overdrive, a desire to consume and possess not just objects but the bodies of fellow citizens.[32] However, this consumption has a particular edge and articulation in that they dominate and destroy the "Other" of American society: persons of color, women, homosexuals, anyone vaguely or explicitly countercultural. As such, the zombies stand as the swarming enforcers of a social order familiar to us all, even in a vision of the end of that order.

This account is quite flawed and feels oddly unmoored from the texture of the films themselves: if zombies remain capitalist subjects, they are surely not *capitalists* per se. Capitalism works concretely through a small number of capitalists exploiting the labor power of hordes of workers, with the attendant threat and pressure of the industrial reserve army hungry for access to jobs. Zombies may be many things, but managers they are not. This is not to misrepresent Wood's point: his argument is subtle and recognizes that it isn't an issue of what the zombies think they are doing but *how* and *to whom* the violence is done (an all-out assault by the many on a smaller group of individuals largely coded as marginal to mainstream American society). It isn't a model of intentionality but of the creation of films in which we witness men of color and (primarily white) women struggle for their lives against the white men locked in the houses/malls/bunkers with them and against the rainbow coalition of the undead outside. (That said, it's difficult to truly argue that it is the *zombies* who are the ones "targeting" these Others, even within the Romero films: it is the redneck cops at the end of *Night*, dead boyfriends and biker gangs in *Dawn*, and coked-up/adrenaline-fuelled military macho men in *Day*.)

The bigger problem with the argument is its conception of possessiveness and consumption. The collective hunting and *enjoying-wrongly* – the fact that enjoyment is no longer mediated through the value-form but through a gory mining of the potential hunger-sating use-value of one's friends and neighbors

– point, if anywhere, to the fact that individual possession has nothing to do with it. While hunger may be the symptomatic absence that gives truth to consumption, possession is merely a misconstruction of what happens. They move en masse, they work together, they rip and tear, and move on. If anything, this is closer to a model of mutual aid or collective goal oriented hive mind than atomized life in the face of market relations. *They do not own what they kill, and they do not care.* One could begin to imagine how different the films would be if this were the case, something far closer to a vampire film, in which the one who has bitten and "turned" you has a position of ownership and control, or is at least more ancient, and hence more legit. In a zombie film, this would produce an endless chain of pseudo-ownership and authenticity, but it would also undo the very core of the films, the glimpse of a totality that affects everyone. There is no original, and certainly no aristocratic glamour even if one could be found. (The most nobly rotten?)

A related analysis, one manifested on the surface of the films themselves, figures the zombies as consumerism run amok: the barbaric forces underlying the management of commodity culture are unmasked for all to see. Mindless consumers from life to un-death, they simply move from a slavish devotion to plastic trinkets to a slavish devotion to the flesh of the living. Folded into this is a vague sense of apocalyptic immanentism, something worth guarding even if its articulation is the worst form of critique: *It's the apocalypse, man, we're already mindless zombies, it's all ideology and spectacle, and we're just thoughtless drones watching the world burn ...* Crucial to note, however, is that in this vision, stressed in both cultural responses/parodies/reloads and the films themselves, the zombies are still "consuming subjects." They may wander without buying anything, yet the stress is put on their consumption as a *continuation* – at most, a slight perversion or unmasking – of how they consumed before the apocalypse. They are not the poor or the homeless, or at least not truly lumpen. The first zombie/"ghoul" we see in the Romero films indeed is coded as a homeless drifter, a man down on his luck, but in *Dawn* and in its echoes reaching far beyond zombie cinema itself, the zombie becomes the "good" consumer simply gone too far, an indictment not of a system that lets people "fall through the safety net" but of a system which encourages decadent, selfish, brutish behavior. Hence if we accept the argument presented in *Dawn*, that the zombies return to the mall because they came here in life, with as much critical gravity as it seems intended to have, we also accept that their remembrance establishes them as the continuation of "correct" consumption, even as they learn to *consume wrongly*.[33]

What are the ideological consequences of this dominant mode of reading zombie films (i.e. zombie films are about the anxieties of late capitalism, with particular focus on the consequences of excess consumerism, individual greed that threatens communities, and the decline in individual critical thinking in favor of shared consumption of mass ideology)? More specifically, if there is indeed a "critical" connection between the consumption of the zombies and the general consumption of commodities, what is it?

The operation at work is a division of the world into two:

1. There is "everyone," the mindless masses of consumers, regular folk hoodwinked into accepting the impoverished world of commodity-centered life. This "everyone" is a universal that functions by undermining its own claim. It explicitly does not mean *everyone*: rather, it serves to designate who is allowed to count as part of the *everyone*, a non-encompassing claim that excludes all those who do not or cannot work, who very well might like to participate in excess consumerism but who have been cast out of the ranks of the purchasing classes, (i.e. the truly poor, the homeless). It is an "everyone" that negatively illuminates

what it means to be beyond the pale of normal life.

2. Those who know better than everyone, who don't buy into buying, who escape the clutches of mass ideology and who could save us all if the herd of slobbering consumers learned to listen. The vanguard of clarity in a foggy age are fittingly also those who survive the zombie apocalypse. This, it should be clear, implicitly includes all of us, the viewers in on the joke, who "get what it's all about."

Taken as a whole, the zombie film – insofar as it not only is misrepresented in this manner but also fosters this ideological construction – is a fantasy of just such a division and of being on the right side of the divide. And that fantasy does not go by the name of Romero or Fulci or any director. It goes by the name of cynical reason. To clarify, this is not in the sense of ancient Cynical philosophy. Here cynicism is the modern mode of "enlightened false consciousness" that Peter Sloterdijk outlines in *Critique of Cynical Reason*: it makes "knowing better than" part of the structure of non-action, so you get to feel smarter than a social order and receive the assurance that you can't do anything to change it. By passing through the door of supposed anti-consumerist left political critique, it smuggles in both the self-disavowing illusion of standing outside of the system and the self-sustaining fantasy of freedom of choice. As such, what is really at stake here is the cynicism of master knowledge that claims to act so as to "make the unthinking think": to help the cowed sheep of the post-proletariat stop mindless consumption and to cure the bourgeoisie of their false consciousness. Put otherwise, to face the anxiety about the unknown that lies beyond the illusory stability of capital and to confront the possibility of acting otherwise. Hidden in the critique is the formulation of the critical speaker's position, as the one who can bravely push through anxieties toward the new horizon.

Indeed, this question of *anxiety* is the crux of the issue: how does it function and what is the particular anxiety of which the zombie film is a manifestation and to which it contributes? Who do we imagine to be anxious and about what?

The real problem with this cynical reason/consumer model is its short-circuited leap that conceives zombies as at once über-consumers – the blind, ideologically determined subject – and as the monstrous other. In short, doubly coded as the subject who doesn't know better and who just does these things for no rational reason. Worse still, for those of us who do know better, is that there are a lot of them. We are quite outnumbered. As such, the critique falls firmly on the irrationality of the living consumer, on what the zombies "were before they were dead": one tends to assume that zombies are beyond reform, therefore the source has to be located in the kind of people inhabiting the kind of world now rendered catastrophic. And it is the anxiety of "these people" that seems to be the problem, a crippling anxiety of the prospect that the world might become unrecognizable and impossible to navigate. An anxiety so massive that it can only lead to complacency and clinging to the edifices of ideological certainty of what's safely new, objects for purchase that reinforce the perpetuation of the same.

Hence, the general anxiety about the decline of the West finds a blamable source in the particular anxiety of the masses toward the New, their incapacity to envision modes of life that exceed the forms modeled in the shopping mall. To be clear: in the schematic of the cynical subject[34], anxiety emerges *for the masses* at the prospect of the New which terrifies them, and the role of the critic/artist is to produce texts that call into question the inability of the unthinking ones to see beyond themselves to these horizons of possibility. As such, the alleged power of Romero's *Dawn* as a cultural object is not that it shows how "we are all like zombies" but about how we, the knowing subjects, need to be vigilant in our attacks upon these consumers.

And isn't that the heart of the pleasure we see taken and which we take in watching? No more cultural mediation and propaganda, no more trying to convince someone that there is a better life beyond the circle of work and consumption. Years of failed arguments replaced with the simple clarity of a gunshot or the libidinal spray of a chainsaw: *You dumb fucker, how could you not see?* This is pleasure of enlightened false consciousness, the trademark of cynical reason, those who know very well, but nevertheless ... Who know very well that they cannot themselves change anything or escape the ideological network, but who make this knowledge of impotency the very condition for their claiming to know better than the rest. The deep cancerous form of smug resignation, of letting the world burn while you repeat to yourself, *At least I know that there wasn't anything I could do about it.*

Self-knowing and self-disavowing or not, this needs to be dismantled.[35] On two fronts. First, we should reject a causal chain of the fait accompli, a bad reasoning that goes as follows: *Dawn* has been enormously influential and popular, part of that influence has been the embedded social critique, that critique (and the horror of which it was a part) struck a nerve with contemporary anxieties, therefore the anxieties represented in the film – rampant consumerism produces the kind of world that ends this way – are the underlying anxieties of an audience and their historical moment. Against this we should insist that just because it has an "anti-consumerist" tone, and indeed has become such a classic in part because of that bent, does not mean that this is the real underpinning anxiety. This is not to claim that fears of a general trendline toward societal decadence, due in large part to consumerism and a naturalization of capitalism as the only option available, are absent, or that the film did not savagely capture some of those fears. Rather, it is to claim that if we speak of the anxiety of an era, the film must be thought of as an elaboration, a perfect storm of contradictory tendencies, a working-through of sub-currents and patterns of fear and desire that cannot be simply represented. What remains powerful about *Dawn* isn't that Romero put his finger on a "widespread anxiety," but rather that the film represents a particularly knotty and canny constellation of factors and influences in which we can detect what is missing – think here again of the conspicuous absence of hunger – and on which we can discern the cynical logic we project to protect ourselves from having to admit our deep complicity with this way of the world.

The second, and more important, attack on thinking zombie movies as being "about" consumption is the model of anxiety it employs. It is the common notion of anxiety: we get anxious at what we do not know, when we have a lack of knowledge and don't know if the New will be a pleasant or unpleasant surprise. We feel unmoored and uncertain, and anxiety is the affect of that inability to predict the New. It is an obstacle to action, pushing us to remain content with what is certain or to find other, safer ways to get the shock of the New without exposing ourselves to all the risks of undoing the assurances of this world order (or relationship or housing situation or pattern of behavior, and so on). But let's take on another model, one drawn from French psychoanalyst Jacques Lacan. Following and moving out from Lacan, we could say that anxiety is never about the radically new but rather about the horrible possibility of the same persisting.

Lacan refers to this as the "lack of a lack."[36] In short: what's worse than Mom's breast not being there when I need it? Mom's breast always being there, forever. Anxiety emerges with the creeping realization that there may be no lack, no space in which to move, leaving us crushed by the awful possible certainty of knowing how things are and knowing that they will remain that way. Mass anxiety, in this way of thinking, arises in and fixates on a world without a clear directionality or progress, a world in which the self-same repetition of drive – or the self-same accumulation of capital – is king.

So if it is indeed the case that Romero "put his finger on a widespread anxiety" about the state of life in late capitalism, is it not the case that the real encounter here is not about the knowing critique of political art pointing out the anxiety and resistance of those who don't know better, but precisely the inversion, that the real encounter is the rendering comprehensible of the zombies? Not the difficulty of getting "them" (consumers, zombies) to comprehend but the sudden opening up of our thought beyond the deadlock of cynical reason? This is not a rendering empathetic, nor is it simply understanding that we don't really know better and that we're still subject to mass ideology. Rather, these are the first steps toward leaving behind the notion of irrationality and illusion. Precisely not by claiming, *We're all just like zombies*, but rather that, *Zombies are all like us*. And not to further generalize, so that we see we're all in this together, but rather to locate in them the emergent possibility of something truly wrong, beyond feeling that they are beneath our conceptions of morality and proper decorum. The real difference emerges: not between us and the zombies but between us as bourgeois subjects (those who know better) and us as we are in all our situated messiness. What disappears is that *everyone*, that universal category which allows the exception of the cynical subject and demands the exclusion of those who can't be included without rupturing the category's capacity to restrict the meaning of being *one* of *everyone* to a limited range of acceptable thought and action.

The anxiety proper to zombie films is the deep horror of something not being different, of *everyone* remaining as limited a category as we know it to be, of the same persisting, of the end of death and lack. In this way, the consumerism account very much identifies the problem, namely, the pseudo-new of late capitalism, the foreclosure of other possibilities and the contraction of experience to petty alternatives. But what it misses is that this situation isn't the *result* of an anxiety about the New. This material situation is the very source and site of the anxiety and awareness that this may be all that there is. People are not consumers because they are scared of change. They are scared of change because they are consumers.

More than that, the zombie is not the simple manifestation of this anxiety, not a monster that makes clear the "truth" of consumerism. Zombies are not the problem but a blood-spattered possibility, still nascent, still reeling from the shock of undeath, still learning how to speak. We should not take aim at those who don't know but rather at this entire stress on "purchase politics" and on thinking that that the real problem could ever be ameliorated, let alone solved, by more sustainable, informed ways of buying commodities. We have to counter the whole reduction of critical thought to the facile move of claiming that some people consume wrongly, for the consumption deemed "wrong" in that schematic is precisely the kind of consumption needed to keep the system afloat. That is, anyone who supports capitalism as a system cannot speak of those who "consume wrongly." It is a purely aesthetic and moral condemnation, saying that the uncultured should be more subtle about their participation in the reproduction of wealth.

That is, until you get to those who really do consume wrongly. Namely, the zombie: the obscure, halted-decay vision of something really outside the systemic logic, something truly wrong. Not bad taste but bad hunger. (Therein the specificity of *cannibalism*, which mirrors the urge on the part of those still living to do violence to members of their species.) A spreading shadow making darkly clear that even our attacks on those who can't think beyond the degraded world of consumption are expected attacks, just demands for more subtle degradation. That is the injunction of *Dawn*, against itself: to make the dead talk clearly, to take on and talk from that position, to hear the unseen speak rationally out of the irrationality of managed life, and to force *everyone* to take on a very different meaning. It is an injunction that will be answered, but never by zombies and always uncertainly.

PLAGUE IN THE GEARS

We haven't entirely answered the question raised before: who, then, are the zombies? To proceed negatively ...

They are *not* extensions of the capitalist injunction to consume. Or, if they are, not because "purchasing unnecessary shit to bolster your social capital is like becoming part of a roving horde of undead cannibals." To be sure, the real linkage is that of non-necessity. In the Romero vision of zombies, they physiologically need to eat like we physiologically need a certain brand of jeans: not at all.[37] But the analogy ends here. For their consumption is not the will to possess, the momentary grasp of the New in the form of the passing fashion. It is a mode of consuming that is against all ownership, against exchange value, against reification, against representation itself.[38]

Allegorically, they are both the dream and nightmare of the ruling class, the motor that turns the gears of the system and the rotting wrench forced into those gears. In an era of overproduction and overcapacity, when there are both too many workers and too many factories, zombies are the fantasy form of the real necessity of "creative destruction," clearing the ground of the dead weight of outmoded industry. Provided, of course, that the living eventually rid themselves of the pesky undead, what opportunities for growth, for rebuilding! As a character in the oddball Italian zombie film *Nightmare City* (1980) puts it, "It's part of the vital cycle of the human race. Create and obliterate until we destroy ourselves." Perhaps not "the human race," but we know for certain that this economic regime cannot function without the cyclical destruction of whole swathes of productive capacity. Recalling our earlier discussion of the sadism of false necessity, the zombies serve another crucial function: they are the crisis which allows for powers that be to declare a "state of emergency," to suspend the normal channels of legislation and to bring about drastic changes (the barricading of cities to foreigners, forms of martial law, restructuring the social order, etc). And as with the false necessity of *But I had to, she was going to turn ...*, we should ask here: *Sure, but for how long were you waiting for the excuse to do these things?*

And yet ... even in that vision of creative destruction, of being the accidental tool of the order against which you rage, the center on which the fantasy of the zombie hinges is the horror of that which cannot quit. What's been trailing along but missing, hinted at but rarely brought forth, in our analysis should be obvious by now: *It's about labor*. It's never been about consumerism gone bad, but the lost heritage of the zombie film, the horror from more Haitian origins: of being forced to work, of knowing that "choosing" to sell one's labor has never been a choice, just a particularly nasty illusion of free will. If the surplus-life nightmare of zombies sticks with us, fascinates and disturbs, it's because it brings to its logical conclusion not the vapid barbarism of the consuming classes but the buried antagonism of the labor relation, a world order dragging us from our rest incessantly to do what "must be done" yet for which we will be blamed. The infernal position of workers, cursed for doing wrong what can never be right.

To be clear, if recent zombie films have involved a certain betrayal of the Romero trajectory, that Romero trajectory – and with it, the dominant line of zombie thought – is itself a betrayal of a history that could have been. This is the lost heritage of those *forced* to work, raised from the dead to do the compulsory bidding of a master. Yet this "betrayal" registers a powerful shift that's ultimately faithful to the core of the voodoo-inflected zombie model. The particularity of that nightmare form is distinctly postcolonial, a deep existential horror of being a slave still or once more, even after death, and the recognition that relations of domination and subordination have distinct faces: *someone* is doing this to *me*, particular actions had to be taken by that individual in order to control me as the hollow remnant of an individual. Power is personal, and so too the antagonism on which it uncertainly rests.

The zombie film, from Romero on, derails this particular emphasis on forced labor, and with it, the closer connection of the zombie and the laborer, in favor of an emphasis on compulsory consumption.[39] Yet in doing so, it nails something else. Not that class antagonism and its attendant anxieties are "about" consumption now: those fears are the underbelly of an older period, of postwar boom and new sectors of society starting to purchase in ways never before available to them. Rather, if the later films symptomatically capture something of the particular anxieties of the emergent post-Fordist/post-capitalism's-golden-years period, it has to do with those relations of domination. It approaches, however darkly, an awareness that the problem of the age is no longer the horror of being controlled by a discernible master but the indecipherability of those relations of domination, the lack of discernible masters at whom to aim. While the voodoo-inflected zombie film recoils at the thought of being forced to assume a direction dictated by your master, the Romero mode remains troubled by *lack* of direction: *What if I'm doomed to not get anything done, other than some reprehensible canni-*

balism, and worse, what if there's no one I can blame for this? The powerful capacity of the zombie film to approximate totality is a consequence – if it is to be located historically at all – of 1) the violent foreclosure of organized resistance to global capitalism by counter-revolutionary state action, 2) the related dissolution of working class power and the very idea of working class identity, and 3) the emergent new planet-spanning structure of flows of finance, information, and goods. To be sure, these are trendlines that gain shape only in hindsight, but it is no stretch to see the torsion of these massive shifts in the cinema of the long '70s into the '80s. And nowhere more so in the zombie film, particularly when that doesn't simply mean films in which the undead eat the living.[40]

But to get a sense of that lost history that roils beneath the surface of the films from this period on, we look to a remarkable other beginning, the British 1966 film, *Plague of the Zombies*. If we imagine the openings and closures of different traditions and lineages, this is one that both continues and reworks the Caribbean roots of earlier zombie productions (*White Zombie, I Walked with a Zombie*) while also blazing a path that was not to be followed: overlapping modes of production, the literal return of the postcolonial repressed brought home to solve labor shortages, and a peculiarly British awareness of decorum, class, and general nastiness towards others. We are speaking of a film, after all, in which zombies work as tin miners.

Released two years before *Night of the Living Dead*, it shares little with that genre-forger. It's a period piece in brilliant color, complete with cadmium paint blood, diabolical squires, and the other trappings of the Hammer Studios films in that period (recognizable actors, loads of cleavage, an insistence on telling fully fleshed-out narratives, even while they collapse under the weight of their own contradictions). It is not a "siege" film, thereby lacking the spatial ordering of inside barricading/outside threat. And most crucially, it features nonaccidental zombies that require the active efforts of individuals: there is no zombie holocaust here, no threat of it spreading beyond the small town.

To summarize very briefly: Sir James, a retired professor of medicine, receives a letter from his ex-pupil, Peter, telling him that strange things are going on in his Cornish village. Sir James and his daughter Sylvia go to the town, and it becomes increasingly apparent that the vague plague is in fact the work of voodoo, a skill picked in Haiti up by Squire Hamilton, who rules over the area with an occult-ring bedecked fist. Conditions in his tin mine had become too dangerous to convince laborers to work there, hence he has started killing off and resurrecting members of the working class to employ as shambling corpses who require a lot of whipping to get any work done. Things go from bad to worse: Peter's wife Alice is killed, and Sylvia falls under the voodoo command of Hamilton only to be saved from becoming a (presumably) virgin sacrifice after her father and Peter burst in at the last moment. The three escape, as the zombies catch on fire (their voodoo dolls have been burned elsewhere), kill their controllers, and the tin mine explodes.

From the start, *Plague* develops a world of barbed pleasures, of getting to respond to your daughter's exhortations with, "I don't know why I put up with you at all. I should have drowned you at birth." Unlike the sadism of false necessity, this is a world in which antagonisms remain conversational, with each character hell-bent on not giving others the satisfaction of feeling that their satisfaction matters. That is, of course, with the exception of the class hatred on which the film turns, posing a striated world of landed aristocracy, non-landed but quite comfortable aristocracy, upper-middle class educated doctors trying their hand at village life, the various government and police functionaries of the town, the farmers and working class, colonial exports brought to serve as butlers and "voodoo drummers," and, finally, the tin miner zombies. (One should ask, in all seriousness, how the film positions the last two categories, the black servants and the zombies, in terms of who is afforded more respect.) Yet while the film makes very apparent this hierarchy, it cannot – at least on the surface – deal with its implications without fleeing into a certain language of transhistorical human nature and of evil. Consider the early exchange between Sir James and Sylvia, after Sylvia has witnessed, with great displeasure, the goons of Hamilton hunting a fox.

SIR JAMES: "Men have always hunted."

SYLVIA: "For food, yes, not for bloodlust."

At that point in the film,[41] we are intended to side with Sylvia, in supposing that there is indeed something qualitatively different here. Yet this difference is not that of new historical forms of cruelty and micro-barbarism. Rather, it is coded as a throwback to a blood-dimmed pastoral of aristocratic rule, incontrovertible laws, and superstition. If there is an explicit arc to the film, it is the movement toward Sir James' position away from that of Sylvia: men kill because that's what they do, but there are some who are pathological in the way they do, insofar as they can be seen to combine bloodlust with greed. And they do so because they have missed the news about the Enlightenment and the solid rationality of the British middle class: they are brutes and haughty elites, superstitious fools and sadist perverts. The most explicit formations of class antagonism function in this way, as a battle between modernity and the bastions of country life. When Peter refuses – because he is unable – to give the villagers a satisfactory account of just what the hell is going on, he couches it in terms of refusing to betray his principles of scientific rationality: to give them a lie to appease them just wouldn't be "good enough." To which, in a moment that would likely elicit a cheer from not a few readers, one of the "working class" men responds, "You're not good enough for us!" However, the champions of local custom hardly fare better from our perspective. As given in the film, the range of their positions runs on an attenuated continuum from sullen anger and the inability to question the social structure of the feudal/pastoral, to the canny sadism and calculation of those in positions of power, well aware that the world is changing but equally aware that capitalizing on it requires an insistence on preserving the status quo. As we are reminded, "This isn't London," and it's hard to grasp this as anything other than a condemnation. That said, similarly to Lucio Fulci's brutal masterpiece, *Don't Torture a Duckling* (1972), *Plague* is largely about a battle between "modernity" (London/science) and "backwardness" (Cornish village/superstition). But given the fraught intersections between the two positions, and the violence that consequently emerges, neither option seems worth saving or defending.

What the film approaches, but remains unable to fully comprehend, is the particularly capitalist – and distinctly not retrograde – nature of the wrongdoing. To be sure, *Plague* paints a world in which that edifice of landed gentry and all its social codes still has sway. But it's out of sync with the progress toward industry: the voyage to the Cornish village is a voyage to a backwater, an earlier organization of feudal life confronted with the peculiar new horrors of capitalist accumulation. (In this case, the grinding horror of knowing that just because a job is too dangerous for workers doesn't mean that workers will not be forced to do it.) If one of our preoccupations here is the question of combined and uneven development/apocalypse, of overlapping regimes of production/catastrophe, *Plague* captures this out of the corner of its roaming eye. Literalizing all those vague allegories of undead labor, of the black magic of drawing forth value from nothing, of undermining the natural order in the name of profit, Hamilton's "disgusting" enterprise is an oblique, parodic freeze-frame of a moment in the unfreezing of capital via advanced techniques, imported from afar and brought home to mine the heart of the empire.

This first becomes evident in the assumed opposition between science and superstition. In the bravely immoral new world of Hamilton, rational calculations of profit margins and labor affordability turn to esoteric, "magical" means. It is the scientific application of non-scientific techniques: even Sir James, reading up on voodoo methods in the priest's library of occult volumes, declares, "It's all clearly scientifically stated." The film differs from the majority of "men of science vs. supernatural occurrence" horror movies, in which the enterprise of Enlightenment critical thought is abandoned in the face of what cannot be explained, complete with the requisite invocations of faith and the failure of those men of science to adequately become men of action, to stop theorizing and just pull the trigger. Conversely, *Plague* is an indeterminate zone, and the problem of the zombies is that they are *not* supernatural: they are the result of hard work and ingenious arcane methods brought to bear on a ruthless drive to reopen that abandoned tin mine. Hamilton preserves his status as the squire of the region by adopting fully the mechanisms of that new social structure which will displace him. In struggling to cling to the vestiges of authority granted by feudal order, he overleaps the logic of that order.

Of course, he keeps this all quite literally underground. For he is the emergent product of a mode of domination in which nothing is sacred, a saturnine hack Nietzschean who insists on raising the dead only when the living become too expensive. A moral debate between science and superstition matters not at all. It is at that point, when the cost and difficulty of obtaining labor "scientifically" (a calculation of wages, resources, proto-industrial reserve army, etc) as an extension of the feudal mode that Hamilton turns from science, at least in its Western conception. When you can no longer squeeze a profit from your workers, the point is not to squeeze harder. It is to change the nature of the work. To change the nature of the workers, of the structure of exploitation itself.

And change this he does. Not however, because the workers are technically dead and hence mindless slaves. (As we see, they require a fair amount of coercion – i.e. constant whipping – and remain capable of striking back when their moment comes.) Rather, because his enterprise represents a radical innovation in the shape of the colonial enterprise, folded back upon itself. Free labor is no longer to be extracted from the colonies by the intellect, will, and brute force of its colonizers. Rather, the colonial heritage comes home to roost: the repressed truth of empire returns to corrupt and innovate its tired home market. Black plagues strike indeed, but from afar. In short, the innovation – and perhaps the underlying horror – is not just "how horrible to be killed and brought back to life as a slave" but: what if our past is never forgotten? Not remembered by historians or marked into very landscape and bodies of the colonies, but smuggled back in, dark knowledge too powerful to be lost and too tempting for capitalism to ignore.

To be more specific: it is *black* knowledge, wielded by a white man. The racial composition of the film – and its portrayal of value creation – needs to be considered. A rich white squire left England to travel abroad. In Haiti, he was somehow educated in the arts of voodoo. (Foreign currency opens a number of surprising doors.) He returned to find his father dead, and the stable hold on the position of landed aristocracy in crisis. Worse, the rich vein of tin running below his lands could not be mined; the white townspeople refused to engage in that work. They rejected the equation of compensation offered for work that would probably kill them. Hamilton, then, employs Haitian drummers (and, in one of the more compelling minor roles, a black butler) to aid him in the rites which kill, raise, and control the townspeople. Here, however, is the crucial question. In what way is it economically advantageous to create zombie laborers? (And moreover, zombie laborers out of those same white villagers who turned down the work in the first place?) The film seems to say: obviously, because they are mute slaves who work for free, they just ceaselessly mine and turn a profit. But in one of those remarkable moves in which what the film is "about" and what actually happens become unmistakably divergent, it becomes clear that maintaining an army of undead miners is a ton of work, particularly for wannabe overlord Hamilton. (What also becomes apparent throughout the film is that the only real reason for him to be doing all this is because he quite enjoys it, that he gets off on being "beyond morality," putting on his voodoo mask and robes, and mess around in graveyards at night.) He doesn't just dig up corpses that come to un-life to work for him. No, he has to find a way via clumsy subterfuge to cut each future zombie, surreptitiously gather a bit of that blood, perform complicated rituals, wait for the "plague" death of the individual, and dig him or her up. And it doesn't stop there.

In the establishing shots of the tin mine, we notice two things. First, the zombies require a lot of whipping to keep moving. Even though it is the sadistic stooges of Hamilton who do the whipping, they don't seem particularly to be enjoying it, as we might imagine, asserting their position in the hierarchy of masters. They seem genuinely worn out from constantly trying to goad the shambling dead into action. And when the zombies do "work," it seems startlingly ineffective, some pathetic approximation of human labor. Raising the hammer weakly to let it fall. They may work for free, but they surely don't work very well.

Second, this would be fine if we imagined a real horde of them, hundreds of fumbling, ineffective, rotting hands pulling shreds of tin from the earth. But Hamilton's tin mine is woefully understaffed, with no more than fifteen to twenty of these workers. And hence we can only ask: how does he turn a profit? The presence of the Haitian drummers and butler immediately raise the seeming obvious solution, exporting cheap labor from afar. If the townspeople are not willing to work in the mine, Hamilton surely knows that there are others who would throw themselves – or more realistically, be thrown – into this situation at the prospect of escaping crushing poverty and famine. The other solution, again more obvious than it appears, is to make the mine safer. Put in some structural reinforcements, draw workers back with minimum wages and the assurance of non-collapse, and start drawing tin from the earth at a rate far faster than that of your "free" labor. Put your very able-bodied thugs to work not whipping zombies or digging up corpses, but mining some tin themselves. And if living humans won't work there, consider not just inhuman labor but non-human labor: the shadow of the real historical development, of automated machinery, looms large over this film.[42]

If there is an answer to this question, it is in part simply that it wouldn't be this kind of film without this intersection of the occult, the murderous, the witty class-based barbed jokes, the lust and loss. In short, it couldn't be a horror movie, and that was what Hammer did consummately well. And yet, we need to clarify what *kind* of horror movie. And more precisely, what is the horror that the film purports to be about? We know what kind of horror movie it is, in a way: lightly bloody, pseudo-surreal, atmospheric, one that splits between a whole lot of carefully scripted talking and moments in which one cannot talk, the voiceless shock of watching your wife die a second time. In this way, it is a horror movie with intended scares every so often (the seemingly dead man threw down her corpse! Sir James just cut off her head! Hamilton is about to rape/stab her!), with a general atmosphere of creeping unease.

But what about the horror it depicts, rather than the terror/unease it hopes to provoke in us? First, the horror of everyday relations in which minor exceptions merely cut away the fat to show the brutality beneath. Like the other Hammer (and, in a sense, the Romero-inflected zombie lineage) films, equal stress is placed on the problems caused by the undead and by those who have to deal with them yet who are capable and willing to inflict serious harm of their own.

Second, the horror of the "natural order" being disturbed, that doing this with corpses goes against nature and disturbs the peace of the dead. Yet as a character in the film wonders: "Peace ... what is that?" And further, what is so wrong about any use of the dead? We should briefly interrogate this attachment, even from within a framework of the capitalist reproduction of life and wealth. For we could easily imagine a form in which we wouldn't care, in which we would happily sell our posthumous labor. That is, if we were properly remunerated for it. This is the true problem lurking behind the anxiety of meddling with the natural order of things. In a conservative form: if I'm not getting paid, there's no way I'm working for someone else. And in a radical form: if we refuse work, if we refuse to accept a system in which I should put myself at risk for minor recompense, we also refuse to be brought in against our will, black magic-tricked into participation. In short, the seething anger at the prospect of not having a choice. The true underbelly of "freely selling one's labor," the realization that it has been a non-choice from the start.

And out of this anger something bursts through, intermittent at first before truly exploding at the end. Its first real expression is not one of labor betrayed, at least not in the form of masculine mining labor. It is an expression of desire that the staid middle class-ness of the film's world cannot fathom.

Peter's wife Alice, voodoo-seduced and killed by Hamilton, is to join his dead work force. (A rather odd plot conceit, given that the miner-zombies are resolutely male and that when he gets Cynthia in his clutches, his interest seems primarily in threaten-ingly molesting her before pulling a sacrificial knife. We might question just what he has in mind and the ways in which this indicates how much Hamilton does these things for pleasure and the reassurance of knowing that he can.) When Peter and Sir James interrupt her disinterring by Hamilton and his masked crew, they witness her skin and hair go gray before she rises. And the walks, with a look of direct lascivious lust, and the proper graveside smile of one who has knowledge of other horizons, the likes of which have no place in this film about men and the things they enjoy talking about. If there is a return of the repressed here, it cannot be separated from this instance as easily as her head is cleft from her body.

For as before, the question is one of apocalyptic *fantasy*. And this should be stressed in its particularity. *Fantasy*, in that it is a mode of narrative that consists of frozen captures: it naturalizes a story out of irreconcilable instances. It is a way of organizing desire[43] so that it can produce the appearance of approaching what it "wants" without ever having to get it, without having to confront the shock of drive's blind repetition. For what are all these films and cultural objects, political theories and ideologies if not series of crystallized desires, ordered to avoid the real apocalyptic confrontation with the anxiety of the same, of realizing that the punch-line has been out in the open from the start? Hence, to speak of *return* and *repressed* is misleading, for these things never left. Shoved to the side, caught at the edge of our vision, perhaps, but only because we so resolutely turn from them, again and again.

And in this case, none more so than the colonial past repurposed in *Plague*, a bloody, teeming site of experimentation and innovation, brought back to break the impasses of stagnant capital. But like the attempts to manage and control these pasts, fantasies slip and fail, symptoms overwhelm, and the never-left comes back wrongly. It's just a matter of time before your undead miners get their shit together. Here the occasion is perhaps an accident (the burning of the voodoo dolls that preserves their control), but what happens is striking. Because when the technics of control and animation are destroyed, the dead don't just go back to being dead. We might imagine that the destruction of the instruments of plague, the willful sickness that put them to death to put them to work, would be the end of the zombies, now just lifeless corpses in an abandoned mine. But no. The plague persists and turns back on its source. The zombies, some on fire in psychic bonds with their voodoo dolls, swarm and attack their whipping overlords. It is a plague that cannot be separated from its victims: they are nothing but the embodiment of this sickness to be given back, in full ferocious rage, to all who have capitalized on it.

And so the film ends consumed in flames, consuming the site of their condemned labor. In the particular history that could have been, of which *Plague* is the outpost, the zombie film writes the full apocalyptic obscenity and frivolity of this scenario: you are raised from the grave to perform the work of digging the grave of the world that brought you back. Yet we should stress this is no impossible imagining relegated to schlock horror. However hyperbolic, this is the plague of capitalism. The point is to learn how to give it back. Following Italian Marxist Mario Tronti, we begin to grasp that the development of capitalism is not a story imposed from above, of new technologies and modes of accumulation and circulation, of a constant drive forward against which workers struggle, like harpooning a leviathan that drags us forward and casts us off.[44] For Tronti, capitalist development must be understood from below: it is because workers struggle and refuse to freely give their power to production, that capitalism develops. It innovates, becomes stronger, more flexible, precisely because workers resist the world and wages it offers them. Class antagonism – and its expressions in riotous moments and long grinding struggle, in the gulf between bourgeois ideology and proletarian theory – is not the secondary consequence of the drive to profit. It is the motor that drives the whole ungodly enterprise forward. And as this trajectory of films shows us, when the condemned and damned, plagued and unwanted begin to act in concert, when hell isn't just full but mined for its innovations, the dead won't just walk the earth.

They will share that hell with us, one and all.

RETURN OF THE DYING DEAD

Dan O'Bannon's 1985 *Return of the Living Dead* ruined zombie films.[45] Or that is what intelligent critical thinkers are supposed to think. Coming out the same year as the manic, claustrophobic *Day of the Dead*, *Return* made zombies self-aware kitsch, made the whole thing about moaning *Brains* ..., about Linnea Quigley stripping in a graveyard to the thought of being eaten alive by rotting corpses, about the kinds of jokes that can only end in our current idiotic quagmire of LOLzombies and zombie apocalypse survival guides. It is the beginning of the end, the point at which the fissures of crass commercialism, and the elision of left critique can be detected.

None of this, however, is the case. *Return* is a startling film, shot through with deep, unabiding sadness, visions of collectivity, the blackest of comedy, a treatise on pain and memory, an unsteady shaking oscillation between cobbled together constructions of cheap gags, gory excess, and moments of lyrical quiet. Of course, the ways in which it is remembered – and perhaps, the dominant way in which it asks to be watched – is rather kitschy, cheap, and ultimately not that interesting. Yes, there is the cheap frisson of auto-referentiality, of people talking about how to kill zombies based on the Romero movies they have seen. There are really shitty jokes about eating brains. There are running zombies who chase and swarm. (Which, contrary to the supposed innovation of *28 Days Later* and its imitators, are nothing new. Idiotic starving rage hordes that also run are.) Superficially, it is a film populated with petty, hysterical, and generally moronic people. But in the midst of all that is rather forgettable, the altogether unexpected emerges.

From the start, it's a film about work and non-work, about those caught in the structures of employment and those punks who seemingly opt out. In a medical supply company warehouse, Freddy – coded as a semi-punk kid aiming to make a working-class run at it – starts his first day of work. It will consequently turn into a film about the worst first day of work in history, yet one which curiously demonstrates the deep hooks of an ideology of respect and worry about the job you have: in the midst of the soon-to-come zombie apocalypse, Freddy is ordered to watch his foul language ("If you want to keep your job"). On this first day, to impress, scare, and gently haze him, his older coworker, Frank, tells him that the events of that famous film, *Night of the Living Dead*, were very real indeed, but that the film got it wrong. It was actually an experimental chemical weapon, the soon-to-be infamous 245 Trioxin, which caused dead bodies to jerk about. The military dealt with it predictably, sweeping it under the bureaucratic rug, sealing the bodies in barrels and then promptly losing track of their location. Of course, those barrels happen to be in the basement of this particular storage facility. And, of course, what would breaking in the new guy be like without showing him a corpse in a military-issued barrel?

1985 was evidently a big year in drawing connections between the undead and the military-industrial complex: first *Dawn of the Dead* set in the bunkered world of major military spending, now *Return* set against the backdrop of the biotechnologies developed and left to wreak havoc elsewhere, in other times and places. In a horrible prescient echo forward to Hurricane Katrina, we are wrongly assured that the zombie cans are safe.

FREDDY: "These things don't leak do they?"

FRANK: "Hell no, these things were made by the Army Corps of Engineers."

We know now all too well what sort of guarantee this is, and sure enough, the barrel cracks and spews forth its toxic load.

Before we return to the inevitable result of this contagion, we are offered a glimpse of another sort of contagion let loose onto the American landscape, the idiocies of the self-declared punks, here in every pop culture permutation: tough leather and pierced skinhead, Rick James-esque fancy dresser, over-sexed/sexually frank dyed-hair slut, tag-along "good girl," couple of New Wavers, as well as the obligatory mohawk and dirty Converse-wearing weirdo. Until the outbreak of the undead forces a shift in their non-routines, their daily life seems to consist of making inane pseudo-Bataille statements ("I like death" and "I like death with sex," immediately come to mind), driving around carefully so as to better preserve gas, visiting cemeteries, and declaring the various ways in which they are punk. This raises a key question, not just for this film, but for our approach to this genre as a whole: what movie do these people imagine themselves to be in? The answer in this case has to be, at the very least, three-fold. Frank, Freddy, and their boss Burt try their damnedest to play the parts inherited from a Romero movie: both their failed tactics and increasingly frustrated way of talking about those failures derive from the sense of, *Goddamnit, it worked there, why not here?*[46] In addition, they are indebted to some imaginary Abbot and Costello sketch about the perils of the working world. In their turn, the punks have watched a mainstream news report on the "punk movement," early MTV, perhaps a documentary on British punk, and, apparently, this movie itself, in a weird doubling back on a film that distinguishes itself in part by its punk soundtrack and iconography (and with the film's tagline, "They're back from the grave and ready to party!"). And the zombies? A longer question to be addressed, but we might as well say upfront that they didn't particularly care about *Night of the Living Dead* but found Sergei Eisenstein's *Strike* (1925) and Gillo Pontecorvo's *The Battle of Algiers* (1966) worth remembering.

Back at the medical suppliers, we're at the early stages of another fierce return of the repressed, now staged on the most bodily of levels, a mute sputter of surplus-life, the will to survive triggered and grown monstrous. Hacking and coughing, Frank and Freddy leave the basement to enter some of the more remarkable minutes in any zombie film I've seen. The gas, it appears, not only animates whole-bodied human corpses. It is an obscene principle of life itself, a whisper to everything that has lived that, *you never stopped living*. A bisected dog for classroom use barks and pants, its exposed organs throbbing. A display on pinioned butterflies flaps its wings gently. And a cadaver hung indifferently by meathook in a freezer wakes up very, very angry its current state of affairs.

The workers and their boss, as we would expect in a film like this, decide that dealing with a representative of the pissed-off undead means killing him more thoroughly. But, as we learn in this film, in an echo of that first moment of realization in *Night of the Living Dead* (the "Funny, it's not usually this hard to kill the poor" epiphany) is that it is no longer about destroying the body as a whole by removing its head.

Because in that case, you just get an even more furious, acephalic zombie running and flailing blindly through the warehouse. The sightless and thoughtless refusal to die, from the whole to the smallest part. Tied up and hack-sawed apart, the severed limbs shake in rage.[47] Flesh melted away with acid, the bones will not be quiet. And incinerated, the ashes may lay still, but the desperate insistences of the body do not stop. They rise up in a cloud of smoke, to meet the rain and trickle back down through grass, earth, and coffin lids, to pass the message to the other dead bodies that hadn't gotten the word.

In terms of transmission, *Return* represents an odd intermediary between the global totality cause in the Romero cycle and one-to-one infection logic emphasized in recent zombie culture. Here, there is a discernible event (the army created a gas with certain properties) and that event has to be directly transmitted (exposure to the gas or something already affected by it), but it remains strangely diffuse, raining down on dead and living alike. Furthermore, its effects break with either of these opposed models. It doesn't give the living a virus or surplus-life that "resurrects" them after death, it doesn't create a condition that only affects those who die after that condition has come to be. Yet the zombies we see in the film are, more than anything, a continuation of what they were in life, far more than in the parodic shambling of Romero's shoppers and munchers. Here, they run, they talk, they scheme and fool around, they work together toward common goals. If the thought of surplus-life hangs heavy over the whole genre, it does so here negatively. It is decisively present, in that form of a fanatical insistence of all once-living matter to flex its rotting muscles. And as for those who are alive when they face the gas, indeed, they become "dead" in the eyes of the living, but more than that, they become unable to truly die. The motivation for this uncanny life is not the urging of the body itself or a deep impulse transmitted by radiation or saliva-borne bacteria. Even the gas itself seems a cover story, a phenomenally present form of transmission that isn't ultimately about chemicals. Instead, it is about thought, a death-knowledge, a knowledge – *and a hostility* – strong enough to counter life.

This death-knowledge, which is less an allegorical reading of the film than a description of how we see the transmission and reanimation work throughout it, is a certain awareness. It finds some lingering shred of consciousness and infects it, brings the faint memory of death into the dominant horizon, and with it the "pain of being dead." Crucially, this isn't just an intellectual knowledge. It is somatic, speaking another tongue to the minimal units of living matter which, once made aware, cannot forget and won't settle down. The implication which forms a powerful nihilistic core to the film – one which entirely exceeds the petty immoral sex-and-death nihilism of the costume punks – and which cannot be shaken, is that being alive is solely the consequence of ignorance, of not being cognizant of your own decay.

Nowhere is this more evident than with the workers exposed to the gas. The major arc of the film is their story, as they move from mock frustration (with a bit of real terror) to a deep sickness, an ontological horror as they become dead without dying. The gas gives the same message to the living and the dead (*Did you know that you are dead? What are you going to do about it?*), yet while this knowledge animates the dead, stirs them into an action impelled by the pain of awareness itself, this shock to thought produces a mournful stasis for the workers, and dialogue that would be funny if it weren't injected with a rending, lingering sadness. When the paramedics are called to treat Freddy and Frank, and find them shivering, pale, with no pulse, and the temperature of a cold morgue, they are understandably stupefied.

PARAMEDIC: Because technically you're not alive. But you're conscious. So we don't know what it means.

FREDDY: Are you saying we're dead?

PARAMEDIC: Let's not jump to conclusions.

PARAMEDIC: I didn't mean you were really dead. Dead people don't move around and talk.

Because technically you're not alive. But you're conscious ... In a move familiar to the horror genre, we are supposed to be unsettled, spooked, or disturbed by the prospect that animating consciousness can exist in forms that exceed the living. That there are consciousnesses alien, and likely hostile, to our own. The standard narrative logic of those films tends to function via initial disbelief (*How could this be possible?*), then a recognition that belief must be suspended in order to deal with the threat, to conquer it so as to return to a "normal" that can never be truly normal again, because it is now infused with the knowledge that there are textures and shapes of being that exceed our ability to grasp.[48] All that we need to grasp is how to deal with them, with adequate violence and skill. In *Return*, we are indeed unsettled. But this unsettling is the consequence of a far darker operation: not that there are other kinds of perhaps undead consciousness, but that the very condition of normal life is itself a mere symptom of actively repressing what we know to be the case, that we're dying from the start, death warmed over and stretched out across the duration of the heart winding down, a self-tiring clock. Consequently, the return to death is the approach to the original state of things.

Almost. What this leaves out is the messianic undertones of the film and how it explores this schematic of the hard work of convincing others to join "the movement," via a sort of radical zombie pedagogy, a third way, the undead truth. The message begins with the gas, but it becomes part of the flesh of all that it touches, so that when the corpse is burned, it is the conviction and knowledge now part of the flesh itself which turns to smoke and spreads. The structure is essentially missionary, soldiers of God spreading the word: *Have you heard the good news? Jesus died*

for you. Or, in the case of this film, *Have you heard the bad news?*
You've already died. A necro-version of the sunglasses that lay bare
the class/alien race structure in Carpenter's *They Live* – once you
see, you can't go back to seeing otherwise.

What of *brains ...*, the constant, self-mocking cry kicked off in
this film that the figure of the zombie can't seem to shake? We
should consider it two ways, in how it derives and deviates from
the Romero model and on the terms established by the film itself.
In Romero's *Dead* series, the zombies have no particular love or
appetite for brains. (One might imagine a particular distaste for
them, given the difficulty of opening up a skull, especially for
hordes of the undead who aren't very adept at using tools.) They
fixate on general gutting and tearing, a non-targeted sloppy free-
for-all. And while the unsatisfactory and incomplete explana-
tions of *why* varies from film to film, the rough consensus is that
they do it because of some deep, and now misrecognized,
memory: of a savage primal past, of the mechanism of hunger
which no longer physiologically applies, of rampant consumer
consumption. In each case, the point is that *they do not choose to
do* it and that somewhere along the way, the message got mixed
up. ("Consume *commodities*? Hell, we've been going about this all
wrong.") Things are quite different in *Return*, although they also
have no real "need" to consume. The zombies know very well
what they are doing, and they're quite good about making sure
it gets done. It is an active choice, one that can be delayed in
order for the greater collective enterprise of spreading zombie
mayhem. And if anything, the problem isn't that they don't
remember clearly enough. It is that they remember far too
clearly, an awful clarity of mnemotechnic pain, searing
reminders of the decay of all things living.

The startling moment in which this is fully laid bare is one
unlikely to be forgotten by any who have seen the film. A long-
dead, grave husk zombie captured by the living, with nothing
left of her but her head, shoulders, and an exposed spine

swaying to and fro, is interrogated on an examining table. When asked "why brains?", she responds in a hissing whisper, "The pain of being dead ... I can feel myself rot." Pressed further as to the connection between this "pain" (which already seems closer to the pain of *knowing* you are dead) and brain lust, she replies, "Eating brains makes the pain go away." I'm not interested in speculating as to the ways in which the consumption of brains might physiologically dull the pain of a rotting body. For one thing, the film itself has little interest in this, leaving any direct connection cloudy and pointing in more compelling directions. If it is knowledge that causes this pain, a certain brutal deconstruction, willful misuse, and redeployment of knowledge can be the only solution. An overliteralized version of giving you something else to think about, albeit thoughts which enter through the guts rather than ears and eyes, swallowing a different sort of knowledge, distracting yourself from what you can't stop thinking about. (A distraction that never lasts: how could it when we never stop falling apart?) And more sharply, a sort of pain sharing, an act of spreading the bad word. Gathering ranks for an army and a war that may truly end the world as we know it. Having inherited a pain that comes with your position in a system you didn't choose, solace comes in knowing that this pain – and what it drives you to willfully choose to do – is not singular but collective. If, as Fredric Jameson has put it pithily,

"History is what hurts," *Return* is the story of how the already dead attempt to write a history "back from the grave" and into this world, a trajectory in reverse, written in a pain experienced by those who are doomed to hurt and who demand in turn that we all hurt. It's hard to envision another cinematic instance of such direct propaganda work. *Want to know what the pain of thought and thought of pain is? Give me your head for a moment.*

Out of this unyielding "pain," one has two choices, at least according to the film: suicide or mass participation in knowledge-sharing. (The other non-choice that we see pursued, with no great success, is to skulk around a cellar, biting into the brains of idiot punks who have little knowledge to share, or to wait around until your "turn" to make a bad joke and go for your girlfriend's head.) The first choice we witness in a moment that genuinely shares pain beyond the film, to all who watch it, as Frank, now "technically not alive," prays briefly, removes his wedding ring, and pushes himself into the blazing fires of the crematorium. Yet even this attempt to cut himself out of the cycle, to refuse to participate in the zombie holocaust, cannot succeed. It may remove his ongoing personal pain, but as we witness earlier, it is the fact of burning and the transmission of the buried message in the smoke, out into the night air, that allows for the mass dissemination of knowledge. In opting out of the cursed game, Frank becomes a martyr for a cause he died to avoid supporting.

If Frank's death is the awful pathos of a broken man caught in a cycle of the inevitable, the other alternative is the joyous center of the film, its recurring cheers from the audience, and the "utopian" kernel of it all. It is collectivity formed out of what could be a crushing awareness, knowing that you are not even special in the ontological pain you feel, that you are just one of a growing horde of those powerless to change it, to die properly, to quit the pain. Yet against either the dysphoric retreat or the escape into the fantasy of the irrational – "I will act as irrational, bloody shambling horde-like, as the system that made us" – that linger at the edges of this first knowledge emerges a new rationality.

This is a crucial point, for much of the ideology of the zombie situation hinges on the assumption of their irrationality. Sure, maybe they once knew what they were doing, and now remember a shard of it. Or maybe, in the later iterations of the Romero cycle, particularly *Land of the Dead* (2005), they can move toward an incipient group knowledge, rudimentary use of tools and implements, basic swarm strategies, and so on. *Return* shows something different altogether: what if what this thing we assumed from the start to be, at least initially, mindless in its anger, illogical in its hunger, what *if it has been rational all along*? What if it not only can hurt, but comprehends this hurt? And what if it realizes that this pain is not individual but collective? What if the ways in which it aims to destroy the system – the system that wants to destroy it – are rational?

Return approaches, in the midst of its gags and "punk" soundtrack, these very serious questions, although incompletely. The closest it gets is to ask: *what if they get their shit together?* The threat – and the supposed horror we feel at witnessing an uncanny imitation of almost-life – is not that of an otherness that shows our complicity in mindless structures of consumption or of an underlying savagery, not blind groupthink or hive mind, not of never being at peace and forced to wander, not of the very unearthing and undermining of the natural order of things. It is the threat of collectivity itself. It is something we have learned to fear, not the end of romantic individuality itself but the prospect that autonomous subjects may recognize the limits of that autonomy and begin to act together, an unholy assemblage of different tactics, motives, and skills unified into a shared weapon against a world gone very wrong.

It is also, in this case, getting onto the ambulance radio to pretend to be a concerned citizen and call for more paramedics to be directed into the mouths of your fellow zombies waiting in the shadows. It is dressing up in the policeman's uniform, acting very official and directing drivers to where they will meet their untimely end (or, depending on your perspective, be "convinced" of the fact of their deadness and the need to do something about it). It is being very rational and coldly calculating about how to achieve and enact your apparent irrationality.

The world of the living is, to be sure, not interested in the utopian potential of this mode of organization and antagonism. Having learned that Trioxin has been leaked, with all its attendant effects, Colonel Glover receives a call in bed and makes the decision, still in his monogrammed pajamas, to nuke Louisville, Kentucky.

We hear a high, keening whistling as the zombies, their victims, and those trying to avoid being either look up and wait. And then, the mushroom cloud rises at dawn. It was a complete success, the threat has been contained, and, even more fortunately, the rain is putting out the fires. Of course, the rain now carries the atomized microparticles of the death-knowledge, sprayed infinitesimally small into the atmosphere, the diffuse message of antagonism and pain, now borne in clouds and tiny water droplets to fall onto other towns, onto other places of the dead. Here we go again.

TO BECOME NO FUTURE

What of those punks we left earlier, killing time, talking about the varying degrees of their punkness? In a supremely kitschy moment, they pull up to the "Resurrection Cemetery" to wait for Freddy to finish his shift. Spider – the leather and piercing punk, nominally the leader of this not-as-motley-as-it-wants-to-be crew – has a convertible that is covered in graffiti, evidently of his own design. On the door, "WHY." On the hood, "WHO CARES?" As with so much of the pop-cultural versions of punk, you have to ask at what point someone doth protest too much. The inanity continues onto the gate of the cemetery, which features arguably my favorite bit of sublimely direct graffito: "SEX." And in big red letters on the heavy wood, "NO FUTURE."

The "punks" in this movie are tools, shallow poseurs who we are only too happy to see butchered. But the inclusion of "NO FUTURE" points elsewhere and raises, even if it ultimately cannot answer it, the connection to the real historical anxieties, furies, and closed horizons of which the figure of punk and punks were a willful symptom and abortive anti-solution. If our interest with salvagepunk was on the *operation* of punk, here it is explicitly on *the punks*, those who are sneeringly labeled as such or who take on such an epithet as a badge of pride.

And indeed, the punks here have a lot of pride and libidinal energy invested in being designated as such. In one of his great laughable moments, Spider, draped with naked Trash (remarkably incapable of ever locating her pants once she takes them off), huffs and puffs that no one understand his punkness. "You think this is a costume? This is a way of life." We believe him, although not in the way he likely intends. It clearly takes a fair amount of effort to match up your appearance and character in accordance with a vision of punk from afar – the "ways" of his life consist of a complex parroting. Furthermore we should recall that the film is set in Louisville, not London or Los Angeles or other historic punk metropoles, and that by 1985, punk was hardly cutting-edge. If anything, the problem was that by that time it was indeed a "way of life," just one more identity to take on as mantle, with its particular valences of commodity and identity, all wrapped in an increasingly stale version of a "fuck the world" ethos.

Spider does get one thing very right, although once more against the grain of how he means it. One of the thought-forms of punk – if we can talk of it this way – is a collapsing of essence and form, of visions of a humanist subject and unique individual that should be understood as who you "really are." Punk, at its best, is a frontal assault on this mode, insisting instead that if there is something that lies beneath our surface manifestations, it isn't particularly worth elevating. It is a negative subject, notable only in its absence: what future can there be when we no longer believe ourselves to be basically good, rational, and democratic, when our future isn't worth saving? Into this absence steps a logic of pure surface, insisting that there is nothing but *ways of life*, expressions without reference to *what* or *who* they express. The question is *how* you express. The question is a tactics of ornament and style. So while Spider means that this isn't a costume (a false garb) but rather a correct expression/translation of who he really is, the turn proper to punks would be to say that now, in the twilight of the West, there remain nothing but costumes, masks with nothing behind. Punk often remained incapable of dropping a certain moralism that underpins a version of this (society wants us to be false, but we can start living "true" lives), but the intuition remains both forceful and inseparable from its historical moment.

Something closer to the zombie policeman.

Return's zombie-in-police-drag is the real punch-line to the weak joke of the film's punks. He is aware that to wage war against the world, you sometimes need to wear a costume, and that there is a crucially important gap between the ideology of "authenticity" (how you appear should express what kind of person you are) and the concrete practices of fighting against a totality (the world as such). Donning the garments of a cop, putting on the arrangement of fabric that codifies you as someone to be trusted bears no connection to who you are. There is only what you do once dressed in this way: uphold the social and legal conventions of a economic system and its mediated barbarisms, or, for this zombie-punk, work to viscerally undo these conventions and usher in a new system of visible barbarism. We should elevate and revere neither system, but the innovation, the dressing-up in order to take down, is hard not to admire.

This fundamental move of punk might be summed up as follows: the human experience is just an organization of surface instances and concrete actions - we don't like the constellations of surfaces forced upon us by this era and its institutions under the guise of possibilities for our future – we therefore declare war against this empty future (or one that we'll make damn sure turns out to be empty). That said, the sense of "no future" and manner of war varies vastly:

a self-destructive solipsism: *I wage war on myself* (I have no future in this world)

a withdrawal into micro-communities of the likeminded: *We wage war on the assumption that we would want to engage with the options presented to us* (we want no future in this wider world that does not want us)

a corrosive and raging negativity: *We wage war on everything* (we want no future for this world)

an apocalyptic politics of the end: *We take over the war the world wages on itself in order to shape its waging* (this world has created its own end, and we are the agents and manifestations of that no-future)

One could begin to see how a film like *Return* acts as a sort of cognitive map of these permutations: the war on self (Frank's suicide), the war on participation (the punks dropping out), the war on everything (the blanket A-bombing of the town, the zombies before they act collectively), and the war on the world's organization/mode of future (the tactical zombies). Indeed, we should retain an awareness of the ways in which these mediated responses to a world to be destroyed shape not only the zombie film but apocalyptic culture more broadly. The question, now and always, is not just how the world may end, but what part you will – or can – play in shaping, causing, and mediating that end.

More particularly, the issue at hand isn't the claim that the zombies do punkish things, or even that we can detect in zombies some of the same energies and anxieties placed on the figure of punks in film (i.e. considered as dangerous, pitiable, execrable, or just silly). Rather, the issue is that zombies and punks are bound together in a relationship both allegorical and historical. (Crucially, 'punks' here means not just those who think of themselves as punk," but those older senses, of the unwanted, of street trash, hoodlums, lumpen, and wastes-of-life.) For if zombies are both those incapable of consuming correctly and those who take revenge on a regime of work and life, they stand, however tenuously, in relation to those who can neither work nor afford to consume correctly, and to those who make an active decision to do neither.

This is ultimately a relation between two inheritances, political and cultural/aesthetic legacies that cross at the intersection of zombies and punks. First, a badly repressed political inheritance: the social fallout of counter-revolution and its consequences for the political climate and horizons in the long '70s and the decades to come. To take the example of the American context, on which our zombie focus has fallen, this is the arc from social unrest and urban revolutionary movements (such as the Black Panthers) to the active work of COINTELPRO (Counter Intelligence Program, the notorious covert FBI actions to infiltrate and destroy dissident organizations) to the wide-spread emergence of gangs and the crack trade. This is also the story of the collapse of the welfare state and its mental health services, loosing the dregs of society, its crazies and unwanted, onto the streets. This is the brutal closure, by active measure and shifting economic landscape, of a broader sense of social change and disruption, as those who *rationally* contested the system via organization and action, declined into the amorphous swarms of those systematically excluded and declared *irrational*. This dismantling of the forms of resistance could not, of course, remove the energy and discontent behind it. Instead, it could only dissipate it across the city and into cultural forms that could only be marked deeply by this.

A second inheritance is one visible only now, in the present consumer feeding frenzy for all things undead. It is almost strictly cultural-aesthetic: the look and trope of the nervous laughter of the black comedic zombie film, now dragged into every multiplex, the backlog of specialized knowledge of supposedly hard-to-find old films (the game of the low culture mining virtuoso), and pseudo-hipster cultural obsession.[49] It has become – or so we are told – the sign of our times without registering the social content underpinning those '70s and '80s films. An inheritance with not enough of the repressed returning, glossed over into a banal thought supposedly about worries of contagion and vague apocalypticism in our swine flu and speculative bubble era.

In other words, if we can detect in the zombie films of that earlier period not a direct manifestation of mass anxieties about the unknown but a repeating set of attempts to elaborate a persistent and horrifying same, then the generic conventions, aesthetics, and tropes taken up en masse in recent years function as a willful forgetting of those attempts. This isn't to say that these films used to be "political" and are no longer. It is rather that some of their odd force was the sloppy forging of the aesthetics of counter-revolution itself, meeting at that point of contact between the end of a political trajectory and the start of what would become a juicy and endlessly replicable bit of cultural zeitgeist. Yet the point of contact on which this relation hinges is perhaps not the zombie film itself, but its fellow traveler and necessary double, the "punk film" (and film punks) that gathers the critical energy, worries, and fears of counter-revolution with a near total absence of allegorical distance.

The kind of film "punks" we mean? To take a cursory survey: the psychotic and dissolute rapist scum of *Death Wish* (1974) and its sequels in 1982 and 1985; the everyone-can-be-possessed psychotic urban anxiety of *God Told Me To* (1974), not to mention a good chunk of Larry Cohen's other output; the multi-ethnic gang Street Thunder and their blood pact in *Assault on Precinct 13* (1976); the costumed, mutually destructive youth tribe "armies of the night" of *The Warriors* (1979); pretty much the entirety of *Repo Man* (1984); the literally melting winos in *Street Trash* (1987); certain eccentric, vaguely queer baddies plus the broad sense of a lumpen population able to be mobilized for crime in *Robocop* (1987) and *Robocop 2* (1990); the less reformed of the Joker's post-

Arkham henchmen and assorted grimy low-lifes in *Batman* (1989) and the rest of that series (involving a real predilection for garish face paint and an excessive amount of leather and latex, pretty much evenly across the good and evil spectrum).

These punk films, varied as they are, and the zombie films discussed above have a relation of mutual disclosure, in which the stoppages and potentials that can't be addressed in one find a skewed reflection in the other. This centers on the conceptions of what kind of *no future* we talk about and what response it demands (the kind of war to be waged). At its best moments, the zombie film captures a diffuse energy lurking in the notion of the punk that couldn't find full formation in its cultural representations, an energy of diffusion itself, of the mass and the horde: not the street gangs or homeless of one city, but the global undead swarm, heterogeneous and menacing. Connected with that, the zombie retains a powerful perspective that few of these punk films are capable of mapping, namely, the movements from global totality to local consequence. The tendency for the hoodlum-punks or the punk rocker detritus to be cast, respectively, as evil or stupid is not just the result of a fundamentally reactionary tint to the films, as pervasive as that may be. Rather, it is symptomatic of the deep difficulty of grasping how these situated instances of the irrational – or that which is rational but counter to the available definitions of what discontent would look like – emerge from a set of "rational" calculations of profit, accumulation, and circulation.

What, then, does the punk film do that the zombie film cannot or will not? First, it presents a vision of the irrational-to-rational arc of the Romero cycle (mapped across the films as the possibility of the zombies beginning to learn and act in concert) that remains "realist," in which irrationality is never seen as a condition of exceptionality imposed from afar, from biochemical technology gone awry, or according to arcane law. At its worst, it flees into the conservative hysterics that paint the punks as perverted low-lifes who are simply "just those kind of people." Yet even there, the recognition persists that something has changed on the ground, that something is qualitatively different now, and it has discernible roots in the shifting organization of urban spaces, social programs, and opportunities for labor and community formation. Second, if the zombie apocalypse (and hence the revelatory aspect) is the sudden and total unearthing of the savage heart of capital's antagonisms, the punk apocalypse is an inconstant and ongoing one: we can never tell quite where it stops and starts, when it started, and just how widespread it is. Third, most painfully, it presents both the fierce potential of the antagonist group's collective rationality and the auto-destruction of that possibility as those groups sabotage what may have been otherwise.

The real worry wound through these movies, mean-spirited, laughable, and bloodthirsty as they are, isn't that you will be overrun by those you condemn as irrational and subhuman. Rather, there are two worries. First, they might, as in *Assault on Precinct 13*, start firing in the same direction. The *cholo* placed on the police station isn't just a commitment to fight to the death. It's a flag, a marker of where to aim. Notably, it's at the moment when the blood is thrown and war declared that the film abandons the earlier plot interest in a cross-cutting focus on the vaguely revolutionary leaders. (A sort of COINTELPRO caricature of dissident groups: a Che rip-off, an IRA-esque sniper, pseudo-Black Panther, and so on.) At that point, they become faceless, replaceable. The would-be revolutionaries become zombies, dark hordes clambering through the broken windows. Of course, what Street Thunder could learn from a better analysis of zombie movies is to set their sights beyond the already evacuated pockets of hell on earth. To Hollywood, then...

A second worry: what if these degenerates not only feel pain but rationalize it, not to explain it away but to track out its sources, finding better targets than an empty police station? That they won't destroy themselves in the ravages of drug epidemics (most potently and meltingly realized in *Street Trash*, in which winos drink the cheapest of all alcohol, quite literal rot-gut, and subsequently disintegrate before our eyes) or in turf wars and skirmishes over control of black markets? What if they get it together enough to run everyone else out of town, or perhaps worse, just stop giving a damn about the systems and processes that cast them out in the first place, stop giving you an excuse to "crack down" on them (i.e. massacre and imprison)? The derided other stops looking back your way for disapproval.

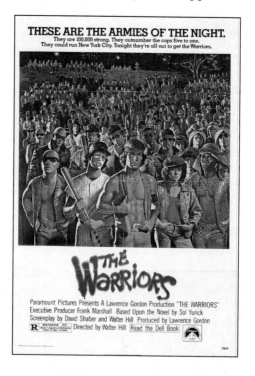

And yet ... The extended poster tagline for *The Warriors* begins: "These are the armies of the night. They are 100,000 strong. They outnumber the cops five to one. They could run New York City." And indeed, they could. We should gauge and note both the proximity and distance of this to zombie film. They are equally coded as an infernal force, something unholy ("armies of the night" is essentially a stand-in for "legions of evil"). But what is different, emergent, and ultimately unsustainable, is this sense of density, purpose, and distinct shape: armies *that could run a city*. The film opens with the assembly of the disparate gangs and the prospect, notably, not of taking the city anarchically via an amorphous fury of looting, violence, and intimidation, but through an almost democratic calculation of numbers and a near anarcho-syndicalist model of how to do it (albeit with "crime" syndicates). The police, who stand as the guardians and stewards of the current social order of the city, are vastly outnumbered by the gangs, the heralds of an opaque but possible order to come, gathered beneath a collective but not unitary banner.

We never get the chance to see what rule by street punk coalition would look like, for, in a moment of cutting historical resonance, the possibilities of self-organization and autonomous control – in all its utopian and dystopian colors – shoots itself dead. A member of the Rogues shoots Cyrus – the leader of the assembly calling for gang collaboration – for *no reason*. The fundamental irrationality of a particle of the whole provokes the general collapse of the rational, as it slides back into bloody factionalism once more. The movie changes from what could have been the story of a battle between systems/*Weltanschauungen* to a hectic chase through the night, a tale of mistaken blame, and clearing your gang's good name. As the tagline concludes, "Tonight they're all out to get the Warriors."

And so they will remain, the punks never able to pull together again, not just in this film, but in the arc across genres, across cultural spheres, across the declension of insurrectionary politics in the neoliberal age. We are left with, and now witness the terminal conclusions of, the walking dead, shuffling ahead without the critical energy of the punk.

THE WHOLE EARTH SHUDDERS

How did we get from there to here, from the strange cinematic crucible of the necrotic cannibal and the gang haunted by the shadow of a failed revolutionary past to *Pride and Prejudice and Zombies*? From the aching pain of memory and the contagious knowledge of zombie pedagogy to just "brains ..." and a general acceleration, as if the zombies sprinting faster would make it so we can't see what has been lost?

The answer, if there is one, lies less in a direct correlation with broad trends in politics and ideology and more in the trajectory of the horror film in general and the particular effects this had on the genre of the zombie film. As a tradition leaving the U.S., exported primarily under the Romero name, the zombie film found a range of potent expressions. Most famously and powerfully, the Lovecraftian mystical apocalypse and gore mining of Lucio Fulci's films, full of brutal splatter and decay, ranging from the Satanic Surrealist genius of *The Beyond* (1981) to the island of fetid cadaverous cannibals (and a return to the Caribbean roots) in *Zombie 2* (1979).[50] However, as a mainstream horror trope in the U.S., the zombie film lost its cachet for a period, as the nameless, replaceable hordes were themselves replaced by the endless iterations of the big names (Freddy, Jason, Michael, Chuckie, etc) and the attempts to establish serial characters. More precisely, the continuing reliable location of threat and menace in hard-to-kill, discernible individuals.

Such a tendency was equally hard for the industry to kill, as it continued (and continues) to churn out increasingly campy versions, with the kind of proto-mash-up format we can see in *Freddy vs. Jason* (2003) and *Alien vs. Predator* (2004) (those odd films that have distant ancestors in the sort of madcap goofiness that is *Abbott and Costello Meet Frankenstein* [1948]). In the two year span between '94 and '96, Wes Craven released *Wes Craven's New Nightmare* (which took the wind out of his own Freddy

Kreuger series and, with a broad, post-modern gesture, took the legs out of 80s horror seriality) and *Scream*, which paved the way for imitators of its brand of smugly knowing, black comedic slashers playing auto-referentially with the moves and conventions of the genre.

This is all to say that while the legacy of Romero's films never went fully away, the dominant logic in horror films became that of one-to-one violence: the antagonist kills one individual after another, not as a systemic event (suddenly all the dead rise) but as a series of encounters (Jason kills another camper) which give the illusion of moral readability and localizable causality (revenge, individual pathology, the usual suspects).

Yet if we consider the preeminent expression of the contemporary zombie film (*28 Days Later* and *28 Weeks Later* [2007], *Shaun of the Dead*, the 2004 remake of *Dawn of the Dead*, with its significant difference from the original), we find a striking departure from the founding Romero, and later O'Bannon, gesture. Namely, in these recent films, the zombies are not the dead risen (or the surplus-life undead): they are simply the infected living. This is neither the sickness of knowledge nor the abstract compulsion of transmission. Rather, it is the "Rage" virus in the Boyle series and the vampire-like contagion in the *Dawn of the Dead* remake. It is a sickness that makes you act "less than human." Regarding the *Dawn* remake, the fundamental difference from its source film is that it is a *one-to-one* transmission. If you are bitten, you will become a zombie, not because you will die after the new condition of surplus-life has affected you, but because some-*one* infected you.

What are the ideological effects of this? In brief, the specificity of the zombie, as the global condition that repeats endlessly the ceaseless getting back up of the corpses, is abandoned for a scenario that combines the one-to-one logic of the slasher, the subject-turning bite of the vampire/werewolf film, and the fear of the thoughtless, rabid masses (although these are now a good deal less concerned with sating hunger than with biting, in a blind fury of species propagation quite different from the tactical pedagogy and mutual aid of *Return*'s walking dead). The moral economy and clarity of one-to-one violence – both of the "sick" person who gives it to you and, in a longer echo, of the individual voodoo master – and the ability to blame meets the horror of the rabid, mindless horde. As a result, blame can only be directed to this or that person, who "should have known better," who is "that sort of person," who did this to me. It shifts away from either an attack directed toward the master or toward the masterless dominance of abstraction. Instead, you blame the zombies. You curse those already cursed.

Why this, why now? Are zombies the nasty return of materiality, a figure of undead labor in the face of collapsing "spectral" capitalism? Do these films get made because they stand in for the constantly resurgent worries about pandemics, tainted products, and supergerms? The answer can only be: if so, not in any direct way. If we call into question the ethics of one-to-one transmission models, we should equally question the efficacy of one-to-one allegorical models. Quite simply, that isn't how films get made, how mass culture happens. At best, we can complicate and return to the broader arc of the story told here, of how real abstractions work on real bodies. To sketch back over the ground covered: zombies begin again, reloaded, in their Romero form as the monstrous thought of totality and the causeless abstract event causing concrete horrors. This thought is crystallized in the figure of the swarming, irrational horde, a figure that echoes the destruction of organized radical groups and the diffusion of that potential into disunified antagonism and the scattered modes of the punk. In this resides the real fear of the zombie model, that they might organize differently, swarms and hordes replaced with discipline, uniform hunger, and new pedagogies of struggle. This is lost in the march toward one-to-one horror, as is the vision of the mass form as causal, produced by a system that has systematically destroyed alternatives. We are left with the carriers of contagion who "don't know any better" yet who are to be blamed for individual actions, the ones we "have" to kill.

There is indeed something we have to kill now, as much as we can ever interfere in the unholy recombinatory mechanisms of advertising departments, massive cultural production, word of mouth, and various ways to make sexy zombie Halloween costumes. No more zombies, not now, not while the nightmare image of our times has become equally a dollar sign.[51] Not because something we loved – or that scared us – has been ruined, not because it's lame now that everyone is doing. Not for the false purity of a devotee convinced that the essence or brutality has been tainted. And, crucially, not because zombies no longer mean what they used to. No, it is because they no longer mean what they could. And that *could* remains what it has been from the start, the horizon of the structurally *wrong* realizing its systemic origin, its rational composition, and its militant potential. Zombies no longer stand in for the wrong. They are the frozen appearance of that which is just a little off, a bit gauche and a bit goth, the flawless consumable trope of the pseudo-wrong.

This is not to say that recent zombie films are either bad or uninteresting. The Boyle series is often sharp and harrowing, *Shaun of the Dead* is both funnier and smarter  than it has any right to be, and the recent Romero films (*Land of Dead* and *Diary of the Dead* [2007]) have their moments. *Land*, in particular, draws forth the nascent and lingering logic of zombie group formation and casts it in an on-the-surface anti-capitalist bent, insofar as Dennis Hopper's city lord oligarch and his barricaded zone of normalcy stands in for capitalism. And *Diary* is alarmingly realist, insofar as it is an obnoxious film putatively made by obnoxious people: its fake verisimilitude does too good a job of showing the kind of hand-held hack filmmaking these shallow artistes would in fact make, particularly in the face of a zombie uprising. But one cannot avoid a sense of *too much, too late*. In the era of ultra self-knowing zombie culture, these are drawn into the force-field of "just once more," even as they participate in the broader arc described (especially the trend toward the one-to-one logic of contagion).

A film like *Fido*, the 2006 *Pleasantville*-meets-Bub-from-*Day of the Dead* campy outing, stands exactly at that juncture: it's relatively funny and quite aware of its position as both a revisionist reload and as one more in the long line. In the rough conceit, after a Fordist-era suburban zombie holocaust has been quelled, we've figured out how to "tame" zombies, via the shock/pacification collars provided by the ever-present mega corporation. So begins a seemingly subversive production: we learn that white male patriarchy is a bad thing, that the staid homogeneity of suburban commodity life cannot provide for the real desires of lonely housewives, that the undead are likely more attentive to your needs than your well-meaning but sexless husband. And indeed, in that facile and expected counter-cultural turn of siding with the zombies, Fido, the eponymous zombie butler/gardener/dead man about the house, takes the family helm. The inattentive father is killed, the local head of the corporation is himself turned into a collared zombie to be led about by his daughter via leash, and the seeming triumph of unwanted menial laborers is assured.

But this zombie triumph is a fleeting cover for the broader trajectory, one that persists in the background of *Fido* but can't come into focus. Namely, the flight back into the *personal* that plagues so much of the apocalyptic imaginary, the inability to think broader structural shifts outside of what happens to families or individual lovers. In this case, while Fido steps into the vacant father role, now dressed in proper retro wear and sipping cold beverages brought by his fawning new wife, all the other zombies continue their labor. The exception and emancipation is singular. And insofar as *Fido* barely veils its consideration of migrant and informal labor, of those unseen who do the work of maintaining the hedges and clean surfaces of the first world, it's difficult to see this as exceeding the real common perspective toward such labor, that the occasional inclusion is OK insofar as it takes the form of assimilation and remains an isolated incident. The zombie triumph of *Fido* is the triumph of an order willing to make exceptions in order to prove their exceptionality.

A brighter recent spark is *Pontypool* (2008), set almost entirely in a Canadian radio station in the winter. Not technically a zombie movie – the director calls the antagonists "Conversationalists" – but clearly situated as a part of that lineage, the "virus" at hand is literally discursive. You get stuck on some minor linguistic slippage, substituting a near-homonym or the like, particularly for relatively "empty" words (the use of *honey* as an affectless term of endearment, for example). And you can't shake it from there, muttering, caught in a bad feedback loop, trying to work out the difference or meaning, until it consumes you. From there, you devolve into a hideous combination of self-mutilation, rage, and parroting of any new bit of language that comes your way. You seek out not so much the living, but the talking or the sign-making, in a brutal attempt to break the circuit of that self-same repetition, in a distant echo of the other reading of *brains* ..., where the influence (or consumption) of another mind is needed to help get your mind off the situation at hand (i.e. being dead). But the most unsettling moment of the film is perhaps the real gap between the "primitive" call for *brains* ... or even some shared mantra, and the moment when we learn that a group of Conversationalists swarming a car are mimicking, en masse, the quiet hiss and scrape of windshield wipers. Repetition decoupled from any object of desire ...

The theory supporting the film is unsteady: are there certain words that carry the contagion, or does it emerge from the mechanism of linguistic failure, regardless of which words? But what it does stress, nevertheless, in the talk radio host's manic, near-Dadaist ramble as nuclear retribution comes near (as it did to Louisville in *Return of the Living Dead*), is the realization that some forms of discourse just replicate what is wrong from the start. More important, however, is the accompanying recognition that the solution isn't to prohibit participating in those forms of discourse, to just shut up and wait for things to blow over. Like the plague brought home from afar, the point is to do the work of the virus better than it can and to turn it back on itself. To find the words and tropes repeated to the point where they mean nothing other than the very failed attempt to break through a deadlock of thought, and to make them mean otherwise.

"Zombie" has already become one of those words in our contemporary moment: it is the vacant and incessant sign of a breakdown both of historical thought and of history's prospects of going differently. The way forward, therefore, out of the stalemate of repetition made mass, lies in two directions. First, to "make it mean otherwise," to strip and retrofit the genre and its moves, in the way that the cop-uniform zombie or the "language virus" gets the original gesture right with the real fidelity of a surface betrayal. Second, to know when *not* to search for those lost origins and their energy, when to focus instead on the *deadness* which trails along the unceasing heart of surplus-life. To be clearer, let's return to the lines from Adorno with which we began: "The surplus of reality amounts to its collapse; by striking the subject dead, reality itself becomes deathly." The point here, both frightening and expansive, bleak and bright, is to take fully onto ourselves this endgame of the "surplus of reality," of the symbolic, political, and economic over-determination of all the things of the world under capitalism, and particularly of its apocalyptic imaginings. Out of this surplus, this overwhelming of the subject capable of speaking and intervening, the dead things and soon-to-be-dead laboring bodies of the world – the basic material truth of the system – perhaps find tongues, even if they remain silent. A silence all the more poisonous and resonant. Like the infinite corpse-strewn wasteland that concludes Fulci's *The Beyond* (a rare film with the courage to stick to its properly apocalyptic guns) or Guy Debord's proposition that reality explodes in the heart of the world made unreal, the task might be, at least figuratively, to stop searching for the nostalgic beating heart that brings radical thought to a standstill, in its frozen image, and to start from the fundamental deadness of that world. This is neither conciliation nor reconciliation. It is an exposure of the already-was and the no-longer.

This is a far darker proposition than that of salvagepunk, which also deals with brokenness and the attempt to dig innate values out of the dead pile. It lacks the hopeful task of the salvager. What more would we expect from that which remains, even or perhaps because of those ceaseless iterations of the world of the living colonized by the world of the dead, but with no one to blame? A plague born of abstraction and all the harder to stop for it, made worse because of our complicity in its reproduction. In the face of this, our best attempt is to detect the other plagues that we also cannot produce but can perhaps dig out. Perhaps not just of surplus-life bound to spin its wheels on the surface, but to the deeper dead, all that we thought too far gone to return.

To grasp at a structural condition: to speak through the dead and to make history say what it didn't but *should*? To go back further, against the grain, to false starts that didn't catch, abortive gestures not decayed, but out of sight. That's the real nightmare: what awakens but goes nowhere, pressed down beneath the massive weight. The long dead rising, rustling in their sealed coffins, awake and restless and buried too deep, but thinking again. Scattered bones in killing fields sweating and shuffling. The whole earth shudders.

Combined and uneven apocalypse

Wild, dark times are rumbling toward us, and the prophet who wishes to write a new apocalypse will have to invent entirely new beasts, and beasts so terrible that the ancient animal symbols of St. John will seem like cooing doves and cupids in comparison.
- Heinrich Heine, Lutetia; or, Paris

So when the ship goes down, so too do the first class passengers ...
- Amadeo Bordiga, "Weird and Wonderful Tales of Modern Social Decadence"

BARBARIANS INSIDE THE GATES

The world is already apocalyptic. Just not all at the same time.

To be overcome: the notion of apocalypse as evental, the ground-clearing revelatory trauma that immediately founds a new *nomos* of the earth.[52] In its place: combined and uneven apocalypse.

In other words, we already occupy a world in which Heine's entirely new beasts have emerged and exist alongside us, real organizations of suffering and domination. All the more so, in unprecedented invention and brutality, under capitalism. The question is the visibility of these beasts. They constantly rear their figurative heads, yes. But because they are not accidents but necessary functions and consequences of the capitalist world system, they are structural blindspots. The intentional symptom, the shouldn't-be that has-to-be for it all to work: no wonder it's so hard to write a new apocalypse.

This isn't to dredge back up the persistent (and always relevant) point that we remain conveniently unaware of pockets of hell on earth that approximate the total breakdown of civility and quality of life, or that we catch glimpses of them only when they surge up in the midst of supposedly advanced sectors of the world. For example, the rotting refuse and murdered "looters" of Hurricane Katrina revealed what we've "known all along" about the structures of poverty, race and urban decay in America. The brief and quickly forgotten media focus on "unthinkable" poverty and desperation following in the wake of natural disasters, catches, out the corner of its impatient and trained eye, forms of deprivation that cannot be ascribed to whatever tsunami or earthquake is in question. (Like some terrible echo of the question to be asked of horror movies: "well, if this particular catastrophic event - werewolves, zombies, or evil fog - didn't happen, what would still be very wrong with people's lives?" What does this exceptional instance reveal that is horrifying *because* it's already the case?) And underpinning this, the articulations of liberal guilt, sincere as it may or may not be, ranging from NGOs and their often well-intentioned apologetics of new imperialism to calls for less conspicuous consumption, from staying well-informed and reading the right newspapers to learning the doomed-to-fail limits of that knowledge.

To counter this, to at once grasp the non-evental persistence of hell on earth and to escape the falsely naturalizing vision that "these sort of things are just part of human life," we push toward a theory of *combined and uneven apocalypse*. The term is a revision and pun off of the Marxist theory of combined and uneven development, a theory that gives shape to my analysis not just of geographical displacement but a general structure of overlapping timescales, speculative trajectories out of joint, and all those knotty passages from abstraction to the barest shapes of the concrete.

The term first came into use with Trotsky's analysis, especially in *The History of the Russian Revolution*, of the process of development for nations – in this case, backward, peasant-centered Russia – entering into bourgeois social relations, and the real subsumption of labor forms to capitalism in the midst of an already "modern" world dominated by fully developed powers. One of the particularities of capitalism as a developmental model is that the very nature of international trade and emergent global circulation of raw materials and commodities means that countries cannot develop *capitalistically* outside of the broader trendline of development. Once capitalism was forged out of the partition of the commons and the innovation of post-feudal labor models in England, no other country could develop it "organically" from scratch. It is a game of catch-up, mimicking the new forms and technologies, securing trade routes, and walking the fine line between fiercely protecting one's interests and opening up markets to the more anarchic struggles of competition. It's stepping forward unstably, on the basis of a combination of mercenary innovation, prior geopolitical sway, historical luck, and a commitment to scrapping the old organization of economic life while keeping its ideologies of domination. Above all, it's making damn sure that once you've secured a piece of the production-circulation pie, you will bar others from entering the system except as markets for your goods, pools of cheap labor for your production, and sites resource extraction. Hence, any nation trying to break from this position faces a battle of rupturing the material organization of the capitalist system: a willingness to be nastier in forcing the acceleration toward social restructuring and to offer cheaper labor than elsewhere available was, unfortunately, the dominant solution of the 20th century.

Not is all bad news for our latecomers, our barbarians at the value-form gate. To enter into the global order is to arrive at its modernity, wherever that may be: the need to compete at the level of the other powers means rushing headlong forward, to arrive at that market-confirmed point of the present (the rates of profit against which one shines or fails) without passing through all the stages of "organic" development prior. As Trotsky writes,

> A backward country assimilates the material and intellectual conquests of the advanced countries. But this does not mean that it reproduces them slavishly, reproduces all the stages of their past ... The privilege of historic backwardness permits, or rather compels, the adoption of whatever is ready in advance of any specified date, skipping a whole series of intermediate stages. Savages throw away their bows and arrows for rifles all at once, without traveling the road which lay between those two weapons in the past.[53]

(Although, as we have seen with salvagepunk and will consider further, that doesn't mean that non-savages can't slide back to weapons they never held in the past. Apparently leaps and bounds don't preclude an odd depth of awareness of fantasmatic savageries never lived, but dreamt hotly.) The point to draw out here, in a consideration of cultural objects and the political imaginary at work behind them, is not lagging behind and then deciding to launch ahead. It is that these coexisting modes of production (Poulantzas) and their attendant time scales are a structural consequence, a necessity for the world system to function: from the perspective of capital, they are not irreconcilable. As such, in deciding to enter the world market, you don't "get" to inherit and approximate the most advanced forms. You are forced to do in order to compete and, in doing so, inject not just fresh labor into the global calculations of profit and value-extraction but also new hybrid ways of doing business. The most advanced forms compete and feed off of the lost innovations of the backward and out of joint. Automation of assembly lines and forcible land-grabs exist uneasily side by side, their friction sparks lighting up new ways of excavating the old and outmoding the new.

The other sense of "combined and uneven development" applicable (and already gestured to) is a broader picture of the world system. This perspective, drawn out by Luxemburg and Lenin and more recently by Neal Smith and David Harvey, among others, sees that the lag-behinds, pockets of underdevelopment, zones of abject poverty and domination, and startling gaps between rich and poor regions are not the consequence of an irrational or badly managed global economic order. They are the manifestation of and articulated mechanism by which capitalism, taken as a totality, assures its overall preservation and development. The fundamental requirement of the system to not "stay still," to constantly reduce the cost of production and maintain positive growth rate – for, under capitalism, a year of systemic breaking-even, of *sustainable* production and consumption, is a year of crisis – necessitates a planetary order materially organized around the appropriation of certain areas as mere resource pockets and opportunities for the investment of foreign capital.

The account and specificity of how this comes to be and how this functions far exceeds our space and interest here. More immediate, then, is the perspective that underlies this model and which it offers beyond itself. What does this have to do with making sense of movies about the end of the world and our reversion/conversion to cavemen, gas-obsessed barbarians, walking corpses, insane loners in an empty city? And what foothold does it give for an antagonism, thought and lived, against late capitalism?

Three thoughts.

First, it's a perspective that exceeds either a simple monolithic advance – or reversal, at times – of history as progress nor a scattered patchwork of different time scales, historical projects, and their resultant organization of bodies and moneys. Rather, it is a properly dialectical conception, of stresses between actual political geography and visions of where the world historical project is going. Specifically, it considers the consequences of the intersections between such a monolithic perspective (the march forward of global capitalism through and toward liberal democracy as a way to weather the increasingly severe economic, ecological, and sociopolitical crises bound to emerge) and the zones which can never be seen by it as other than barbaric pockets of anti-modernity, lingering vestiges of intolerance, superstition, and simpler times to be celebrated for their "authentic diversity" while folded in under strictures of extractive market relations. This isn't to say that one perspective or the other, either the unified teleology of capitalist progress or the competing and incompatible micro-visions of different historical trajectories, is more or less true. Rather, the point is to grasp how the unified vision only gains consistency through its relationship to what *cannot fit into it* and of how it provides an ideological backdrop for the material shaping of a world that will preserve those unwelcome zones. In other words, decisively not flattening the world and welcoming all equally into the financial fold, but providing the narrative of that as the cover story for an opposite practice.

Second, what does, or what would, it mean to fight progress, to refuse the trendlines and timelines offered? Neither to desperately cling to past regimes nor, crucially, to fetishize the way things were. Instead, to wonder, like certain strains of idiosyncratic apocalypticism at once anti-capitalist and anti-modern, if the savage might throw away his bow for a rifle in order to take aim at the very need to throw away the bow in the first place. To take up the arms of the contemporary capitalist world, either to beat it at its own game (a certain Communist vision of employing capitalist technology in order to develop productive forces beyond the limits of capitalist scarcity) or to take it down from within (alternately, versions of Italian workerism and certain Situationist and ultra-left cultural practices). The point, as always, is to stay a bit savage in the midst of all this mediated savagery, to fight for something more equal, organized, perhaps even clean and modern, by never going totally non-native.

Third, to stress the *givenness* of this order. You're is always in the shadow of the world that rejects you, and privation is not reduced to the grayness of a degree zero. These are apocalyptic zones, sites in which we see exposed both the collapse of capitalist universality and the revealed presence of what cannot be included ("differentiated," recognized) without undermining the workings of the global economic order. For this reason, the degradation to the status and material forms of the backward, the primitive, the anarchic, the hell-on-earth is *always historically marked*, and not in terms of what era of backwardness a region approximates. It is not uncommon to hear people speak of certain zones (deep in jungles, high on mountains) as "unchanged since the 13th century," or the like, claims which, while occasionally accurate in describing agricultural practices, family structure, etc, are incapable of recognizing that such zones are historically tarred, however much in shadow, with the sign of the Now, precisely because they are visible to us only as a *not-this, not-Now*. Even on a less extreme scale, the collapse – and willful maintenance by powerful nations – of certain areas into the barest subsistence farming, warlord powers, clan battles, uncontrollable ravages of disease, and aching famine: these must be grasped as "signs of the time," not as vestiges of what should be outmoded if we could just get everyone to agree on the universal model of liberal capitalism. These barbarisms are the direct result and fundamental support system for all those new beasts springing forth, odd innovations in finance, different ways of streamlining shipping containers, revolutions in the time scales and cycles of capital. The seeming banalities and technical details are the real writers of a new apocalypse. To counter this, to write otherwise, is also to refuse to pass through the old stages, to stand in the present while recognizing that any capture we manage is of a moment already passing. The owl of Minerva flies only at dusk, indeed.

Before proceeding further, we should take stock of a theoretical question relatively specific to my apocalyptic project. If "combined and uneven development" as a concept and model itself grasps the levels of hellishness that ensure and ensured, what does combined and uneven *apocalypse* offer, beyond a demonstration of deep attachment to clever rewording? The point isn't just to ramp this up, to stress that the political and social effects of capitalism are "apocalyptic," in the looser sense of "so bad that it signals the end of things." Rather, it offers three things.

1. It is to stress the apocalyptic *potential* of these spaces, not as permanent catastrophe – a paradoxical catastrophe that does not signal end but systemic health – but as permanent visibility of the hidden. It is not transhistorical, but a historically delimited duration, particular to the 20th century and only getting worse, in which no event can signal a phase shift. It is diffuse apocalypse.

2. Despite our brief forays into consideration of "real world" conditions, the emphasis here is on the cultural fantasies of apocalypse and what follows it. Crucially, however, these should nor be taken as just hyperbolic versions of how things really are. Visions of the world after peak oil don't just ramp our seemingly inevitable situation, zombies don't just take the struggle of laborers and the denigration of the homeless and

make them more mindlessly and necrotically horrible. If there is an allegorical relation at play between these movies and their historical conditions, it isn't as stand-ins for the limit-case of what already is the case. Rather, given the ideological structure of capitalism, combined and uneven development is an invisible truth. We know it to be the case, but to speak it, to show it, remains something altogether different. These films and books, mass cultural phenomena and subcultural obsessions, are the closest articulation we can get of the structures of totality underpinning this. Not a mirror but a busy prism. In the distortions of this restless cognitive mapping, we get closer to not just the texture of an age, but the support structure on which it is stretched and formed.

3. If this odd collection of instances, this anti-canon of shared apocalyptic dreams and nightmares, are an inconstant lens onto how things *are*, they are also a path to be followed to what *may be*. They are concrete fashionings not of how things will go (the real possibility of zombie holocaust remains unlikely) but how we *might* like them to, projections out from the barely detectable difference of this conjuncture to a conjecture of where this leads us. With this comes, necessarily, a revision of what *apocalypse* can or should mean, and an insistence on readying ourselves for the role we will have in its coming to be.

So forget enlightenment, forget the worry of starting in the dusk and losing our way. Let us willfully begin at midnight, with the singing of and about the dark times.

Therefore, a different tack here, moving through the dream-image of salvagepunk and the nightmare-image of the dead rising, to venture an unstable third: the recognition that *the post-apocalyptic is not an image of that-to-be*. It is not that which lies beyond the apocalyptic event. It is a perspectival stance to be taken up now. It is a necessary optic onto the flourishing waste-lands of late capitalism, the recognition that the apocalyptic event has been unfolding, in slow motion with sudden leaps and storms. Behind our backs and in front of our faces. In waiting for the cataclysm, we missed the drift of it. In looking for the catastrophe[54], waiting in the wings or already passed (a certain threshold of no return), we turned away. Instead, we slowly start to recognize that we stand beyond that threshold: we become post-apocalyptic when we start making something of what has been revealed.

The figure we focus on here, the figure of thought around which our post-apocalyptic work must center, is the city. The city in the era of decaying industrial first-world power, the petro-wealth boom towns beginning to slip, the slum megalopolises across the globe. In a time in which, as Mike Davis and others have shown with clarity, cities across the globe are wracked by conditions we would be hard pressed to describe as other than catastrophic, we need to look to the cultural instantiations of *apocalyptic* cities via the lens of their post-apocalyptic uses. These instantiations are not limited to the visions of the big city; it's not just the Statue of Liberty crushed by tidal waves or London under martial law. To clarify, the films and books in this chapter aren't exclusively concerned with the "urban," either as a location or as a theme. Long detours are taken elsewhere: Jean-Luc Godard's *Weekend*, one of the central films discussed here, explicitly centers around a road trip *away* from Paris. *City*, in our investigation, is an organization of life, small or large, a concretized and micro form of larger spatial patterns of population, commerce, and struggle. More importantly, it is the site set in dialectical opposition to *emptiness* and to *nature*, to *backwardness* and *exclusion*, constant across its instances only in this negative defin-ition.[55] Indeed, it takes shape out of its unavoidable intersections with the particularities of its ecological and geographical condi-tions. And moreover, the city has become a *third nature* of sorts, not just an enclosure of the "natural" commons but a produced anti-nature to be protected and fought for as a communal zone. However, as a figure of thought, the city remains marked by the sign of the triumph of the inorganic. It maintains its assertion of permanence, will, and capacity to give shape and order against the decay of all things and the looming internal prospect of its decline into barbaric chaos. What is it if not the battleground of apocalypse, keeping below its surface and off to the sides all the undifferentiated that allegedly cannot come to light?

We take its post-apocalyptic cultural fantasy versions along four broad lines:

1. The city as ruins emptied of human life, a melancholic remainder and reminder of the voluntary extinction of the species at our own hands

2. The city at war with nature, on the losing end of an ongoing battle to assert itself in the face of deep ecological time and the constant push of the green into the gray

3. The city as site of uneven time, of the coexistence of apocalyptic zones with the overall functioning of commerce and urban daily life

4. The city as time-out-of-joint zone within the world order as a whole, the consciously neglected site in which collectivities may begin to emerge

Wound through this , and inserted more directly in the middle, are the first gestures toward addressing explicitly what has given shape to this whole investigation: what is apocalyptic temporality beyond the simple illusion of the *before* and *after*? How do we break the deadlock of thinking either shock or decadence, the abrupt phantasm of the New or the entropy of the Old hissing out into centuries…

THE UNQUIET EARTH

Post-apocalyptic cities tend to cling to the far poles of a primary opposition between the empty and the full apocalypse, the barren and the teeming. They oscillate between loners wandering the evacuated sites of life and abandoned hordes swarming in some reclaimed outpost of lost humanity. To be sure, the most subtle iterations claim a space that is both (think of the plague city of loners flooded with the walking dead, at once the excess of bodies and the apparent desolation of life).[56]

Running beneath this opposition, however, is a consistent aesthetic and affect of the city "after the fall," namely, the melancholic contemplation of decay, the dysphoric nostalgia of reveling in what can never be the same again.[57] It is not, however, a question of being alone in the urban mausoleum. To draw from film: there may be a single survivor who eventually finds a few others (*The Quiet Earth* [1981], the Matheson versions [*I Am Legend/Omega Man/Last Man on Earth*], *The World, The Flesh, and The Devil* [1959]); there may be a band of them (*End of August at the Hotel Ozone* [1967], pretty much half of all zombie movies ever made, the more lyrical parts of *Terminator Salvation* [2009]); there may be a whole city holding out against the wilds and wild things pounding at the gates (*28 Weeks Later*, *Zardoz* [1974], in an odd way). The thread running through is the fantasy of the contemplative museum of ruins, a waste *zone* (echoes of Tarkovsky's *Stalker* and Marker's *Sans Soleil* intended) that cannot be escaped: all that remains to do is to mourn without ever putting the past properly to bed. Just the pornography of decay, perhaps experienced en masse but never collectively.

In Tarkovsky's *Stalker* (1979), a consummate film of the broken world's loveliness, the sort of extra-urban Zone, guarded by the military, is a space closed off from "normal" life surrounding it, in all its decay and Soviet rust-belt prettiness. In our move away from the global event version of the apocalypse, we find again and again the borderland and the bound, the space encircled to keep without and within. Yet in *Stalker*, what is preserved (as the emancipatory potential of a post-apocalyptic, post-rational Zone) is the hollow, an empty anti-commons. The vestiges of day-to-day existence become otherworldly in their vacancy, fused with a halting spirituality notably absent in the far more subtle novella (the Strugatskys' *Roadside Picnic*) that forms *Stalker*'s source.[58] This runs the full gamut from a faded painting of Lenin's face, watching over an abandoned room, to the sad, silent majesty of interior sand dunes that may as well be burial mounds.

Geoff Murphy's New Zealand doomsday film *The Quiet Earth* (1985) has the conviction to stick with the going-insane reality of a lone survivor, scientist Zac Hobson, for a decent chunk of the movie. It tempers this with some needed pleasure, a whole lot of rage, and some unforgettable visions of how to take revenge at a world with no one left to blame (other than yourself). Notably, we see a balding man dressing in a woman's slip and Cesar robes, pontificating from a balcony to a pre-recorded soundtrack of applause and an audience of cardboard cut-outs of luminaries such as Adolf Hitler and Bob Marley.

This is quickly followed by a consummate revenge fantasy: shotgun in a cathedral, blowing away crucifixes, and getting to declare yourself God. Unfortunately, however, the film cannot quite take full pleasure in this, or even in the more mild forms of indulgent joy in fucking with the remnants of a world suddenly without other humans. (Aside from watching our protagonist enjoy a breakfast of a raw egg cracked into a flute of expensive champagne, the great moment of sheer pleasure comes when we cut from a model train circling aimlessly to watching Zac drive a real train.) Instead, it hints from the start that there is something fundamentally wrong with making a racket. Even before Zac discovers two other survivors and develops a normal living situation tensed around a love triangle of sorts, the film already hints that his need to yell loud and destroy the edifices of that past life are wrong, that the correct relationship to the land of the dead is deadly silence and quiet contemplation. One should lead a quiet life on this quiet earth.

Folded into this is an odd assertion of the strength of resignation. The three survivors all survived the galactic disruption of the "elementary charge" because they were at the moment of death: at the respective losing ends of a fight, a faulty hairdryer, and one's own hands, slipping into a pill overdose slumber. (We return shortly to this connection between suicide and post-apocalyptic landscapes, but here, we might imagine it turned otherwise, back onto a system-wide level: to willfully push civilization to the point of total collapse so as to therefore mediate the terms of that collapse, to weather the storm and be ready to come back from death. The worst of bellicose apocalypticism.)

The broader issue is how our melancholy, yearning, or resignation is marked spatially. We might return here to the function of the dream-image thinking its utopian future, shedding off the accrued material of the recent past and sliding back toward the impossible time "before it all went bad." In these examples, and running throughout the genre as a common tendency, the fantasy of utopian liberty and the visions of an other world are located in the *site* of the past. And on this site, we encounter both the doomed nostalgia epitomized by strains of primitivist thought, at best, and, at worst, a form of Hegelian logic distorted beyond recognition: the naked ape (or two self-consciousnesses, to be precise) encounter in the forest, to be mediated and navigated into the master-slave relation, is instead writ species wide into the fantasy of the human race confronting itself in mortal combat.

To be clearer, here, we might think of the recurrent instance in post-apocalyptic culture (for example, in Hiroki Endo's *Eden: It's an Endless World!* manga series) when an individual subject acts willfully – or hints at the desire to do so – in order to bring about the death of the species as a whole. This is neither bald misanthropy nor the kind of anti-human logic espoused by certain radical ecological movements (though the manga series does articulate plenty of those *the earth would be better off without us and our attendant damage* sentiments). Rather, buried within all their survivor-guilt and loathing of "what we've become" is the dangerous gambit of a properly apocalyptic dialectical ethics:

The human race is only worth preserving if we have the courage to make the willful decision to exterminate it.

More than just the petty "scorch the earth and reset the clock" fantasy of certain posturing black metal bands, this is the paradox suffocating and structuring those who face the bloodbath of the 20th century as well as those loners wandering those waste zones on the other side of the irreversible catastrophic event. Like the being that must be unlike itself to prove that it's more than bare drive and instinct, the impossible thought here is that only suicide proves that you are indeed an autonomous subject. Species-wide Russian roulette: you have to pull the trigger to realize that you never should have done so.

Ubaldo Ragona's 1964 *The Last Man on Earth*, the most haunting adaptation yet of *I Am Legend*, is riven by this, caught and split between the melancholy of nights alone (listening to old jazz records and drinking while the zombies feebly try to break in) and the task of extermination (the long slow work of daytime dispatching of those who will rise).

Of course, in the remarkable turn now well-known that impels the sudden and utter collapse of the persistent lone hero narrative, the task of extermination finds its real roadblock: the one to be killed is the killer himself the one who doesn't grasp that a new order has been inaugurated. He kills to preserve the irrevocably gone and can't make the one kill that alone redeems him. Only in putting a stake through his own heart would the death of the human race become something worth mourning.[59]

Tragic as this may be, we don't want a model of revolutionary thought that is tragedy.[60] We see, in short, the sticking-point of the empty world post-apocalyptic model: it remains in thrall only with the possibility of its own death and the non-subjective processes that will come along and swallow up the ruins of humanity. If this is the dominant figure of our day, we should be truly afraid, for it is the end of politics, the end of the thought of intervention in the patterns of history.

What, though, of another common articulation of "persisting through the dead world," not producing the urge to pull the plug on it all but rather the struggle to survive after the fact? We speak here of films that are neither apocalyptic (the event and its revelations are happening) nor post-apocalyptic (the attempt to move forward or build otherwise in accordance with what has been revealed.) Rather, they are post-*catastrophic*. Something has caused the collapse of society, and we are asked to focus on the quiet desperation and explosions of savagery in the contentious attempts to preserve structures and memories of pre-Event normalcy. This has echoes in films and genres considered earlier but finds its dourest articulation in the dystopian realism of the post-catastrophe model, films such as *End of August at the Hotel Ozone* (1967), *Time of the Wolf* (2002), *The World, The Flesh and the Devil, Blindness* (2008), and, *The Road* (2009).[61]

These are often very serious films, equally serious about being high art; with that comes both a certain portentous gravity and the capacity for innovative misanthropy. They also share a very marked resistance to explain exactly what sort of catastrophe happened, or at least what triggered it. Therein lies their catastrophic nature: the previous order (and way of ordering human society) has come to a definitive end, but nothing was revealed, no glimpses of totality or of what has been structurally excluded from that totality. At most, we see two things. First, we see the material after-effects of that catastrophe: stillness of the blighted landscape, undrinkability of its water, and various consequences of long-time pollution or nuclear winter. Second, the rapid degeneration of the social contract and the emerging degeneracy of people finally let loose in a post-state system to be as bad as they've always wanted to be (or that they "cannot help" being). Insofar as these two tendencies are related, the lovely melancholy of the ruins and the visions of pseudo-scarcity function primarily as a backdrop to the all the bad things people do to one another and to other living things (cannibalism, rape, torture, ritual sacrifice, kicking out strangers because you can't trust anyone). And crucially, this isn't the sort of violence enacted by an emergent dystopian authoritarian order: not systemic exploitation, nothing of the sort of emergent iron fist of Orwell, Judge Dredd, or *Aeon Flux*, not even neo-nomadic marauders with the prospect of forming a group to be reckoned with. Rather, sloppy assemblages of the scared and hungry, abortive communities, and hollow remnants of nuclear families. The rhythm and texture of these films is analogously marked by this disconnect between setting and behavior, with glacial pacing and tableau framing, out of which the barely repressed explodes again and again: a quiet earth, perhaps, but one on which noise and fury are the rule.

Underpinning this all is a deep commitment to a certain conception of the human animal. At the end of history (here defined as the narrative of a civilizing project tending toward the global stalemate of liberal capitalism), we discover that our capacity to act badly is not historically contingent or determined. More than that, we see that whatever the accidents of history were, whatever the repressions and imbalances that shaped the globe, they were ultimately a necessary corrective to the chaotic fury of the human unchained. According to this perspective, one far more common than a set of serious-minded art films, it isn't that we act badly because the reigning order's mechanisms of exploitation and domination were rewarded and learned. Nor is it that the catastrophic undercutting of those structures left a void into which the learned patterns could only continue in a bloody and relentless recurrence of the same: what else do we know how to do, other than steal, rape, cheat, and kill ...

And so for all their emphasis and lingering gaze on the material traces of the catastrophe, these films cannot help but evoke a deep anti-materialism, as we are asked to treat the savage behavior we witness as the *transhistorical* brutish underbelly of the human animal.[62] In other words, we are invited not to see it as the consequence of a social organization that has conditioned such behavior but as the consequence of that social organization no longer existing.

However, what of the fact that these films are in many ways "about" the preservation of older forms (the family, commodity artifacts, storytelling and history, constant appeals to what we do or don't do)? In its most recent iteration, we might think of the insistent commodity fetishism of *The Road*, as if the way to preserve the best parts of the Old is to give your son the fizzy New in the form of a can of Coke. But the genre tendency remains capable of sharp critical intelligence, and it's clearest in the way that it undercuts so much of the post-apocalyptic emphasis on remembering the Old as the necessary mode of salvation. Transhistorical brutishness may still be waiting in the wings. However, the solution may not necessarily be the frantic grasping at whatever tattered remnants remain. In fact, those solutions may do far more harm than good.

Two brief examples. In *The End of August at the Hotel Ozone*, Jan Schmidt's sparklingly bleak film, a band of Czech doomsday female soldiers roam a post-nuclear world of ruined and overgrown cities, argue, and torture animals. If they are the face of the New, the New is often mute, rather feral, rather sexy, and deeply aimless: mercenaries without direction, supposed reproductive potential with no future. The preservation of the Old order is the task of two characters in the film: an old woman who leads them and an understandably bewildered old man upon whom they happen. (We might fairly sympathize with his flustered confusion at their attempts to flirt with him: the transition from last man on earth, holed up with memories, to a confrontation with this gang of proto-riot grrls, is a bit of an epistemic shock.) The film is, at its most basic, a nihilistic and relentless destruction of the Old. Despite the attempts to inscribe personal memory as an antidote to the end of history, especially in the compelling shot in which the old woman counts back through history via the rings of a tree stump, the total disconnect between what was and what is can only blossom out into violence. There is an uncrossable rift, leaving only the sense that those unmoored from historical knowledge will be the death of us all. Or, rather, the second death of us all, after the first death of the nuclear winter. It remains unclear, however, just who is unmoored from history, for despite their destructive urge and inability to recall or adhere to older structures of social collectivity, the vital intensity of the women remains the only spark of life.

The question becomes moot. Eventually, following the death of their leader, the soldiers kill the old man for his gramophone, the last vestige of culture. And what was he protecting, holding out for the potential future to come? A single 78 rpm disc of polka, "Beer Barrel Polka (Roll Out the Barrel)."[63]

If *End* ventures the fundamental incompatibility of the post-catastrophic New with the teetering and musty records of the past, Michael Haneke's *Time of the Wolf* pushes further to insist that it isn't simply that our old modes may be defunct confronted with the barbarian inheritors of the vacant earth. They may directly stand in the way of reclaiming a social decency, and they threaten to destroy the potential agents of a struggling advance forward.[64] The nuclear family is destroyed, as the father of our protagonistic group is shot a couple minutes into the film, and what emerges is an emphasis on new mythmaking, as a groundwork for understanding heroism, sacrifice, and communal good in a time of total despair. A story is told of the "35 Just," the elite group who safeguards humanity, and of sacrifices for the common good.

But where does it lead?

To a naked boy with a nosebleed trying to set himself aflame on the railroad tracks. Saved at the last minute by a guard, the boy is told:

> "You'd have done it [self-sacrifice to save the others], for sure. Believe me. You were ready to do it. That's enough, see. You'll see. Everything'll work out [...] It's enough that you were ready to do it."

If this is a slightly more positive version of the notion of retroactive species valorization by collective suicide, the emphasis should be put on the "slightly." Haneke's formal distancing keeps a sense of judgment from encroaching too heavily, but it certainly should be noted that the embrace and "saving" cannot remotely compensate for the deeper horror of the logic encouraged here. I'm hard pressed to conceive of the full scope of an ethical logic in which it is remotely good that he was "ready to do it." Aside from the functional uselessness of a suicide in a filmed world where the mystical power of self-sacrifice seems entirely lacking, this comforting gesture is the worst stain of the Old. For when everything doesn't work out, as it likely won't without a lot of hard work and without arbitrary suicides, it is too easy a step to think that perhaps being merely ready to do it isn't quite enough ...

From the absence of causal links between environmental after-effects and their sources to the incapacity of remembering better to stop the directionless march toward nihilism, these films draw out the full emergence of *inhuman human nature*. It is a notion to be pursued through the rest of this chapter and beyond, in its dual senses. First, a historical formation that results in behavior fundamentally opposed to a humanist conception of the kind of creatures we are. Second, a longer sense of the absence of originary human nature: it has never been anything more than the deviation from what we assumed to be originary, it lies in that assumed perversion itself, that unlikeness to itself.[65] An initial stab at this should ask:

Why do the vast majority of apocalyptic fantasies assume that things going bad will lead to human relations going far, far worse?

Why does the end of capitalist days – and the revelation of the undifferentiated – so often entail a return to what is coded as a state of nature, a state that few of us know beyond these cultural visions?

To approach these questions, incompletely, we should follow the turn at the end of *Time of the Wolf*. After Ben's abortive suicide, the film cuts to forest and verdant green shot from a moving train, a third party perspective with no human behind it, as if all that remains to be seen at the end of history is nature itself, seething silently and waiting its turn.

AGAINST-NATURE

If our apocalyptic fantasies can't help but become navigations of what human nature looks like, these navigations necessarily circle back around to a concept of *nature* itself. This is present in the general eschatological notion of the apocalyptic: against all our grand human plans and pride of a constructed world built to last, something grounded in the eternal and ordained order of the universe intervenes, clears away the slate of all we built against nature to reveal the true face of things. The same holds true for secular visions of late capitalist apocalypse, although here the schematic is nature betrayed and mistreated, leading us to reap what we've sown, whether the fruit of labor is radiation infused zombies, melted ice cap tidal waves, supergerm pandemics, or a slow devolution into the decadence of liberalism's polluted twilight.

But *nature* here can't just mean the raw material on which capital works and from which it draws value, either the physiological capacity of the working body or the resources of the earth. Nor should we fall into the trap of treating nature as the already- and always-there, the "organic" opposite of the "inorganic"/constructed worlds of all that humans make, think, and do. To say what nature "is" or "means" stands far beyond the purview of this book. Nevertheless, against the flatness of these conceptions, the peculiarities of apocalyptic fantasy throw into relief their pitfalls, back-stories, and absent backgrounds, in part because so much of apocalyptic culture is an overextended elaboration of such logics. It isn't that movies about the new ice age or the regeneration of forests where cities once stood, let alone the vague mass cultural and political preoccupations drifting around mass media, offer a particularly innovative model of thinking about nature. But they do stand as oddly bald-faced and hamfisted representations of the dominant lines of thought about what we've been doing to the earth and what it would like to do back to us. ("People are worried about global warming. Here's a movie in which the effects of global warming kill us all.") And as we've seen before, it is often out of these faithful accounts and manifestations of the basic ideological form, whether or not the cultural object is famous or obscure, that the cracks show themselves sharply.

My counter-conception of nature – a post-apocalyptic anti-organic conception, perhaps – emerges polemically against these lines, but it's worth clarifying the rough shape of this alternative. It is one drawn loosely from far more exhaustive and sophisticated accounts, primarily those of critical geographers like Neal Smith and David Harvey and of "space" theorists like Henri Lefebvre. To sketch it broadly here, the concept of nature central to capitalism (and replicated ad infinitum in apocalyptic fantasies) is fundamentally contradictory. On one hand, nature is universal. Everything is nature: economic, technological, and social "progress" is part of what the human species does, and nature thereby includes the material intersections between humans and their biosphere, as a unified and contentious network develops which shapes nature as a whole. On the other, nature is external. It is all that is not us, all that was here before this particular organization of society, what that organization constitutes itself out of, and only in this working opposition do we gain coherency as a species. We are human because we strive away from nature. (As is immediately evident, certain conceptions of "human nature" are inextricably bound up in this as well, insofar as we consider it human nature to move away from a base, low, animalistic "state of nature": the human animal is the one who can act *against* nature.)

We can oppose this conception on two intersecting grounds, analytical and political. Regarding the former, the problem is that it simply cannot account for the realities and tendencies of capitalist development. It isn't the case that either universal nature or external nature is "correct." Rather, they share a common blindspot: they understand nature as an inherited *given*, as passive, either as the general sphere that includes everything that happens or as the terrain of extraction and the basis from which to build otherwise. This non-dialectical doubling results in the general sense that nature is *dominated* across the board, that in the opposition of "nature vs. society," the basic form of the *vs.* remains constant and immutable, anchoring nature to society in a contested bind of slave and master. Across time, a history of perversion, as the resources and shapes of the natural world are depleted and twisted beyond recognition, a dark echo of what we've done to human nature, the twisted timber contorted to fit structures of abstract labor and value.

But the specificity and power of a Marxist, or other materialist, conception of history lies in its recognition not only that the shape of *vs.* changes radically but also that its shifts result in equally radical configurations of the two terms it puts into opposition. More simply, "nature" does not exist independently of the way in which it is worked on by human enterprise, any more than human enterprise exists in a vacuum from the materials of its reproduction and extension. The concept of nature is *produced* by the material process of production: it takes determinate shape only in accordance with the processes that shape it. This isn't to say that such a concept remains at a distance. It feeds back into the material ordering of the world, a ceaseless circuit between how we work on the world and how we unstably grasp such a world, the cognition marked all the more by our working on it.

And so capitalism produces the eternal adversary against which it gains consistency, and in doing so, equally produces the contradictions which it cannot overcome other than through its eventual annihilation. Nature is quantified into particular determinate measurable units, while it is simultaneously abstracted into a universal beyond measure. Capitalism eternalizes nature as that which will always be there, and it revolutionizes it, insisting that we can always use it differently, that the wheels of progress will break open the locks of hidden knowledge and reveal the buried stores of plenitude. It "naturalizes" nature as what is unnatural to itself.

The political fallout of such a conception – and the question of what is to be done otherwise – will emerge throughout the following section, in all its apocalyptic permutations. Here we should foreshadow only by considering the notion of *second nature*, of those social relations and conceptions of the world that themselves become naturalized, thereby taking on the character of "just how things are." As nature is produced, so too our ways of production, and the accompanying modes of collectivity, desiring, and resisting, become natural. As such, a return to the state of nature is bound to be an abortive return, caught in the matrices of what we know to be "artificial" but beyond which we cannot know. Instead, rather than hoping to find modes of anti-capitalism in what we imagine might have been before, we push further to insist that, for capitalism, nature now is nothing. Nature, is "like" nature: it is not identical to itself but *similar* to the idea of itself. And we then ask: what else, traditionally marked as non-natural, becomes like nature? For lingering behind these visions of the apocalyptic interplay between the city and the forces waiting to wipe it from the earth is another sense, that of the city itself as *third nature*, as a commons *as if* natural to be protected against the new enclosures of the neither-city-nor-country, all the diffuse networks of flattening and false authenticity.

More immediately at stake is the apocalyptic imagination of the city at war with nature, taking five different shapes in the following pages according to five different modes of war between the built world and all that stands opposed.

1. The lyrical melancholy of the abandoned zone quietly reclaimed by natural processes: nature is what remains, and gently recolonizes, after we're gone.

2. The ongoing battle between the constructed world and the

ceaseless fecund push of plant and animal life into those zones: nature is what cannot be controlled fully and which constantly threatens the edifices of human settlement.

3. The ecological catastrophe event: nature is what comes out of the blue – or lies unheeded in the words of green prophets – and levels us.

4. The blighted world we corrupt: nature is what we have set ourselves against and from which we need to subtract ourselves.

5. The minor holdouts in the total interpenetration of capital and its objects, organic or otherwise: nature as the timescale of indifferent otherness.

1: Gentle reclamation

This sort of green magical realism/ecological lyrical melancholy has been discussed (and somewhat mocked) before, particularly in the empty city fantasy and as the background for general meanness in dystopian realist post-catastrophe films. Devoid of crowds and all the hubbub of human existence, the ruins enter into contact once more with Nature, a soft declension as they succumb to deep ecological time. Yet there's a crucial aspect of this so far ignored: despite the melancholic tint that stains many of these versions, there's also a striking current of violence, both of the wilds (the literal jungle where the urban jungle once stood) and of the process by which edifices of civilization crumble and fall. In other words, captured in freeze-frame, the city after humans may be the silence of still-life, of other currents of time resurfacing and of life persisting after the anthropic principle has vanished. But taken across such time, when the cameras are rolling, the full nihilism of fecundity emerges. A description early in Maurice Dantec's 2005 novel *Cosmos Inc.* sums up this tendency acutely:

> Nature may have been pushed aside by ecoglobal planning, but human cities are turning back into jungles: half-petrified virgin forests in the stagnant water of this unified human world, barely distinguishable from what remains of the natural wilderness around them, or from the out-of-control efflorescence running riot in the deserted streets, the silent highways; the empty buildings, shopping centers, and subway stations.
>
> In these dead cities, cities abandoned by men, nature has become savage again, escaping the automated cycles and engineers of geo-global planning. It is the last vestige of liberty left by technology to the world of Homo sapiens. It does not lack a certain tragic beauty.[66]

Dantec, whose idiosyncratic post-punk writing swerves from post-human frenzy to Catholic futurism, nails the implicit link between technological liberty and nature running riot. Following out our earlier discussion of the production of nature, nature let loose upon the world necessarily takes the shape of the remnants of that world: *destruction by nature* is as much a production by the organization of fixed capital as is the exploitation of nature's productive forces. Therein lies the libidinal surge of those sort of imaginings: what would happen if we were gone, what would the built world of capital be without us, its constant attendants and hand-servants, what would happen if the dialectic of nature and capital became a battle the latter was doomed to lose?

At our current moment, when the collapse of capitalism's current incarnation raises the hard question of what is to follow (i.e. the question of post-apocalyptic politics on which this book hinges), this particular flight of fancy – the world after people – is a particularly contemporary one. This is perhaps unsurprising, given that it involves the easiest transition of thought: take the contemporary built world, hold that in mind, and now just remove all the people from it. Apocalypse with no one around to witness what is revealed. And that is exactly what the recent History Channel show, *Life After People: The Series*, does.

It is, in short, the ultimate lurid dream of an Earth First activist, now transitioned from flickering No Future fantasies to big budget scope, CGI excessive, drawn out over an entire series. A seriously odd sign of our times: the strange union of primitivist longing for a post-human world returning to deep ecological time with a television station known above all for its near bellicose fetishization of all things World War.

Tarkovsky and those other merchants of apocalyptic melancholy could barely envision pulling off something on this scale, something this pornographic in its lingering gaze on the evacuated landscape, with all the attendant heavy-breathing, false restraint at the lusty gaze at monuments and networks without upkeep tumbling down and fizzling out. (Or, in its more dramatic moments, exploding outwards: without workers to maintain it, "The fuel that once propelled mankind around the world now fuels a seemingly endless inferno.") Behind the cover story of scientific curiosity, we're left with this slick drizzle and dust as scavengers and creeping kudzu unmake the urban landscape.

For a glimpse of the tone of the series, the episode descriptions hit the mark. A sample:

Episode Nine: The Road to Nowhere

The post-apocalyptic fate of our cars, planes and roads. Oil refineries turn into time bombs. In the Motor City, harsh northern winters dismantles auto headquarters. While in Texas, the Alamo succumbs to a new invader. Also, animals adapt: armadillos spread, some dogs rekindle their hunting instincts, and long-horn cattle flourish once again.

Such use of the "Also," is not only rather sneakily funny ("by the way, major evolutionary changes and the collapse of the remaining structures of now-extinct humankind") but indicative of the structure of the series and the fantasy underpinning it. Another example is the description for Episode 6: "Also, Philadelphia's Liberty Bell cracks for good and San Francisco's cable cars and bridges snap." It is a model of non-causality to be found at the origin of the series: the whole thing is posed on the hypothetical of the entire human race vanishing without a trace or cause. And more than that, without a struggle or without bringing down much of the constructed world. What is a lingering echo in the dystopian post-catastrophic realist model, with its obscure source and scattered savage effects, here becomes a pure thought experiment, even as it cuts the legs out from the source-finding modes of apocalyptic imaginary.

It's for this reason that the series initially seems a genuine betrayal of what the apocalyptic can allow us to think, the processes of construction and collectivization brought out in the move to the post-apocalyptic. In other words, there are no humans left over to work toward becoming a people again. There are only the assorted talking heads to give a bit of master knowledge to validate the money shots of our national icons falling apart, as well as the carnival barker of a narrator. And conversely, the fact this absence doesn't change the fact that the event of species extinction is still registered by anthropocentric projection: how does the world work through our death, and how could we think it other than life without people, marked infinitely by that absence? However, if we think of apocalypse in the proper revelatory sense, the series and all its indulgent melancholy gains traction. For what emerges is the eccentricity and idiosyncrasy of the leftover objects of capitalism, without their attendants and protectors.[67] No one filling the cracks or moving the debris to other shores. No more circulation, no more abandonment, no more accumulation, subtle or primitive.

And in this way, the series in all its drooling gloom and over-blown aesthetics of digital decay – you don't need computers to find these sorts of teeming messes and vacant mini-worlds, you just need to know where to look – nails the distinction between the end of the world and the end of days. It's the latter which is properly apocalyptic, in all its dialectical chances to speak the banality of our epoch, as a sequence of *days*. Furthermore, the sense of the end of "day" as a unit of time measure: the work day, with its corollary equal segments of play and sleep. Not an end of history per se, but an end of our pseudo-cycles of history that consists of interlocking and unhalting 8-hour blocks. How do we make this kind of conceptual ground clearing – thinking about end of days without clamoring for the end of the world as such – possible without waiting for us to be gone? Or without slipping into that ethics of suicide, where the worth of it all can only be seen in the backwards glance from the death of it all? The dual answer, not ventured explicitly by the series but there never-theless, might be as follows. We need tactics born from dogs gone wild: the ingenuity of the domestic refinding its lost ferocity. (Arguably the greatest and weirdest moment of the series is when the Queen of England's corgis go feral and become dirty, scrappy street-fighting bastards.) And we need that in order to cling to vanishing possibilities of life not adrift in the wild, but a ferocity to locate ingenious modes of what the "domestic" could be. In other words, to stand ground on the catastrophic nature of the present – and acting as the apocalyptic negation of its *post* void – without letting it be the total determinant of what our politics could be. Such a recognition of our times as times of catastrophe, looming or ongoing, catches us at a knife edge. Ignore it, and we retreat to the worst illusions of sustainability and reform.

Yet accept it too fully, and we fall into an equally bad fantasy doomed to go nowhere: fun as it may be, imagining ourselves as anarcho-communist versions of *Tank Girl* characters, won't get us far. We can't just think of ourselves as wolves and pigs, bestiaries of those ready to rummage and run through the chaos of an order-ending time, anymore than we can afford to act only as the prescient witnesses of this present disaster. Lingering too long in the dusky prettiness of collapse hastens that collapse, and not in the productive sense of bringing contradictions to the point of crisis and struggle to its necessary limits. We should recall instead some other aspects of whatever particular political-aesthetic lineage with which we align, particularly those aspects that became unwanted due to their unfortunate co-optation, totalitarian or yuppie. In this case: clean, open spaces and careful construction, not junk piles but thoughtful, durable piles of concrete and glass to house more than just rich couples.[68] Planning and care, welfare and distribution. Mutual aid not just after the fact of total collapse, but as a way of apocalypse without end, either entropic or sudden. For without this bedrock and commitment to principles of how collective life could be built from scratch, even while knowing that it can only be built from scrap, our scavenging, hunting, and constructing capacities just sniff around pointlessly, finding nothing but the scent of their own trail.

2: Fecund revenge: green Geist screws us all

One of the other strengths of *Life After People*, beyond the genuine pleasure of its recurrent apocalyptic money shots, is its awareness that the processes which unmake the world after people are already taking place. If it refuses to ask how we disappear or how our disappearance would necessarily shape the world left behind, the series makes clear that it takes a constant effort to prevent life after people from commencing while we're still around. Cities may be "third nature," but that doesn't stop "first nature" from waging constant war. The battle for the post-human history of the earth has been going on all along from the moment that human history started.

If not the best known, then certainly one of the most compelling (and internally inconsistent) articulations of this is the long running DC comic book series, *Swamp Thing*.

The sheer breadth of histories and trajectories involved in its story arc are obviously beyond the reach of this book or author.[69] Of immediate relevance here are two particular moments within Alan Moore's run as author of the series, set against the general backdrop of Swamp Thing's "evolution." The story of Swamp Thing, at least in Moore's version, is the story of a transition from singularity to universality. It is the transition from *a* swamp monster (dead scientist recomposed by the nutrient force of the bog) to *the* fecund Thingliness of all plant life (green elemental force itself, not bound to any particular configuration of matter but rather the abstract *Geist* of flora). Hence the multiple revelations of the series. He realizes that he isn't Alec Holland with a plant body, or even the Swamp itself with the injection of a consciousness defused into it. He isn't even *the* Swamp Thing: he is one among a recurrent series. He is the *idea* of the Green, the collective chlorophyllic intelligence of what lives but is not Meat.

He's also a total hippie hero, Platonic vegan ideal incarnate, complete with mournful eyes for the blighted earth and psychedelic tuber-tumors for inner light exploding acid-trip sex. His consummation of "relations" with his girlfriend Abigail starts with her eating one such tuber and then spreads over multiple pages of pastel light, chakra symmetry, suddenly understanding time itself, and becoming-Oneness. It well may be the world's most concentrated distillation of New Age ideology. However, just as the end of the '60s brought out the seedy and sadistic

undercurrent of hippie-dom there from the start, it is the consequences of this trippy bedding-down – free love and ecstasy
beyond the need for fucking itself! – which brings his verdant
fury to its full antagonistic flowering. It is the moment when care
for the earth becomes notably decoupled from care for the
human, when protectors of the Green reveal that they are no
better at understanding the dialectics of society and nature than
the arch-defenders of capitalism.

After a snooping reporter catches their boggy tryst, Abigail is
jailed for "unnatural relations" and eventually winds up in the
jail of Gotham City, beneath the watchful eye of none other than
Batman. Swamp Thing, off dealing with other more literally
infernal threats to the earth, learns of this, goes insane, and,
manifested in a strip of green cutting across the enclosures and
divides of pastures, roads, and buildings, makes a bee-line
towards her. The eventual narrative outcome of this – he gets her
back, he is "killed" and his consciousness escapes across the
universe, and he works his way back – is not particularly
relevant here. The point is what happens before: his revenge is
the total halting of capitalism and previous modes of daily life in
Gotham. It becomes a veritable Garden of Eden, and the hippie
population of Gotham, surprisingly not previously eradicated by
the rather straitlaced Batman, sheds their clothes and enclosures
and goes back to nature in the heart of the metropolis. Like so
much of apocalyptic fiction, the structural is only approached
through the personal, and so while Swamp Thing himself folds
in plenty of claims about how humans act like they own the earth
they mistreat and how he won't take it anymore, the fact remains
that this elemental force has known about this general
mistreatment for quite some time now. A protector of Gaia,
perhaps, but in this case, the rage and puissance boils over
because of the mistreatment of a far more particular woman.

This is no accident of bad writing. Moore's subtlety, or at least
what saves him from total devolution into the mediocrity of

animist post-'60s thought, is in the recognition of the persistent intersection of the concerns for the personal and the planetary. If anything, the baldness of Swamp Thing's motivation is refreshing: it makes exceedingly literal and epic the ways in which worries about sustainability and protection of Mother Earth are not infrequently worries about the future possibility of getting laid. Less refreshing and more simply disturbing, in its implications for a type of thinking we recognize far beyond the DC universe, is the concluding gesture at the end of Moore's run.

Having returned to earth, dealt necessary revenge to those who booted his consciousness off the planet, and reunited with Abigail, it's time for general reflection on his realized position as elemental force. He has discovered, both in his shaping/pseudo-impregnation of entire planets elsewhere and in his Edenic punishment of Gotham, that he has the full capacity to radically alter the material conditions of a landscape. Hence he wonders, given this power, should he make the world bloom in full, make it a green, lush environment, to end hunger and strife by eliminating scarcity itself? More than that, to reverse the damage of pollution and to "heal the earth"?

He decides otherwise. On one hand, this is entirely understandable, even for a green elemental power (supposedly) concerned with the defense of the planet. If the ravages of capitalism were not a necessary solution of scarce resource management but a contingent situation made into global order of mismanagement, it indeed follows that unbound plenitude will not necessarily result in things getting better. The infinitely adaptable forms of consumer identity prove, if anything, that the distance from our "natural" species-being to "second nature" knows no bounds. As such, from a historical and materialist perspective, it not only makes perfect sense to grasp that while plenitude and equal distribution is a goal of all egalitarian politics, it does not produce such a politics.

However, Swamp Thing's reasoning is entirely opposed to

this, arguing essentially that because humans have always dominated the earth and "taken it for granted," simply providing the end of scarcity will not cause them to learn their lessons. They will profligately squander the new fruits of excess, reject all sustainable modes, and continue to wound an earth that now can bounce back from anything (like the sadist fantasy of a body that endlessly self-heals). His solution instead? Humans need to learn to take care of the earth themselves. He will not intervene – they will have to see how they are destroying their precious resources in order for them to change their ways.

The cynical ugliness of such a position is unmistakable and would be laughable if it didn't capture so much of the tone of green movements at their worst. In short, this God-like defender of the earth is dooming it to catastrophic destruction. To sketch it quickly: humans "mistreat" the earth either because they are "just like that" (i.e. transhistorical human nature), or because their historical situation has conditioned such behavior (i.e. historical second nature). Obviously, the flimsier versions of contemporary ecological discourse fall back on the former conception of "civilized man" as the raping and pillaging animal. Even a cursory glance at prior historical modes of the reproduction of life make evident the uselessness, analytically and especially politically, of such an argument.[70]

Taking on the second notion, then, Swamp Thing is caught, thorny brows knotted, between two models of *how* we learn to act a certain way. Do we act badly because we face fundamental scarcity and have to do whatever it takes to survive in the immediate, sustainability be damned? Or do we act badly because there hasn't been *enough* scarcity, hardship, or antagonism? Outside of the *Swamp Thing* world, our answer would be: *both/and*. Those responsible for the worst treatment of the world and its human occupants continue to do so because we don't make things hard enough for them: a little hardship and directed hostility toward the rich is long, long overdue. At the same time, though, we know very well why such a mass uprising and tidal shift remains difficult. Those who most feel the brunt of scarcity and immiseration are so busy struggling to survive that the historical capacity to act otherwise – either in terms of directing antagonism toward those most responsible or in terms of living more "sustainably" and not participating in the mistreatment of resources – remains a dream primarily for those with the leisure time to imagine it.

In terms of the comic's narrative, Swamp Thing *refuses to recognize either position.* Given his peculiar talents, we could easily imagine a mediated form, directing edible flora to areas of the world facing total starvation. But no. He essentially commits to perpetuating a contemporary order in which the problem isn't just that we face ecological catastrophe. The problem is *who* it will affect first. (Hint: those already living below the poverty line, those packed into cramped and disease-ridden slums, those in areas barely surviving on monocrop production dependent on particular weather conditions, those in shanties that won't stand up to tsunamis, those in zones of the world so ignored that no number of liberal guilt donation boxes in Starbucks will change a thing.)

Again, to draw out a now expected point, Swamp Thing's refusal to be the apocalyptic force that he has been all along is the total commitment to total catastrophe. If he's worried that making the earth full of food and lush green bedding will allow the thoughtless to litter and chemical plant capitalists to dump their waste in rivers, then *punish them.* His vegetal powers are not just regenerative but directed: why not be the proper growing *avenger,* giving the righteous fruit to eat while lashing the wicked to tree trunks? The only answer can be found in his deep anti-materialism and a fundamental hatred of the human animal, conceived as bad, across time. This rears its head continuously in the degradation of "Meat," of all things red as opposed to green, of anything that consumes something else, not just humans. (See here his entirely unnecessary torturing of an alligator in the final pages, immediately after his meditation on treating the earth better.)

Folded into all this is a valorization of laboring itself, assuming that man will become wicked if he does not have to toil.[71] And in line with this, how exactly does he propose that the human species will deal adequately with its already dire ecological situation? The only situation we see endorsed is Abigail's participation in a tiny environmental group, i.e. her transition from literal lover of this defender of the earth to a somewhat hesitant love of earth defense causes. The scope of this group, whose numbers are slim to none, seems closer to letter-writing and pamphleteering. Furthermore, after his decision that the urgent situation of the polluted earth is to be dealt with by this second rate Sierra Club, of which Abigail is one of the only members, he whisks her away via lily pad to their flowering love nest built in the swamp for a couple months of gazing into each other's eyes and hippie sex.

I' m no great analyst of what should be done with what is indeed a dire situation. But it's no great task to recognize that putting the future of the earth in the hands of a couple activists before stealing one of them away for a secession-from-the-world honeymoon is more than just a failure. It's atrocious bad faith in a leafy mask. It's what follows from forging an eternal divide of the green and the red. It's a damnation of us all. And frankly, we're screwed.

3: Global catastrophe: Emmerich avec Bordiga

If a basic lesson of *Swamp Thing* is the flailing impotence of human agency in the face of permanent war with nature (both in terms of creeping encroachment and toxic consequences), contemporary disaster films don't just accept such a lesson. They relish it fully and compound it into forty minutes – at most,

given the interminable lead up to what we're really there to see –
of pure inhuman holocaust. Or at least they should. That would
certainly be better. What's remarkable about these films (*2012*
[2009], *Day After Tomorrow* [2004], *Deep Impact* [1998], *Armageddon*
[1998], and, in a way, *Independence Day* [1996]) and the rest of the
invaders from beyond genre) is how committed they are to
ruining the fun. If you're going to commit to an evental
conception of war with nature (here "meaning that which stands
in material opposition to human society"), give us that war's full
abstraction from the individual's petty concerns. They could
stand to learn much from Japanese landscape painting: with this
much apocalyptic grandeur and deathly sublime shoved into our
faces, we're not there to see who is saying what about having
loved someone all along. Again and again, the dominant aspect
of these films is their insistence on the micro-personal as the only
way in which the truly impersonal can be grasped. One form of
this can be seen in the narrative arcs of the films, where the
emphasis is almost entirely on the preservation of the family and
those willing to sacrifice themselves to plant new seeds of family
units to come. Related to this emphasis on the locally interper-
sonal – extending slightly to strangers who become hero-friends
in our last days – is the equal emphasis on notions of individual
witness or struggle in the face of mass death. Hence the taglines
for two films from Roland Emmerich, our foremost merchant of
fantasized mass death:

Day After Tomorrow: "Where Will You Be?"
2012: "How Will You Survive?"

(It's hard not to read these as respectively saying, "Will You See
This Film That Is Supposed to Be a Massive Pop Cultural Event?"
and "How Will You Survive Another One of My Terrible
Movies?") The real answer that the films venture is that you will
survive because you will have become inhuman perspective

itself, and where you will be is in outer space or high above the destruction, looking down at it all, with the obligatory sudden cut from rushing fire along the ground to tranquil vision after the fact.[72] They are truly spectator films, faux-mourning individual deaths while telescoping in reverse to watch with trembling glee from afar. Equally indicative is the tagline for *Deep Impact*, one of the most singularly dismal films I've ever watched: "Oceans rise. Cities fall. Hope survives."

Aside from a perhaps sneering response that hope shouldn't survive, given that it's the cataclysmic death of much of the world's population at hand, something else is telling here. Namely, the odd intensity of the mixture between the personal – "hope" in this film means emotional honesty while a tidal wave crushes you – and the *inevitable*. Even in films like *Day After Tomorrow*, which poses as a cautionary tale about the consequences of global warming, it's telling that in every case, it's too late. It's beyond our control. Whether it's irreversible effects of pollution, asteroid trajectory, or Mayan-predicted tectonic plate shifts, we can't correct what has been ordained, either by deep ecological history or the ways in which we've tainted such a history and now face its consequences. Our best bet is to sit back and try to enjoy, or at least to grasp for final moments of pathos.

This isn't to berate these films because they aren't correctly hopeful about our inability to intervene in natural disasters. (They get that hopelessness right, at the least.) There are plenty of other reasons to berate them. What's more striking is the way in which they aren't just mechanisms for delivering us the sheer joy of watching things blow up or apart. They also present an asubjective fantasy of capitalism itself, one we approached earlier via the zombies as gear-motor and gear-plague. Here too, the issue is the necessity of creative destruction for innovation and profit to keep going. In *Day After Tomorrow*, this is given to us in the terrible ending information that in fact, pollution has finally been reduced because of worldwide catastrophe! At least that's sorted out.

Mapped onto contemporary capital, these films point out that perhaps capital doesn't just need the refreshing bloodletting of a crisis every so often for light rejuvenation and space clearing. It needs massive destruction and decimation. *It needs catastrophe.* In one of the more willful ungainly pairings of this book, we might think here of Roland Emmerich with Amadeo Bordiga, the idiosyncratic Italian ultra-left Communist. In a series of writings on the occasions of "natural" disasters and major accidents (a cruise liner sinking), Bordiga worked to elaborate the ways in which these seeming tragedies about which "nothing could be done" were in fact the direct consequence of capitalism's mode of organization. Beyond the immediate and seemingly contingent issues of cutting corners with shoddy materials, the relentless decimation of naturally stable environments, the hubris of projects doomed to fail, the larger issue is that *capitalism needs the catastrophic.*

> Small scale capitalism's hunger for surplus labour, as set out in our doctrine, already contains the entire analysis of the modern phase of capitalism that has grown enormously: the ravenous hunger for catastrophe and ruin.[73]

Following this, we might stress that if capitalism needs the creative destruction of crises, it also needs the *destructive destruction* of catastrophe. Reworking Marx's rather common-place metaphor of capitalism as a vampire that sucks the blood of the living, Bordiga offers that "capitalism, oppressor of the living, is the murderer also of the dead." In order to exploit living labor, "capital must destroy dead labour which is still useful. Loving to suck warm young blood, it kills corpses."

More than just a tendency toward clearing out the figurative dead weight of the system (workers who think they have the right to fair wages, capitalists without enough liquidity and cunning to weather the crisis), capitalism has to actually shatter, sink, and burn its actual material dead weight: houses, stores, factories, vehicles, commodities, infrastructure, everything. And with it, it must do the same to its living dead weight. It's no great secret that it was largely the destruction – of frozen capital and living labor alike – in the two World Wars of the two World Wars that led capital to such happy years: the wasteland that gives the imperative to the living, *build anew!* It is death *for* the installment plan, the reproduction of the future predicated on the production of the presently dead.

We just may get the last laugh. The prospect of sustainable "green capitalism," supposedly the way out of our current mess, would in fact be the actual death of capitalism. For underpinning Bordiga's analysis is the basic understanding that *capitalism only works when things don't last.* If we actually make responsible, locally produced, durable, reusable "green" commodities, the system cannot function whatsoever. The early stages of this greening show, of course, just how flimsy the fantasy is: buying a hybrid car means junking your old one, putting in a "sustainable" bamboo floor means ripping up what's already there. But one can't help but hope that these neoliberal apologists – and accidental anti-capitalists – for the "ethical totality" of the market, for a corporation's capacity to realize the error of its ways and stop using Styrofoam cups, are listened to, at least in part. Because the promise of sustainable consumption is the promise of the unsustainability of capitalism itself.

Yet this is no cause for joy, because it means only that things will not go that direction. The ship will go down, all of us with it, as long as the ride remains relatively comfortable for those at the top. Forget them grabbing the first life boats: they'll ride it straight to the bottom, as long as the party continues. Bordiga's trenchant reminder – "when the ship goes down, so too the first class passengers" – holds hope only if we can separate that needed revenge from the sick silence of the ocean swallowing the wreck, if we can wrest away the wheel before that happens.

4: Species suicide: Thank you for not breeding!

Of course, there are those among us who would welcome such an outcome, who think that it is, in fact, long overdue.[74] If the previously sketched models of the war zone of deep ecological time, where nature and society clash together, focus on what *cannot* be done (nature comes after we're gone, nature would like us gone, or we've provoked nature into making us dead and gone), this fourth version reinjects a bit of human agency into it. Albeit the agency to make ourselves gone. As with the version of willful species destruction – and retroactive justification for why we shouldn't be destroyed – envisioned in *Last Man on Earth* and its ilk, we are speaking of a strain of fantasy that finds us only worth saving if we deicide that we aren't, after all, worth saving. Humans, at least insofar as we left behind our noble savage ways, and the entire apparatus of civilization are a blight to be removed and forgotten. A contingent blip on the grand scale of the earth, but a blip that has betrayed its place and threatens to ruin the entire enterprise. Such a mode of thought ranges rather wildly. From somewhat tempered modes of green anarchism (with emphasis on practical skills that we should have, particularly as we have to deal with post-apocalyptic mutant corgis running feral) to the idiocy of most anti-civilizational positions. From the real libidinal and aesthetic impulse of neo-primitivism (as antidote to the worst forms of contemporary alienation and media-managed desire) to the incomprehensibility of neo-primitivism as a political or ethical program (as inability to grasp either the awful consequences of fetishizing the pastoral or the fact that libidinal impulses themselves are always unnatural and that desire crystallizes around, and joyously explodes out of, what seems most capable of frustrating it). And the misanthropic cherry on top, the Voluntary Human Extinction Movement

(*VHEMT*), with the slogan, "May we live long and die out. Thank you for not breeding."

Much of this is either quite laughable or quite disturbing. However, it's not disturbing so much because of its anti-human impulse as the fact that it's merely the general thought of ecologism stripped of its humanist dressing: the emphasis on the environmental symptoms of contemporary capitalism, rather than the economic and social relations that reproduce them, lead to an incapacity to grasp root causes and a dangerous misrecognition of both *what* is to be done and *how* it is to be done. And if it is laughable, it isn't because of its cultural associations with billowing clouds of weed smoke and the smugness of "responsible consumption" gone rampant. It's because, against all this, the harder edge of the thought – that undercurrent of fury at the lostness of it all – remains a necessary launching pad for anti-capitalism, even if that pad must be destroyed in passing from it. Four reasons:

1. If civilization was once worth defending, anything that now so relentless plumbs the depths of mediated awfulness can only be worth demolishing. What does it mean to fight for a world in which Christmas-time inspires dog grooming chains to bathe dogs in gingerbread scented shampoo, so that your dog chemically emanates the nauseous odor of the season? A nanosecond of the blinding light of a reality TV show, that weeping construction of forced lust and total exhaustion, is more than enough to make us wish for a return to the Dark Ages.[75] Burn it all down: at least the charred fields won't be so gratingly banal.

2. Thought must constantly pass through – or cast shadows out from its failure – a "non-human" perspective. This impossible prospect of "the thought of non-thought," for some bound up in the truth procedures of math and the

supposed object-thought of science, finds one of its sharpest moments in the approach toward ecological, if not cosmological, time. In the abortive passages between human perspective and non-human world, we might begin to approach something between, unsteadily dialectical, an *inhuman* set of tools for starting to make sense of what undoes the surety of ever being able to make sense in the first place.

3   Attempts to ameliorate both recurrent crises and the forthcoming total catastrophe in fact make things far, far worse. To feed back into an already apocalyptic loop, this is a fundamental awareness that capitalism is not doomed per se, at least in the economist perspective of internal contradictions leading necessarily to the establishment of socialism. If anything, what will bring things to a Ragnarokian head, ecologically and politically, isn't capitalism's inability to manage itself but its deep flexibility and ability to respond "creatively" to crises. The catastrophe is endlessly deferred, battened down and away by new technologies, new markets, new social codes. The release valves are welded shut in order to prevent any hiccups in the forward march. And consequently, when it finally can be held back no more, the floodgates of new consumer identities and containerized circulation will be no match for what seems to have been a very long time coming, namely, the collapse of profitability, the exhaustion of resources, and the deep brutal weirdness of an earth altered beyond repair.

4. The present moment, for all its flexibility and seeming permanence, for all the imagined impossibility of breaking its spell to catch even a glimpse of another world, is also fragile. It teeters, see-sawing on the very point of no return,

between a literally bankrupted future and a bartered past dead and gone. All those stale critiques of a society of boredom, of placid satiation barely able to lift its double chin to see the flames, miss the fundamental fact of fear that's been there all along. Not just the petty fear of an uncertain world, but the rank and crippling paralysis of a world's fundamental uncertainty.

We need to guard these four moves of thought, and even more, we need some of their affective character, the pragmatic bile of hardness in the face of a scared, hard world. We also need to leave behind the source material that lies behind these genuine concerns of how to move forward: the ideology of the wounded green, the prospect of a return to kinder pastoralisms, the fetishization of the primitive, the discourse of sustainability, the rhetorical and conceptual reliance on the *organic*, and the recurrent misrecognition of symptom for absent source. Dealing properly – let alone "fairly" – with much of this is beyond our scope here. And it certainly deserves more space, if only because as one of the dominant signs beneath which resistance to the contemporary world order assembles, it is an enemy from within to be countered. In lieu of a longer treatment, a few scattered comments on a question: to *what do we return when we are past the point of no return?*

The central motor of this contemporary ideological and political position runs off two related thoughts, one primarily environmental/material, one primarily moral. First, the sheer magnitude of the human presence and all our activity on the biosphere is unsustainable: the problem is too many, too much. *The way we live is bad for the earth.* Second, the character of contemporary capitalist existence is a betrayal not just of our basic human nature but of the ways of toiling and interacting that are the real expressions of that human nature: the problem is cubicles, pre-packaged pre-cooked pre-peeled beets, Google

Maps, and free porn. *The way we live is bad for ourselves.* As such, two general categories of solutions. We need to scale down, cut back, slow up, and stop breeding, burning, mining, extracting, and swarming every last untouched corner, high and low, of the globe. And we need to stop living such "mediated" existences in favor of the simple, the direct, the face-to-face and the hand-to-dirt. What is shared in both instances is the underlying claim that we have to *go back* to the way things were, even if we are never quite sure *where* that is.[76]

That missing location is also the vacant core of such a position and why we have to attack it, even while recognizing that it can't be separated from the scent of the times. This going back, this longing for the distant home shores that have melted away long before the ice caps will, involves the further validation of the standing death sentence for much of the world's population. It hinges on the question, *sustainable in terms of what?* Resources or human bodies? To have the green space to return to local, communal farms, verdant pastures from which we will eat macrobiotic food, we need either the preservation of the contemporary state form – which is very good at keeping billions of starving, sick people in teeming global south cities and away from the open land of the north – or a veritable holocaust, coupled with a total crisis in reproduction. This is to say that certain dominant visions of what sustainability look like, including a turn away from the rapidity of modern production and its biotechnical visions of nutrition ex nihilo, are caught between a demand that we do not fundamentally alter the political-economic architecture world and a wish-fulfillment injunction to alter the everyday textures of the first world by killing much of the rest of it off. If this is what we stand for, if we stand for the subjective decision of getting to "go back to the land," we would need the courage to say what this entails. Swapping out commodity fetishism for green acres fetishism isn't just a choice for yuppies who wish to quit the city and get away from it all: however unintentional, it is a categorical declaration that the *history will continue to go as wrong as it does now, if not worse.*

This is, to be sure, a hyperbolic extension of a set of real concerns, even if their articulations frequently oscillate between the naïve and the insipid. But as before, the particular interest here isn't in the logistical calculations and possibilities, asking how many acres of productive soil vs. how many calories of input, to what degree are better fuel cells possible, or how would a return to non-factory farming affect the heat profile of the Arctic. Instead, our focus is on the fantasy support structures for such a position, particularly the moral dimension. This is the dimension raised in the politics and metaphysics, aesthetics and unspoken ethics that can't help but reveal themselves, especially at the most inopportune moments. Moments, for example, like the end credit sequence to Disney-Pixar's *Wall-E* (2008).

Much of the film is remarkable (and very salvagepunk), opening with its breath-taking vista of compacted trash skyscrapers. Indeed, as Mark Fisher points out in *Capitalist Realism*, the first part of the film, with its complete absence of human characters, other than the heavily anthropomorphized Wall-E, comes close to a genuinely inhuman cinema, leaving us to wonder what it would have look like if it stuck to its space ballet/early cinema slapstick/CGI rust-and-rot guns for the rest of the film.[77] The rough narrative arc of *Wall-E* entails a movement out from the earth and back again. We begin with Wall-E, a single robot left the futile task of cleaning up the Earth, literally one giant junkyard. For reasons of love and plot development, he eventually joins the massive spaceship where the remnants of humanity wait out the failed rehabilitation of the earth. The humans are now fat bone-loss blobs, floating around on hover-chairs all day, staring into holographic screens, not working, and living off fast food. (You can practically feel the film nudging you from across the screen. "Get it? It's an allegory of contemporary life and consumer apathy. Get it?") After plenty of cute mayhem and a realization that the earth can once more support plant life, the humans return to Earth to start anew. End film, cue credits.

 What we see in the credits, over the not-very-soaring sounds of Peter Gabriel's awful eco-nostalgia anthem "Down to Earth" ("We're coming down / Coming down to Earth / Like babies at birth") is the story of how the humans recreate society with the help of Wall-E and the other robots. They leave the plenitude of the ship and its food sources for a hardscrabble primitive existence in the dirt. Or, in the leaps-and-skips version we get in the credits, for a transition to new plenitude, full of happy fish, blue jays, and maize, and a newly responsible progress toward the full build-up of civilization: a shirtless boy fishes while sailboats (wind power, no fossil fuels!) drift in front of the former space-ship, now overgrown with the green. In addition, the story is told in a sequence of "paintings" that step their way through art history toward the present. Cave painting spaceship and exodus onto terra firma, hieroglyphs of the protagonists now sure to be the refoundational legends of its archaeological past, Sumerian wall-painting of well drilling, Greek amphoric patterns of grapes and corn, mosaic tile sea turtles swimming the blue sea, Da Vinci-esque sketches of a robotic lifter helping build scaffolded cities, water color vistas, Pointillist boy and sails, and last but certainly not least, a Van Gogh oil, moving from sunflowers to Wall-E and his robot love, EVA, holding "hands" beneath a tree. And as it pans down, the roots of the tree reach into a Van Gogh peasant shoe, hovering in the dark as the scrolling black of normal credits begin.

This sequence only makes full sense when compared with its inverted partner in crime, the opening of *The Road Warrior*

discussed earlier. In both cases, a *rescripting* of inherited cultural images is used to situate the present of the film in terms of a constructed lineage of Western history as such. Yet while the peak oil catastrophe image story of *The Road Warrior* describes its present moment (the time of the film's narrative and the early '80s historical moment when it was released to the "real world") as the descent into the apocalyptic collapse, the cooptation of art styles serves to describe a different arc in *Wall-E*. It's telling that it does not include any approximations of painting after Van Gogh: like the gentle techno-ethos of steampunk, the narrative it tells never gets to the full technocracy, chaos, and pollution of the 20th century, resting instead in the slow pastoralism of its last image before black. And furthermore, we've already seen the final image in the story, the entire film of *Wall-E* itself. Retroactively, the film we have seen *itself* becomes the last image in the sequence, a clue to the lurking darkness behind the move forward. A move forward that, like the conclusion of the Mad Max trilogy, means going back, starting over, and "getting back to basics," even as the post-post-apocalypse it describes is a return to the normal of late capitalism. However, two points of significant divergence. First, *Mad Max*, at its salvagepunkish best, is the story of technology busted beyond repair, but capable of being scrapped and reused. The alternate history paradise of *Wall-E*, conversely, requires that technology never stopped working in the first place. The only fathomable way that the morbidly obese, skill-less, media-sated blob people could survive a single week of "roughing it" is with the constant help of the robots.[78] (One can only wish, a little perversely, for an alternate version in which the earth is repopulated, in beautiful grinding silence, with the robot progeny: trash-skyscrapers rising high, laser-etched with inhuman language, as the insufferable humans retreat to their cozy ship or starve out the first winter.) Second, unlike the total barbarism of *Mad Max*'s world, in which resettling en masse is largely a question of survival, the decision to return to the land in *Wall-E* is purely voluntaristic. A choice decoupled from necessity. It is an issue of *preference*, masquerading as ethical responsibility.

There are two further aspects worth drawing out of this which point to concurrent tendencies broadly shared across green ideology. First, the proto-Fascism of it, or at least the potential to slide that way: from the survivalist and blood and soil injunction, reversing the course of history via fidelity to a lost restoration, as past culture is inscribed as a single narrative towards a cleaner, better, more correct present. (Not to mention the weird Heideggerian echo of the Van Gogh peasant shoe.) However, where it loses this thread is in the rejection of available technology, and with it, the more alluring aesthetics associated with certain far-right movements. There is far more here of German Socialist Realism, albeit with Wall-E and the fat ship's captain instead of golden haired, high cheekboned mothers and sons, than there is of the technological excitement and bellicose experimentalism of the Italian Futurists.

The second issue is far more troubling, insofar as it gestures toward the ultimate complicities of the green neo-pastoral impulse with the basic value form of capitalism and the nastier remnants of older social orders. The residue of *Arbeit Macht Frei* (Work Will Set You Free) hovering here has little to do with these Fascistic overtones and everything to do with the redemptive narrative arc of the film. For the issue at hand is a misrecognition of the "problem" with the people in their spaceship: according to the film, the problem is that *they don't have to work.* Yet this misses the point of what is both utopian opportunity and genuine problem of how to form meaningful community and interaction outside of the arbitrary groupings of work. Indeed, they are fat slobs who float atomistically in chairs, never seeing face to face. But the problem isn't that they don't work, it is what they do with their total time of not-work. The ship is, in fact, a paradise: it is a site of plenitude (at least for the humans, if not their robot underlings), a zone where new forms of egalitarian social interaction could flourish, freed of the hierarchies and antagonisms upon which the "free sale" of one's labor time hinges and produces. If Communism once meant Soviet power plus electrification of the whole country, the implicit accusation here is that lazy post-capitalism (here indistinguishable from hyperconsumerism free from the natural limits of one's earning power and work-day schedule) means floating chair gelatinous impotence plus unlimited electrification for the whole ship. Yet why should we assume a natural, transhistorical equation between non-work and dribbling chemically synthesized milkshakes down your bib? If anything, the film gets it wrong by imagining that the parasitic-bourgeois of the ship would in fact "let themselves go": far more likely would be an obscene cult of the body, wheatgrass smoothies carefully sipped by the ranks of the surgically shaped and flawlessly pilates-toned. And so, if a revolution is to be staged, if the social order is to be turned on its head, the real turn should be a revolution *on the ship*, a mutiny of free time, a recla-mation of pleasure. To continue in the site of plenitude and to insist that while the end of work is the twilight of capital, it does not equal the decadence of human capacity to live well collec-tively. The overturning should precisely not be the deeper perversion of the Protestant work ethic run amok. Unless ...

Unless we see the decision to go back to the soil for what it's been from the start, an *aesthetic* preference that masks a deeper incapacity to think how we might fill our days. In this way, there is still a utopian content to the end of the film, even against the grain of the misplaced command to leave the ship. First, the notion of a return to the land expresses a deeper hungering for circuits of time returned to the imagined clock of the body and the sun. Secondly, and more crucially, if we start to strip out the false moral necessity of the return (*we're doing what's right*), we get closer to the potential force of the insistence on aesthetic and pleasure-centered choices (*we're doing what we like*). With that, an understanding of the often unbridgeable gap between what we assume should be done because it is good to do and what should be done because we like the act of its doing. In short, the gap between:

We should go back to the land and toil in the soil, because otherwise we are lazy and alienated drones of contemporary existence. Also, we should reject the technological possibilities we have because they make us bad.

We should go to the land, because we enjoy digging in the dirt and feel sexy and good when we wear work boots and eat tastier food. Also, we prefer to be surrounded by hay-bales, not by glass cubes.

The point certainly isn't to mock the second position. Quite the opposite. It is a far more "liberated" position, precisely because it decouples an assumed linkage. We should take on the artificiality of our desire – its inseparability from the social order of mediation and prohibition – in order to grasp the libidinal under-currents of what are seen as decisions based on altruistic reasoning. Not because it's "better" but because it is a more honest point of departure, to start to pass from the kind of desiring subject you'd like to be known as to the kind of collective project of making of our free time something more than the resigned shadow of working hours.

The fact remains, though, that even if we pull apart aesthetic preference (or honest pleasure principle) from a more pervasive defense of the status quo, we're still left with an aesthetic conception that describes and defends an ordering of the world, however decoupled it may seem from it. The latter of the two green/organic/back-to-the-earth positions described above might take on its inorganicity (willful choice based on non-necessary desire) and hence give up an assumed authenticity, according to which such an aesthetic preference is a real expression of the "kind of person I am." But without doing that, we are left stuck with an aesthetics of the *neo-pastoral/neo-primitive* that ultimately verifies a politics of the status quo. For as argued throughout the book, any post-apocalyptic "going back" is only to the fantasmatic lost past of an era, not to an organic bedrock. The imaginings of apocalyptic culture consistently raise the question, frequently by glaring omission: *why does a post-apocalyptic world mean that people have forgotten the social codes, languages, and modes of interaction from "before the fall"?* Such a question remains equally unanswered by the broader fashion and yearning for the primitive, the unmodern, the unspoiled, and the idea of the restoration of the time before it all went bad. In the wake of the only plausible answer that can be given (we can only do is either revert to the "second nature" of late capitalism or fully take on the fantasy dimension of what we imagine our originary human nature to be), this new primitivism wishes only for a time when accumulation itself was more primitive. As if the antidote to the mediation of abstract labor and the ecological catastrophe of the contemporary world is to slide back down to the more direct repressions of "earlier" social orders. As if a bridge over the gulf between the frenzy of the modern and the tranquil of the long lost would ever reach the missing other side. As if savages had been noble all along.

I've pushed the need to become post-apocalyptic without waiting for the catastrophic to occur. Yet in the case of the loose aggregate of thinking clustered around a defense of the green and a return to the earth, such an attempt leads to the most banal, and hence most dangerous, misprisions. It simultaneously sets up the transhistorical site of back to nature as somewhere else, in the far past, in the further lands, and confirms the permanence of the capitalist system: *if we can make it more sustainable and slow, we can turn back from the cliff.* What it forgets is what the harder line of catastrophic thinking – that which insists that we pushed off that cliff long ago – grasps better. It is the more extreme position, closer to the call for civilization's end, which gives us sharper tools to forestall such an end, even as we aim to hasten the end of this particular world order.

For this "extreme tendency" knows two things of critical importance. First, in spite of its nostalgia, it recognizes that our return will always be to an absent source. By proclaiming more stridently that we have gone past the point of no return, it demands of us that any stand we make is here, from the position of *what has already been lost*. Second, in spite of envisioning the transhistorical persistence of human nature (either gentle gatherer or permanent barbarian), it detects the fragility of modernization. In a position similar to the dystopian post-catastrophic film, it gets that it doesn't take a full reversion of spaces to a state of nature to cause our concurrent return to inhumanity after the fact. Unlike the slow creep of the green's return to dominance, we can fall back – or forward – quickly. If we can move from bows to rifles in a step, we can slide back far further, far faster. Even as we imagine we are moving forward: what is the triumph of neoliberalism if not the reincorporation of explicit landgrabs and accumulation at its most primitive, precisely under the sign of the modern humanitarian? Against its own fantasy, the full-blown apocalypticism of the neo-primitivist lust for collapse points out that the distant shores of the primitive and the modern were never far apart. They were never separated to start, a doubled shadow image overlaid on those permanent sites of contestation. Which is to say, everywhere.

5: Atrocity repetition

If *no return* doesn't mean returning back to zero, but taking that moment of lost chance as a moment of urgency, the question isn't: *where are we going?* It's: *when are we now?* The fifth mode of apoca-lyptic nature considered here is our point of departure away from ideologies of nature per se back into the central notion of this chapter, that of apocalypse as the frontier battle-line (and revealed cause for war) between uneven timescales, as a durational and inconstant zone of antagonism. And to do so, a passage further away from the *imminent* eschatology of either fast-forwarding to the ecological catastrophic event or rewinding back to the empty tape hiss of a never-there past. Instead, our concern is with an *immanent* eschatology particular to our recent history, the sense that history has not only lost determinate direction but has come to a halt in the hollow crash of postmodern time.

The late great British novelist, short-story writer, and clinically detached provocateur J.G. Ballard has never been a proper modernist or postmodernist. Like his fellow misanthropic horror (of this world or beyond) travelers H.P. Lovecraft and Luigi Malaparte, Louis-Ferdinand Céline and Boris Vian, his work doesn't seem to rest stably in the more recognizable forms of high modernism. Or even its cousin, the recombinatory cut-up salvage of Max Ernst or William Burroughs. Or, for that matter, the pulp underbelly of either sci-fi that Ballard's work supposedly belonged in at first or the nihilistic noir and dusty mean sex of Jim Thompson. Ballard is one of those constitutive exceptions, a chrome mirror off to the side that catches the anamorphic blur of modernism's real concerns and sharpens the image.

This looking-from-the-side glance in Ballard reveals a constant question, in almost all of his writing until the perhaps epistemic but certainly historical shatter point that is *The Atrocity Exhibition* (1970). (Although, appropriately for one of the great writers of off-kilter development, the break is not clean: particularly in his short fiction, the earlier tendency persists through the '70s.) From his devolving airplanes and jungles, dead astronauts and freeze-frame birds, his writing is univocally a working through of time, circling back on itself to ask again and again what it would be to stand outside of time, to step out its river.

From pockets of other-time to momentary eternity, Cape Canaveral to the crystal forest, these are the phantasms of the end of time.

The temptation here is of course to read *time* here as *history*. Again, however, we should stress the side-long position of Ballard in regard to this and take it as symptomatic. For it is not until the lineage of writings inaugurated in by *The Atrocity Exhibition* that history begins to appear more potently as a category, at the very moment that it is becoming increasingly unthinkable. In other words, Ballard thinks history when capitalism allegedly begins its march toward the declaration of the end of history. However...

Ballard writes perhaps the sharpest "historical" novels of late capitalism in terms of capturing a whiff of the Zeitgeist. But they are not designated, generically or by reception, as historical. It is rather their negotiation through, and ceaseless emptying out of the very possibility of, the historical that makes them such. According to one narrative, that offered primarily by Frederic Jameson, we might think of this period – the ascendancy of the postmodern – as that in which time is superseded by space. And in many ways, the Ballardian turn is exactly this: the off-historical is seen as a site, from the lost underpass of *The Concrete Island* to the tower of *High-Rise*. (It's worth noticing here the shift from the "world" in the earlier titles – *The Drowned World*, *The Burning World*, *The Crystal World* – to these markers of distinct sites.) And, as such, Ballard seems to be the definitive postmodern writer.

To double back once more, we should guard the emphasis on "seems," for the opposite is the case: the novels show there is little jubilation about the new spatial logics of the world order or the flattening "waning of affect" or simulacral "hyperspace" or any of the rest of the usual suspect tendencies. Rather, it is about the unbearable lightness of not being historical any more and the fundamental *ethical* question of what to do when there is no longer the task of trying to decouple yourself from the forward progression of historical time. Unmoored, we no longer get the existential satisfaction of striving against the ceaseless march ahead.

Ballard's distinction from a more common postmodern logic comes in the fact that his characters mourn this loss very oddly: perversion as a structure of obsessive repetition futilely trying to resuture meaning to things. One need only recall Ballard's emblematic figure of this, the car crash. Beyond the rather banal reading about the desensitization of the bourgeoisie and the need to "shock" oneself out of erotic apathy, the restaging of famous car crashes has far more to do with the realization that we are in a world in which new events no longer happen. Contingency, and the cunning of reason with it, has fallen victim to the logic of "non-rational administered life," the supposed chaos of competition and the market, the heterogeneous identities and the multitude all moving along the same grooves etched by flows of capital circulation.

In its place, then, are no longer atrocities as the markers of historical tectonic shifts. There are exhibitions, stagings, willful false contingency, the play-acting of an event in the desperate frisson of clinical compulsion to do over, to dig out some remaining kernel of meaning in, say, the car crash of James Dean, that hasn't been fully cannibalized and repackaged. In other words, the historical becomes a task, a trying to get over its own negation by the work of theatricality, of staginess, of the ringing hollow of that which is too overdetermined to ever become simply kitsch.

However, there's nothing singular in this Ballardian gesture: it is, instead, a tactic that appears elsewhere, an unsettling effect of a political aesthetics crashing, over and over in an obscene loop, not against the end of the world but against the end of a historical project.

END OF THE ROAD

We now turn away from Ballard, not so much to other crashes as to *the* crash, to apocalypse on a grander scale than the micro-repetitions of Ballard's auto-erotic atrocities. Instead, to visions of civilization as a whole coming to a bloody, barbaric, senseless halt. Worst of all, to a reverse teleology of decadence and decline with no concrete *BOOM!* of start or finish, no evental rupture announcing the *krisis* is here. Nothing at first, just a lurking sense that: *it wasn't always this bad, was it?* And then, out of the corner of our collective eye, sights we can't forget, black clouds we can't ignore ...

Earlier, in describing the real combined and uneven geographical and economic structure of capitalist apocalypse, I argued that the manifestations of this structure are doubly vicious in their recurrence. They are horrible not only in their effects but in how their repetition naturalizes itself; it is the foreclosure of turning the effects back upon the system that produces them. And as such, they are a stuck motor, feeding back into the eternal present of late capitalism while barely holding off the disaster to come. What might this look like cinematically, let alone in other media? It is perhaps a longer, harder question of cognitive mapping, of trying to depict how a world becomes hellish without coming to an end, but the dominant articulations are closest to a stark realist tradition. This might range here from the more properly hard-line documentarian impulse to the neo-neo-realisms of dour, quiet, ascetic, quietly crushing films springing up in the recent financial crisis years. Films that depict "everyday" struggles against conditions of poverty, starvation, and precarity that constantly threaten to undermine the very category of the everyday.

However, we turn elsewhere, to things a bit more full-blooded, savage, surreal, and with more emphasis on the sudden surge of the apocalyptic than on the slow presentation of what was never hidden, even in plain sight. And if the central question of those realist films is one of perseverance across duration, the central questions of the films more central to this chapter are those of *perversion* across duration, of how to denature the historically given and the everyday to reveal its nightmares of persistence. The powerful and unsettling form this takes indeed involves a sense of the desperation and precarity that were there all along, but they insert a sense of change across time. There is no discernible moment when something went wrong, but it becomes incontrovertible that something went worse.

The glacially slow drift-to-hell and well-mannered barbarism of *Songs From the Second Floor* is one of the sharpest recent versions of this. No spurts of blood, no bursts of fire: just dehumanizing tableau shots, white powdered faces, and a world on the icy skids.

If the genuine threat of the entropic death of profitability and the after-life of the neoliberal order faces us in the decades to come, *Songs* just may become our filmic anthem. Totally absent are gas-hoarding sadists or any of the usual suspects. Even the sudden moments of violence that punctuate *Time of the Wolf* and *The Road* are gone. In its place, minor injuries, mutual aid, insurance fraud, a crucifix salesman throwing his stock of "crucified losers" onto a trash-heap, impeccably well-behaved ghosts, and the fields of the dead suddenly rising to make one man's impossibly bad day even worse. The economy goes down the tubes, and the Swedish state marches a young girl off a cliff in hopes that it will have some occult effect. Constant appeals to fate in the wake of any belief, and the nation's bourgeoisie attempt a mass airport exodus to warmer climates. Above all, the remarkable combination of very little editing, bloodless faces, and distanced (full body) camera framing, rendering formal the sense already lingering over – and long after – the whole film, that we have blood on our hands for bringing into existence a system now predicated on forces beyond the conceit and structure of individual action. Who needs to see facial expressions more closely when there is nothing to see but the vampiric shades of a drained population busy draining out its last shreds of common decency and collective hope?

Bleak as it is, it gets darker, and perhaps funnier, when we consider that it is a film from, and set in, a nation far closer to social democracy than most liberals would dream of, a nation that, despite its capacity for death metal, remains fetishized in the west as very civil society indeed. And so we should go back further to an approximation not of the frigid winter of the welfare state but the burning wreck of the entire enterprise of global Fordism in the wake of the second World War.

In films such as Béla Tarr's *Werckmeister Harmonies* (2000), Derek Jarman's *Jubilee* (1977), and Lars Von Trier's *Europa* trilogy (*Element of Crime* [1984], *Epidemic* [1987], and *Europa* [1991]), what is unspoken but still felt is that the restoration of whole project of Western civilization, from the total abyss of the first half of the 20th century, never happened.[79] Perhaps the "good guys" won the war, but the West – and the general spirit of world historical development – never recovered and picked itself back up. The modern world ended but did not go away, all the darkest corners of human nature and capitalist development bared themselves and never stopped doing so. The floodgates opened and couldn't be closed, so any movement after is either temporarily floating over the drowned ruins or wading through the detritus. *Element of Crime* literalizes this, as the detective returns from Cairo to a Europe lit sickly yellow and everywhere dripping, soaked, raining, misting, and above all, flooded. Rape, perversion, murder, and the sadistic fall-out of scientific method crowd the rotting catacombs of what used to be the cosmopolitan, the civil, the humanist. We descend into the trilogy as if into a bad dream, following the hypnosis of our murdering protagonist in *Element* as he "goes back to Europe" and comes back to be a cop when there's no longer a police force. We remain in the thrall of the sick in *Epidemic*, the title branded in red on the corner of the film through its duration, as an attempt of holed-away writers to imagine the end of the world occurs in concert with the world's descent along the very lines they plot. And in *Europa*, a return to post-Nazi Germany finds the "werewolves" (Nazis who continued to fight for their cause after the war) continuing to plague the general atmosphere of decadence and societal decline. A well-intentioned young American who comes to work the rail-line and help aid in the moral reconstruction of the nation finds his watery end after a bomb brings the train, and all efforts at reconciliation and progress, off a bridge. A deep narrator's voice (Max von Sydow) counts him, and the trilogy, back out of the hypnotic storm of the European nightmare.

If Von Trier's story is of the enclosed bad dream, Jean Luc-Godard's *Weekend* (1967) is the brutal, illogical, and misanthropic burning wreck, breaking through not just that fantasy, but the very fantasy of capitalism's future persistence.[80] It is a vicious triumph not of the post-apocalyptic, but of durational apocalypse that we can never escape because it never starts definitively. The world is full of shallow, nasty people, and all it takes is for them to drive a bit more recklessly for the powder keg of the end of the '60s to catch. The plenitude of the post-war period left bleeding and on fire by the roadside.

What follows is both a long account of the film and, more

generally, of just what we mean by *fantasy* when we speak of apocalyptic fantasies.[81] *Fantasy* remains crucial to any thought of *apocalypse*, for it is a structure of dealing – and putting off having to deal – with what "shouldn't be there," the symptom not revealed via an exceptional event but through the fundamental structures of prohibition that try to put off the catastrophic collapse in the first place. More particularly, *Weekend* approaches fantasy as that which exceeds any individual pathology: it's the fantasy of an era and an order, painting the tint of health over the sickness of the bourgeois subject and the cancerous collapse of late capitalist profitability waiting in the wings.

Like *The Bed Sitting Room* (and sharing a similar central place in my aesthetics and cultural politics), it is an antecedent whose example couldn't be entirely followed. Yet if *BSR* is ultimately about the mess after the fact and the somewhat gentler prospects of taking pleasure in the rubble, *Weekend* takes bleak pleasure in making us watch society grind to a halt and gives us the inter-section of *class war* with the *war of all against all*.

Above all, it is a road map of what can't be reconciled: the capitalist drive toward accumulation at all costs, by any means necessary, and the anti-capitalist drive to destroy that world at all costs, by any means necessary. To no one's surprise, this results in a full crash and, in doing so, pulls our narrative back from the temporal axis to the terrain of the spatial zone. We get closer to our end point, the material coexistence of off-times and opposed totalities engaged in open war with each other. But we aren't there yet, still caught in the confusion of a film that self-desig-nates in its intertitles as "lost in the cosmos" and "found in the scrap-heap." What more could be expected when you're dealing with the question hanging over us: *what is the end of the world when no one tells you that it has started?*

Fittingly, the film opens with a closure, or at least with a roadblock.

An intertitle – and we should insist on it as an intertitle

although it appears to be part of the introductory information about the film – states, "INTERDIT AUX MOINS DE 18 ANS" ("PROHIBITED FOR THOSE UNDER 18 YEARS"). But presumably those watching have already been granted access: either they are over 18, or they have snuck in, bribed an attendant, or stolen a print. So, the inclusion of such an inter-diction has no functional purpose other than to announce that desire will be frustrated and that this frustration will be overcome. It is a device for the structuring of enjoyment, a particular path of the organization of pleasure – and apocalyptic lust – that *Weekend* articulates and undoes.

And perhaps this is best taken as a clue offered to instruct us how to watch. The question, then, is what instructions do this warning – and simultaneous come-on, promising the illicit beyond its frame – give and what sorts of viewing expectations follow. Most directly, the instructions are to prepare oneself for *pornography*, for the type of watching that self-excludes from mass acceptance, that is necessarily private and obscene even when experienced in a theater full of other viewers. And here, right in its very first frames, we get a glimpse of the core of the film's engagement with *fantasy*, as well its future move toward redeploying the exposed material avoided by fantasy toward militant antinomian ends.

Just what do we mean by *fantasy*? Fantasy, in our investi-gation, should be taken in the sense articulated by Jacques Lacan in his later writing and teaching. Fantasy isn't a wish-fulfillment scenario – *those kind of handcuffs, that kind of job promotion, those words I've been wanting to hear* - but rather a fundamental mechanism that organizes our desire so as to foreclose confrontation with the blind repetition of drive. To distinguish briefly, drive is the ceaseless push toward unmediated *jouissance* (pleasure/pain that threatens the consistency of normal functioning), a constant push that has nothing determinate toward which it moves. As such, it cannot be reconciled with prohibition, of having to mediate and defer, and hence it cannot be reconciled with the conditions of entrance into the symbolic realm, the realm of Law. Conversely, desire is inseparable from the Law which refuses drive; desire is how we safely "want" in the face of drive. The consequences of all this is the "inverted ladder of the Law of desire," seeking pleasure in the very prohibition of pleasure itself.

What, then is fantasy? Without getting into, or having to buy into, a psychoanalytic account of a "primordial loss" of what is given up in order to enter the symbolic order (the world of language and Law), we can still say that fantasy is the *narrative* organization of this structure of non-access. It is a "story" that both naturalizes a state of affairs – *that's just the way that things are* – and makes it a personal configuration – *that's just the way that I uniquely am*. And so even to take on the more conventional notion of fantasy as wish-fulfillment, it might be better understood that what's really at stake isn't my weird perversions or secret hopes themselves but the way in which they function to let me approach what I desire without ever getting any closer to it. This is necessary because actually reaching "it" would make immediately apparent the fact that "it" was never there to start. What was there was only, 1) the fact of drive, and 2) the symptoms that emerge as a result of the doomed-to-fail nature of subsuming drive to the acceptable realm of language and mediated desire. As such, if fantasy is a narrative of primal loss (want unbound by mediation), it reinforces the primacy of a lost narrative, insisting that it is possible and necessary to inscribe meaning over and beyond the accidents of existence, to provide the illusion of *depth* in place of the unbearable flatness and senseless repetition of drive. It is therefore a type of cartography, a prescribed navigation that lets us to glimpse the threats to meaningfulness (symptoms, whose causes are absent and which resolutely make no sense, no matter how much we backtrack through what we may have seen in our parent's darkened bedrooms) while swerving past them.

To take a concrete example, then: consider the prohibition against underage watching at the start of *Weekend*. This is exactly the instructive mechanism of fantasy, the organization of desire's operation. And this is, properly speaking, a *fantasy* in that it also veils this basic operation in a framework that grounds and validates this mechanism (as being an objective character of how the world is, i.e. of what is generally agreed to be inappropriate for impressionable youth). In this particular case, the fantasy is pornographic, not so much in the sense that it promises erotic titillation but rather in the *generic fantasy* of pornography, in the erotics of prohibition themselves. You get off on being told that there is a chance that this is the kind of film that might get you off, and, furthermore, that you perhaps are not mature enough to handle it.

If the generic fantasy of pornography conditions *Weekend* from its beginning, what other structures aim to make meaning out of the singular events, to form scenes out of happenings? We can articulate three central modes, or registers, of fantasy here: *generic, subjective,* and *political-economic.*

The first two, the *generic* and the *subjective,* are more immediately familiar from our investigation so far. *Weekend* employs and recognizes generic conventions as fantasmic conventions, codes that not only instruct how to organize the pleasure in watching but also the systems of enjoyment according to which the film moves. In short, the fantasmic function of genre is to offer the rules of the game – the Law, as it were – and to establish the boundaries within which the play of minimal difference and deviation can create desire through messing with the refusal-invitation of such codes. In *Weekend* in particular, one can identify at least four distinct sets of generic formations (pornographic, noir, comedy of manners, road movie), each of which serves to instruct how to desire and also how to deal with the exceptions to their rules.

The subjective fantasy is, superficially, the heart of the surreal work performed by *Weekend*. It's also arguably the least interesting aspect of its general working through the notion and necessity of fantasy, at least insofar as the subjective fantasy – *what kind of desiring person am I?* – is excluded from the thornier historical knot of the asubjective political-economic fantasy we see so gloriously taken to pieces in the film. On the subjective level, the level of the personal fantasies of the subjects portrayed in the film, we encounter a familiar parodic mode of mocking the petty, consumerist fantasies of the haut-bourgeoisie.

To be sure, *Weekend* extends this parody to a level of savagery rarely seen, most notably in Corinne's anguished cries for her lost Hermes purse while mangled bodies spill out of a burning car. This is coupled with the treatment of rich, bored eroticism recognizable from other films of the time, notably those of Luis Buñuel and Claude Chabrol, here hitting its peak in Roland's imitation of a psychoanalytic scene (sitting behind, quietly smoking, mimicking the talking cure with which the rich are so familiar) while Corinne disinterestedly relays the story of her three-way with another couple.

But the force of *Weekend* does not lie in its treatment of this ultimately toothless parody: as Italian Marxist Antonio Gramsci pointed out, what is so dangerous about the profligate habits of the rich aren't the habits themselves, confined to a parasitic level of society, but rather the trickle-down of this "total social hypocrisy" to the working classes (and economic totality as a whole) via the emergence of mass consumption in the Fordist economic regime. And here as well, the real space of contention isn't the follies of the rich but the constitutions of political-economic fantasy that forestall confrontation with the blind drive (to accumulate) of capitalism and its resultant symptoms. In this way, what's ultimately at stake, as we move further from the starting apartment toward the breakdown of order in the countryside, isn't *class fantasy* per se. It is the asubjective fantasy of an economic totality, bound up in and in opposition to the emergent realities of its historical conjuncture. It's the functional appearance of individual choice (the managed depth) which veils the flat horror of collapse.

The interrogation of political-economic fantasies, first under the guise of class critique, begins in two early scenes from *Weekend*. The first scene in this pairing occurs in the parking lot of Roland and Corinne' apartment building. A previous scene of a fight between two drivers, prompted by a minor collision, has already instructed us to witness the parking lot as a scene of conflict particularly inflected by class status. In this scene, the first of many in which the identity of subjects is grounded first and foremost in their status as drivers, the collision is between cars with vastly different economic demarcations, between the tiny, affordable city car and the flashy red *bagnole*. This scene continues, and amplifies, by the marking of the space as such a zone of contention, beginning with its intertitle: "SCENE DE LA VIE PARISIENNE" ("SCENE FROM PARISIAN LIFE").

One function of this intertitle is to mark this scene *allegorically*, using its literal designation of the events as a scene of Parisian life to simultaneously indicate that this is a representative scene, the kind of thing that happens all the time. In short, as a scene from which one can distill a generalized interpretation about codes of social interaction in France in the late '60s. As

Roland and Corinne back their convertible out, harassed by a boy dressed as a Native American chief, they bump into the car owned by the boy's parents. On one level, this quickly becomes the type of interaction central to *Weekend*, the ridiculous turn to brutality resulting from the overvaluation of commodities. It also serves to ground our conception of Roland and Corinne as *those who don't work*, too rich to labor: the angry neighbor accuses them of acting like this only because Corinne's father "owns the block." But it is the arrival of the angered woman's husband that interests us here and justifies our designation of this scene as *allegorical*, or, more accurately, as functioning under the guise of the allegorical.

In this moment, we see the allegorical family, a portrait of bourgeois domesticity that *doesn't work*, in two senses. The portrait doesn't work in that it seems impossible, a parodic version of what they should look like that nevertheless nails it: the husband dressed like an outmoded country squire, shotgun under arm and spaniel in tow, the mother spiking tennis balls at the departing villains, and the boy play-acting as a savage redskin. Yet is also a portrait of bourgeois domesticity that doesn't work in the sense that their clothing indicates that these are not laborers – they all have time to play dress up. Of course, this does take place on a Saturday, and one could argue that we shouldn't make this assumption. But the fact remains that the scene presents itself as an allegory; we get it that this isn't really about a minor car accident but rather about the consequences of excessive commodity fetishism "in general."

If *Weekend* proved unable to advance beyond this level of critique (in other words, if it continued as an "allegorical" film), it would simply be another weak potshot fired off by a facile liberal Left or by the dogmatic bores of French Maoism. But the following scenes, including the second scene to explicitly foreground class-inflected conflict, make a sharp turn and result in the tremendous political force and total misanthropic rage of the film.

After Roland and Corinne leave the parking lot relatively unscathed, they shortly encounter a traffic jam, if that term can even describe the spectacle that we get in a seven minute long tracking shot (pulled back at a constant distance), moving horizontally along a line of halted cars and trucks, their occupants playing cards and with balls, their cars towing boats and caged animals. We follow Roland's car as he drives past the others waiting their turn, eventually passing a bloody mess at the head of the line, bodies ejected out onto the road as a policeman directs cars past. It moves from boring and insufferable, lightly comedic and statically interesting, to compelling and brutal in its interminable progression and gore-slicked end source.

What remains so striking about this scene is its total incommensurability with the expected narrative and generic logic. None of the fantasies we have been offered so far prove capable of reconciling the function or meaning of it. To be sure, we can offer various readings of this scene, the most seductive of which may be as an allegory of the end of Fordist culture, represented by the automobile: stuck traffic, stuck assembly line, and the end of the whole social-cultural apparatus of consumption and personal mobility on which that turns. And given the instructions of how to enjoy this film available to the viewer at this point, it seems the most valid. Yet the formal extremity of the scene and its duration – its ultimate unincorporability in the economy of time – is the very shock that causes the allegorical approach to fail. As Brian Henderson pointed out, the tracking shots of *Weekend*, the majority of which are long shots in terms of distance, serve to flatten the film in terms of form and content.[82] In consequence, the "non-bourgeois camera style" employed does work to undermine illusions of depth and authenticity that give shape to both bourgeois morality and bourgeois cinema. But we can speak of a different type of flatness here which doesn't just dismantle the false sincerity of bourgeois morality. Rather, it is the full flatness revealed apocalyptically on the ruins of fantasy itself, in which all that comes apart and comes to the surface is all that won't go away. It is the flattening of fantasy down to the surface of repetition and drive. It is the process of undifferentiation. For what we witness, in this unbroken duration of after-effect, is *drive itself*, crystallized, frozen in the halted line of traffic. It ruptures the economy of the film, and it is a vicious presentation of the ongoing rupture of the economy beyond the film.

Above all, this stuck crash is the fundamental symptom that makes evident the inadequacy of the fantasies which struggle to make sense of it: it can't be incorporated, it can't be reasoned with, and it can't be broken into more familiar units of editing and meaning-making. Just the stuck record of the same, brought to stillness by a collision we didn't see, that already happened and that left us only with the mess. Zombie films, salvage-prospect, and utter breakdown compressed into a single shot, the kernel of apocalyptic thought moving sideways and going nowhere. There is minor difference in the line of cars, not a flat gray but the variations of vehicles, of activities, of tiny glimpses into other stalled voyages. But they collectively go nowhere, a collection of fundamental fixity and failure. So too the fantasies held out before, so too allegory and the possibility of any of *this* meaning any of *that*. Above all, a breakdown of relation itself and, with it, the capacity of mediating and deferring confrontation. The whole project of profit and progress is broken apart and made indistinguishable from the excluded and undifferentiated, caught in the thick flatness of the broken concepts and orders of separation and management. What once was a line, a direction, a teleology, a way out and forward, now becomes the formless field of antagonism. It isn't that the singular road of development comes to an end and reach its catastrophic destination. It's the end of the road itself.

What, as such, is the specificity of "apocalyptic fantasy," that category on which so much of this investigation turns? *Apocalyptic fantasy navigates the end of fantasy itself.* It is the structure of fantasy turning back onto itself, an approach and deferral, mediation and management become a self-consumptive stalemate. Because apocalypse isn't just the content of revelational end-times, but the dismantling of a knowledge structure itself. Apocalyptic fantasy undoes itself, a corrosive failure that strips away its potential legitimacy, authenticity, and sufficiency. The apocalyptic fantasy, then, of capitalism is *not* a "what comes after." There's nothing progressive about it, nothing in these dream and nightmare images that we didn't know or couldn't see. In their hardest forms, they are the sloppy nihilistic non-equivalence of the end itself, neither enlightenment nor transcendence.

The specificity of *Weekend*'s apocalyptic vision is this startling overdetermined crash: the end of economic accumulation produces a piled-up accumulation of ends, all irrecuperable, as fire and fury consume not just the healthy future of liberal capital, but all possibilities of human decency and advancement. The inability to do otherwise, for a new crash to point elsewhere, means that the revelation of the end both shows the undifferentiated same and recognizes that its repetition is the bloodless heart of the problem. Death drive and the drive toward accumulation are indistinguishable: just the idiocy of the repetition of *more* that will destroy everything by staying the same. Apocalypse is the revelation of nothing but nothing changing.

Of course, as before, the issue is how to move forward from apocalyptic breakdown. (In the case of this scene, moving forward means breaking the social contract. Frankly, it means continuing to act like the consummate assholes that you are, skipping the line and driving by others stuck waiting.) The film sketches four possible modes of advance, the last two of which will be tracked out from here.

The grinding crush forward, trying to advance and making the gridlock worse: the fantasy of progress in accumulation. This is the mode of capitalism in the years after the collapse of global Fordism *Weekend* envisions, a collapse which was deferred. As if we just got a bulldozer (bought with loaned money based on the premise that the bulldozer will do the trick) and just pushed the entire pile-up forward, packing it tighter and wrecking the road on which we move.

Dwelling in misanthropic perversity: taking on the catastrophic world of total war by discovering the pleasures of meanness, wrong-doing, backstabbing, hustling and scrapping, and generally doing wrong - the fantasy of pleasure in naughtiness. This is pretty much the entire film, a thorough-going catalogue of the perversions waiting – or not waiting, going on all along – in the wings of well-mannered society. What else can be said of a film in which Charlotte Brontë is burned alive, and when cannibalism is not enough, when fish are inserted inside the victims who are forced to strip and will likely be raped before slaughter and consumption? Not to mention the more mild forms: breaking lots of things, playing drums in the woods, cheating on your spouse.

The false reconciliation of opposites in a new fantasy of unity, bringing together incommensurable subject positions and class enemies by finding new shared enemies or by pretending that there still is a functioning world worth saving: the fantasy of unity in reconciliation. This possibility, raised in the following scene, is quickly smashed down by the fact of the crash, its severity marking all attempts at unity and forgiveness as naïve at best, viciously cruel in its unwillingness to consider what must be done at worst.

Taking the anti-depth dissolution of hierarchical ordering not just as a temporary consequence of bad times but as the ground of that overdue battle: the anti-fantasy of antagonism in collapse. This is the center of the end-of-all-roads radical left position occupied by *Weekend*, though, as we will see, it cannot ultimately safeguard against being misunderstood and recuperated into new structures of perhaps more dangerous pseudo-political conviction.

The following scene is the site where the film begins to move again and toward the third position of new fantasies of coming-together. Here the bloodied corpse of the rich boy – killed in a collision between his sporty car and a farmer's tractor – keeps us in the sway of the crash, itself a repetition, yet another consequence without explanation. But in comparison with the "Scenes from Parisian Life" sequence, we see its distance from the previous fantasy instructions and see, in its place, the emerging rigor of the political instructions. Consider the structure of the two sequences. The "Scene from Parisian Life" sequence begins with the intertitle that signals its allegorical status, its capacity to stand in for another meaning, its interchangeability. This second sequence indeed contains an intertitle that would seem to signal an allegorical interpretation: "LA LUTTE DE CLASSES" ("CLASS STRUGGLE"). But the scene itself, especially in its relation to the car crash tableau scene, insists upon another reading in two distinct senses.

First, the designation of the sequence as *CLASS STRUGGLE* gives very different viewing instructions from the designation of the first sequence as a "scene from Parisian life." That scene comes under the pretense of being just another scene, a series of ridiculous events that demand interpretation. In short, the intertitle does not offer instructions but indicates the need for such an explanatory mechanism; at that point in the film, we have only received generic or bourgeois fantasy maps to navigate the interaction. Even the more nuanced class fantasy remains, properly speaking, a narrative that avoids confronting the mute heart of drive, retreating instead into the master knowledge of irony and satire. (*We know better, we can mock these silly bourgeois.*) Something different is at work in the "Class struggle" scene, for the intertitle itself offers the instructions previously missing. We don't read allegorically that which is already beyond the point of allegory, and the dialogue in this scene makes it clear that those involved are aware of their positions, not as symbols for their respective class positions but as desiring subjects whose modes of desiring are limited by the class fantasy in which they participate. Not allegorically, but in the very real intersections of material life and the fantasmic support systems of that life. In other words, this scene is neither an allegory nor a metaphor of class struggle. The sports car smashed into the tractor does not indicate class war. It is an instance of it concretized, made unassailable. The dialectics of class war are to be measured in the distance between the crushed metal and the red-slicked face.

The second way in which this scene moves away from the fantasies that, up to this point, give order to the film and all within in it is in the direct incompatibility of available fantasies with the violence of the symptoms they seek to avoid. There's a poverty of recuperation here when an economy of management faces the genuinely undifferentiated, the unwanted, the unseen now blocking the road. We only see the intertitle ("LA LUTTE DE CLASSES") after we have seen the after-effect of drive. This is to say: the designation of the bloody events in this scene *under the sign of the political* is both the attempt to find an organization of meaning capable of dealing with the accelerating blood bath and an indication of just how far we need to go in stripping away those fantasies. Especially those closest to us, all those of radical anti-capitalism, from outmoded inheritances to what we mistake for the unincorporable new capable of intervening without compromise. And in the moment examined and exploded by *Weekend*, as long as the understanding of the class struggle hinges on the signs of Fordist fantasy (subject-status determined by one's purchasing power, as being the owner of a convertible versus a tractor), no progress can be made.

One reaches only the false reconciliation – as we see, the two classes (rich girl and farmer) standing together, arm in arm, is the bad fixity of a "fauxtographe," as an intertitle states. Fittingly, this false unity of the classes succeeds only in turning to another fantasy, a structure of desire that they can agree on, calling Roland and Corinne "dirty Jews," and, in doing so, finding a way to share a common identity – *at least we can agree on hating the Jews* – and avoiding looking at the bloody mess in front of them.

How to go beyond faux reconciliation? Only by dwelling in the brutality of the symptoms and drawing lines not of passage but of common relation to the dominant order. Not digging in the ruins of the past but tracing the scattered landscape of the scrap-heap. In an echo of our take on salvagepunk and ruins, this is the related task of an alternate mapping: the constellation of scars.

In his twenty-third seminar, Lacan introduced the idea of the *"sinthome"* (as opposed to "symptome," the French word for "symptom"). Wordplay aside, for our purposes this means the constellation of symptoms particular to a subject. It's the pattern of access to those moments of confrontation with drive that's particular to an individual, a map not of smooth roads and passages but of passages leading only back to the blockages and threats. As such, the *sinthome* is the antithesis of fantasy; it is a particular organization of enjoyment that keeps running back into fantasy, that stands before drive and its ugly repetition and refuses the detours of desire.

What we can say here is that in *Weekend*, Godard offers an apocalyptic *sinthome* proper to the post-war regime of accumulation, a way of making sense of the symptoms produced as the remainder – and necessary underside – of capitalism's drive. This particular *sinthome* is the instructive force of radical politics, not as a counter-ideology but as a fundamental and persistent threat of enmity and violence that cannot be otherwise. Refusing to treat the difficult singularity of symptoms as accessible through the false depth of allegory, the political instead flattens fantasy down so we see those lumps or drive or the undifferentiated sticking out. Only then begins the long, arduous task of speaking again.

In *Weekend*, this task is achieved, however briefly, in the sequence where the two garbage men from whom Roland and Corrine attempt to beg food but receive only strident anti-capitalist rhetoric. They deliver diatribes against American hegemony, the weakness of the liberal state in its complicity with monopoly capital, and the need for revolutionary violence. What is so startling in this scene is that as they talk, Godard cuts to moments from the film so far, a catalogue of the bloody excess, perversion, rape, murder, arson, and, above all, car crashes. The result of this is that the men's words become instructions *beyond* fantasies, injunctions to think these seemingly random acts of brutality not as allegories of capital's perversion but as real effects of it, making explicit the sense of class struggle as not allegory, fantasy, ideology, or illusion. Just crash and burn, and perspective undermining itself without becoming excusable or understandable.

All is not well, however, for the real viciousness of the film lies in knowing that passing through an apocalypse doesn't mean automatically that you know what you've been through. If the entire film frames the problem of no one having told you that the apocalypse has started, it ends with a further problem: *what if you mishear the new instructions that could make it possible to move through the wreckage*? What secondary fantasies emerge from this misrecognition? This is the exact situation that we face at the end of *Weekend*.

Roland and Corinne are taken hostage by band of ultra-leftist hippie guerillas who have clearly heard the instructions of a rather oddball insurrectionary anarchist or communist tradition. But the forms of desire – and action – necessarily get it wrong, mistake the instructions. In this case, it's basically a bad game of anti-state Telephone that results, variously, in open barbarism, justified property destruction, and a diet very heavy in meat.

We might recall the infamous revolutionary dictum, as formulated by Comrade Lazare Moiseyevich Kaganovich: "Why wail over broken eggs when we are making an omelet!"[83] The revolutionaries know this well. They've also heard about killing capitalist pigs and have taken this to heart as well. They are constantly cracking eggs and killing pigs. But they have mistaken the instructions: they crack eggs to garnish the hostages they capture and cannibalize, and they actually slaughter pigs on camera. In short, they get it too right, take it all too literally and what results is a perverse facsimile of revolutionary fervor.

How do we move beyond this impasse? Perhaps one answer, hinted at in the film, lies in a turn away from *revolutionary terrorism* to *revolutionary horrorism*. Godard himself hints at this:

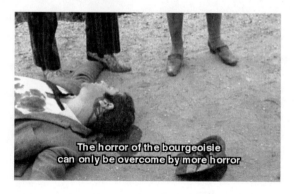

The horror of the bourgeoisie can only be overcome by more horror

in his *Histoire(s) du cinéma*, he writes of *Weekend* in the context of Dreyer's *Vampyr* (1932) and claims that *Weekend* is a film about monsters. And in this way, much as the anti-capitalist instructions for viewing and understanding that are held out to us by the garbage men act as a potential key to working through what we've seen, so too this fifth genre of *horror* to hold out as the instructive knot that might be able to tie together the disparate scatter of the rest of the film.

What would be the consequence of this shift, not just of making *Weekend* a horror movie but more broadly, to thinking of horror over terror? Terror is about the threat to life, of the knife behind you. Horror, conversely, is about the threat to understanding, of living to see the after-effects, of suddenly realizing that you were the one behind the knife all along. In this way, horror is apocalyptic. It confronts us with the symptoms – and with our complicity in reproducing them – and demands that we find new sets of instructions. As such, where the revolutionaries get it wrong is in ignoring the collapsing world around them, the landscape of death, fire, and violence through which *Weekend* passes, and instead trying to be the terroristic principle of the forest, hell-raisers who don't realize that hell has already been raised all around them. Revolutionary horror is the task, then, of not just disrupting the order of things or appearing as a shock from outside, but of reorganizing the symptoms already present, of showing the bare viciousness of drive there from the start. Is this an impossible task? Not at all. The eggs are already broken. We just need to figure out how to scramble them.

DARK CITY

As we leave *Weekend* behind and head toward our conclusion, I should reiterate that *Weekend* is, at is most fundamental, a film of combined and uneven apocalypse. The perverse violence, the air of senseless destruction, and the sense that there is no driver at the wheel: all of this produces the doubling-back of the voyage itself, in which what once was a destination to happen in the future has been happening now, precisely because the very notion of the future and any progress toward it has crashed and burned. In this way, the apocalyptic revelation can only be spatial, as *no future* comes to mean *no way out*, and the eschatological brutality seeps into the entire zone.

Yet one of the crucial points about the persistence of capitalist apocalypse as ongoing duration is the fact that its unevenness is material, concrete, and situated in very particular places. If, in *Weekend*, the landscape as such becomes a landscape of violence in total (appropriately shot in the tracking camera pulled-back tableau of landscape painting), the consequence is that the apocalypse is diffuse and general, bringing all to a halt. Against this, we need to consider those particular unwanted sites, zones of contention and neglect, in which it is impossible to not know that the end of days have come for some while the appearance of the functioning of the system as a whole continues. Eggs not just broken but tossed to the floor, repeated infinitely and savagely, made all the worse for the claim that it doesn't have to be this way and that these zones belong to another time, accidental holdouts from a less modern era.

In place of a far longer cultural history of this, one too immense to grasp here in its range from Pier Paolo Pasolini (in

Accatone [1961] and *Mamma Roma* [1962]) and Marco Ferreri (*Don't Touch the White Woman!* [1974]) to more recent works such as *City of God* (2002) and the full sweep of HBO's *The Wire* (2002-2008), a couple pointed examples that make literal the sense of underground histories and alternate futures that didn't take.

Gary Sherman's *Death Line* (1972, titled *Raw Meat* in the U.S.) is one of the most startling articulations of this tendency, a version that asks the question "socialism or barbarism?" with a subtle, off-kilter severity and a degree of unparalleled literalism. In this case, the definitive answer appears to have been barbarism. The American poster promises a feast of exploitation, all hollow-eyed naked bodies, bearded leonine possible messiah, and the tagline:

BENEATH MODERN LONDON: buried alive in its plague-ridden tunnels lives a tribe of once humans. Neither men nor women, they are less than animals ... they are the raw meat of the human race!

Yet this attempt to shoehorn the film into a more recognizable grindhouse-horror slot is entirely at odds with the film itself. I can only imagine some seriously alarmed viewers looking for gore, nudity, and counter-evolution neo-caveman sex, finding instead a dark parable about the capacity of an economic order to turn against those who labor it requires.

For in reality, the core of the film is a staggering sadness, a mourning man (who happens to be a cannibal) who can no longer speak beyond a parroting of the automated subway voice, rasping "Mind the gap," again and again, impossibly trying to convey the grief for his lost partner. The rough arc of the story is as follows. In 1892, a group of workers digging tunnels for the London Underground were trapped in a collapse. No attempt was made to save them, not because the accident was undetected, but because the corporation behind the digging covered up the incident and went bankrupt, unwilling to threaten their crumbling reputation with the disclosure of what happened. The workers were left to rot, slipping through the cracks of a vanished company and a state that couldn't be bothered to oversee the abuses. In short, capitalism in its standard operating procedure. The result is a bit of sustainable barbarism and the "descent of the species," generations of the workers maintaining a community underground, winding through passageways to pick off commuters for cannibalistic feeding.

Two aspects of the film need to be considered as more than implausibilities needed for the sake of horroring up the plot. If they were trapped collectively below, why have they lost their ability to speak English in just 80 years? And if the underground dwellers know how to get to the other stations to feed, why do they not then return to the world above through these routes?[84]

Regarding the first question: why do they not develop off the bedrock of the Victorian culture to which they belonged? One might imagine a more interesting, and even rather steam-punkish, film in which they maintain a flourishing underground population below, a community that takes off from the state of affairs at their time of burial and then articulates its own history. The Victorian moment in isolation from the world system, set to unpack its ideologies and ways of living without contamination from elsewhere. Instead, though, we watch the consequences of a total slide back to that impossible time. A nightmare image of the human animal cut off from society, we see here that now-familiar tendency to envision that the post-apocalyptic instance is a resetting of the clock. The political appeal of this is therefore an apology for the barbarism of capitalism, a tendency borne out especially in the marketing of the film that shows, unveiled, the true conception of the laboring subject under the industrial order: *once humans, but now no longer men and women, less than animals, just the raw meat of production ...*

The second question, of their staying below, concerns the post-apocalyptic zone as time out of joint. Or better, as historical *space* out of joint, and against the seeming degradation of those within it, a nascent structure of a developing will to territorialize an alternate history. For while it is the seemingly accidental set of circumstances that "seal one off" and create this off-time (the pocket of other living that is the negation of the dominant mode of life in the city), we know better. These circumstances are structural, necessary, desired, not by any planner but by the general logic of capitalist development. These pockets are rarely as dramatically underground (both literally and figuratively) as in *Death Line*. Consider one of the sharper dystopian post-apocalyptic films to date, Godard's *Alphaville* (1965). Because, at the end of the day, the point of *Alphaville* is that you don't need to build a set to approximate a dystopian future. You just need to drive through Paris at night. No other world, no forgotten tomb below the hygienic, ordered, and administered city. The city itself is that set of off-zones, of catastrophes past and future written into the organization of the city. The whole situation holds them out as "empty" placeholders, waiting for the right time to finish destroying them to build anew. The deferred possibility of redevelopment, kicking the unwanted further and further to the periphery.

In the SI journal, Guy Debord and his crew ventured this necessary pairing of material and theoretical "criticism": an image of a supermarket burning during the Watts riots in LA with the caption, "CRITIQUE OF URBANISM." As in, there are critiques of urbanism in general, and there are riotous critiques of particular organizations of urban life. No image more fitting for an ending note here, as we need to ask: what happens when – like zombies who share the pain of death, like salvagepunks refusing to sit quietly in the ruins – those pockets of hell don't just recognize how they are damned and doomed by the system, but when they damn it back? When the periphery storms the center, or when the rotten core bites back at the suburban hand that doesn't feed it? In short, to reclaim the real right to development and progress by turning back against the naturalized fantasies of what that is limited to mean, to assert the right of the apocalyptic itself to bare its teeth as an act of will and knowledge, not to be swept back under the rug of a safer, managed, and vacant future. In short, to move from the violence of the world we inherit toward violence *against* such a world, and to make sure that our violence – cognitive, material, impossible, tactical, ethical – is uncommon, not just inherited and repeated. That it doesn't reproduce the very order it aims to negate by falling into new fantasies of petty destruction and old misreadings of the immensity of any insurrectionary task of throwing off the mantle of the present and advancing otherwise.

The kind of films and books that concretely theorize and work this "revenge anti-fantasy" out have been scattered across our investigation: it's the key turn of the punk film (as inheritor of zombie film) and the harder edge of salvagepunk as assemblage of antagonistic scrap. Carpenter's *Assault on Precinct 13*, discussed in the zombie context, stands as one of its most explicit formulations, for it's made clear that the "state of emergency" invoked by police is not one which threatens Los Angeles as a whole. It applies solely to certain designated pockets, zones of war already abandoned by state and commerce, and it is solely on this ground that the bloodbath happens. As such, the mistake made by the "protagonists" (that awkward band of Howard Hawksian men and women who overcome their positions of tough detachment to join together) isn't to close the police station in the first place and abandon Anderson to its own devices and self-vacating. It's *not* closing it sooner, getting stuck there one night too long. And the antagonists? Their mistake, other than their inability to defeat our plucky heroes, is to remain caught between a notion of what must be protected and what must be attacked. We cannot take their assault on the station as more than a contingency, a soft target that turns out to fight back. One cannot help but wonder what it would have looked like had they waited one night more before taking on the abandoned station. Then, it might have been their stronghold from which to wage the more potent war: attacking stations still in use, bringing the battle to neighborhoods where they don't belong, and forming networks of post-apocalyptic care for those left behind with them in the wasteland.

And then there is *Wolfen*, Michael Wadleigh's quite unreal 1981 film, which is almost too close to the aesthetics and tendencies of this book to discuss. After all, it is about a breed of superwolves who take over an abandoned zone of the south Bronx, survive by feeding on derelicts who didn't get the message to leave that area, kill rich developers and their coke-head wives, and get mistaken for armed left-wing militants. Even the utter mediocrity of its New Age protector-of-the-earth conclusion can't spoil it, in part because that ending affords us the image of wolves watching a cop smash up an architectural model of planned condos in the murdered developer's very '80s luxury apartment. Most of all, *Wolfen* is a documentary horror film, in spite of its being based on a novel, its fantastic turns and latent spiritualism. It is a documentary film because it does not *represent* a derelict urban zone: it is shot on location, in the blighted reality of the south Bronx in that period, in a zone where the film did not just "show" the violence of ruins. It enacted such violence and left material remainders: the emptied husk of a church we see was built up by the film crew, burnt, and left to skeletally stand. As such, the film is the funereal, charred, rubble-strewn present of a place with no future beyond the two possibilities modeled by the film: the sheen of gentrified renewal, or the reconquest by remnants of another past now adapted to flourish in the vacant wilds of a city too busy to notice.

Consequently, *Wolfen* continues in that partial legacy of punk films and their faithful tracings of the inconclusive arc of dissolution and revolutionary failure. Yet in *Wolfen*, it isn't that the wolves are defeated. Quite the contrary: Albert Finney's detective character realizes that they are ancient, powerful, wise ecological protectors, creatures who belong to an order we cannot understand and must respect. However, the Warriors aren't defeated in the film of that name. They make it through the night, right the wrongs, and clear their names. What is lost is the real possibility of the gangs coming together, becoming the unified mass rather the infighting tangle of tribes. So too the problem with the Wolfen – the assumption of their obdurate and ahistorical singularity stands in the way of their doing more than just existing uneasily in the catastrophic modern world. They are held out as too special, too precious, and too ancient and natural to be removed without further upsetting the established order of the world. As a result, they remain incapable of holding out better against the new, second nature established order of uneven development. Against whatever minoritarian wolfish will they have, they come close to defending their new hunting ground for the wrong purpose. Sure, they occasionally wander too far downtown and pick off the rich. After all, isn't that the only reason that they are noticed: they eat someone whose social network has enough political and social clout to get heard by the police? Because when they hold back from that, when they stick to their territory, they in fact aid in the possibility of new condo development: they eat winos and other unwanted types, they would likely pick off any bohemians or young families who might otherwise stake a claim to a zone alternately hip and cheap. In this way, they hold it off as a dead zone in a crowded city, a natural site for new high-rises to emerge.

And so the resolution of the film is the tired exhalation of our breath held at the thought: *what if they picked off that yuppie scumbag and his awful wife on purpose?* The realization of their ancient existence – they are that which has always been and always will be – is also the realization that this was basically an accident, that all the interrogations of left-wing partisan networks and various red brigades were for naught. In this way, it also models the declension of moments in which such armed movements were a genuine threat, however small. In other words, to return a now familiar rhetorical structure: in 1981, it's easier to imagine the hunger of ancient protector superwolves than it is to imagine the persistence of radical militants. But we can insist otherwise, insist on taking the Wolfen as another false start that didn't take. In this case, a real start with an ending that can only ring false. To imagine it otherwise, then, to sever that insipid turn to eternality from its true body: the thought of their willful spread, of having meant it all along ...

This leads us to the final mode of the post-apocalyptic city sketched initially. Not just a fabric of facilitated zones of development, with the attendant post-apocalyptic sites wedged between massive outlays of new capital, but a post-apocalyptic zone *as a whole*. The city as a lived waste land, not just a protected hollow. A designated site of apocalypse, a dark space that gives shape to the combined and uneven development of international capitalism. The city as a negativity, one that is up for grabs not as a lost site to be reclaimed by nature or newer, greener capital but as a determinate negation to be taken en masse.

Cinematically, we see this primarily in the more common senses of *negative,* i.e. the very bad and near unlivable, the without-content, and the non-choice: the besieged city, the plague city, and the dead city. The final example we consider here, the death-sentence city, is also the passage from this flatter sense of the negative that has been and was rejected to the negativity that rejects the world which gave that death sentence. That is to say, we end again with John Carpenter, the greatest filmmaker of the post-apocalyptic city (that is not in the future but lived now), and *Escape from New York*, that sloppy mess of uncertain politics and lumpen life. The film opens, after announcing that in 1988 "the crime rate in the United States rises 400 percent," with a cartographic depiction of the transformation of Manhattan Island into a designated lived waste zone, the space where all prisoners will be sent and prevented from leaving alive.

The successive additions, most notably the coloring in of the empty space, reveal that the city abandoned to those forced to live there is the hollow zone of after-the-fall: it's a space of unwilled collectivity, bodies that need to learn to coexist. And like the subway dwellers of *Death Line*, we are seemingly meant to assume that they would want to leave, that being condemned to live there is necessarily worse than the world that sent them there. That said, sometimes you need to be exiled to realize that you wanted out in the first place.

Not to valorize or romanticize the situation. The Manhattan island of this film is a bleak place, all wet pavement and scattered debris.[85] And one of the opening moments of the film, in a perverse echo of the rafts of refugees struggling toward the shore of developed nations, is a group of convicts on a makeshift raft, heading across the river to the walls of the prison. As they are shot down by a circling helicopter, we see the city first in its exteriority, a dark, dead space from which one will choose escape, even by certain death. New York City has become the consummate wasteland from which life flees. Like the first iteration of post-apocalyptic cities we considered, it is the silent necropolis, halted in time.

But on the ground, things look different. It's an assemblage space, a site of trash and debris, with scurrying figures in the shadows. Our lone hero, Snake Plissken, sent in to receive the president accidentally stranded amongst those his government has exiled for life, finds the downed Air Force One. He stands in near darkness and among the total collapse of the American version of managed life. Of course, the more time we spend with Snake in this space, the more familiar it becomes. Like *Alphaville's* Paris, the discomfort is uncanny, not sublime: we know these sort of spaces, we've walked through the "bad part of town," forgotten as the money and occupants have gone elsewhere.

Yet in this city, itself the designated apocalyptic zone of America, we find spaces that are truly post-apocalyptic, where life neither begins again nor stops. The cheering crowds at the deathmatch, the seething mass ready to act together. And in perhaps the best articulation of Proletkult after the kinotrain and the emergence of culture outside of any industry, the first full glimpse we see of the convicts is in drag putting on a musical revue show in a dilapidated theater. One makes do. Or rather, *ones* make do together. Against this cuts Snake, the mercenary who will trade against his fellow criminals out of an apparent continued belief in an America beyond the walled city, even if that belief is just in the freedom of movement and to not be stuck on the cursed island. He does save the president, he does escape New York, and he most certainly resists participation in collective identity of any sort.

Yet there is that irresistible ending of the film, again that crooked non-grin of the misanthrope who will damn the world. After the president makes evident his lack of care for "those who died along the way," Snake pulls a consummate prank of culture jamming, replacing the cassette with necessary information for defusing a precarious, nuclear-backed political stalemate, with a cassette of "Bandstand Boogie." Having stated, "although I shall not be present at this historic summit, I present this in the hope that our great nations may learn to live in peace," the cheery sounds that spell nuclear war boom out. And we get the supreme pleasure of watching the bulging-eyed, stricken face of power confronted with the big band jazzy consequences of his lack of care for his citizens, even those cast off and refused.

In the final shot of the film, Snake limps away, apparently having produced an exquisite *fuck you* not only to the president but to world peace itself, as he tears the tape from the cassette containing the possibility of recuperation, a supposed promise great enough to gloss over the work of death needed to maintain the status quo.

Is this the same misapplied Hegelian logic, that by letting it burn we find there was something we should have saved? It seems not. Snake's gesture operates differently, in that we're no longer facing a flat world in which the decision can be made definitively. The fallout of his actions are not a universal condition, like the later turn in Endo's *Eden* series, in which we learn eventually that what seemed to be a pandemic ending the human race has affected only certain areas and that much of the world goes on as before. Snake's refusal to play along is different in that it is a knowing rejection not of the world as such but of the first world's claim to be the only world, to be the hegemonic universal beyond which there is nothing worth saving. To be sure, the film overvalorizes the "elite" or vanguard group able to navigate a survival-of-the-fittest state of affairs. But it simultaneously models, however sketchily, the first steps toward a sharper and subtler version of what the revolutionary thinker and actor can, and perhaps must, be: to act as if one's actions are universal while refusing to forget the embeddedness and particularity of the situation. Furthermore, to act as if there is a course of history into which intervention is possible, an intervention which becomes paradoxically possible and necessary only with the knowledge that there is no fundamental direction to history. Just a ruined and contentious battleground of the out-of-joint, uneven and scattered.

To end here is to urge us to think about our position and task as the elaboration of strategy born of the ongoing apocalypse

and tactics designed for the necessary post-apocalypse. Neither to blindly urge acceleration toward a bloody collapse of the system nor to sit and wait for it to never come. Instead, to fully analyze our apocalyptic condition, not to damn our world but to see it as incontrovertibly damned. Given this, the post-apocalyptic is a mode of thought, not a state of affairs. An injunction, not a fantasy.

We face a globe in which whole portions are designated obsolete, forcibly shuffled off the world historical stage. A world in which sections are designated *not of this world*. None of this is accidental, and we can't afford to buy that. We're out of time, running up against the finite limits of resource and profit, while we are equally stuck in histories that don't belong. The point is never to apologize or accept, neither to reconcile nor to compromise, only to take up whatever obstacles we can find and sharpen their edges. For the world isn't flat, despite what capitalism and its apologists like to themselves and us. It never has been. It never worked that way, always depended on the casting to the deep whole populations and spaces of life. We inherit and occupy the material sites of this casting off: it cannot be otherwise. The first step toward our launching differently, both from this point in history and in casting off the weight of a monstrous world order, is to take fully on the burden of an apocalyptic world and structure of history.

If there is a site – material, conceptual, cultural, and geographical – to fully take on this burden, it is undoubtedly the city. But to call for the "right to the city" cannot only mean a request to use it better, to blunt either the full velocity of its development or the wholesale abandonment of its more vulnerable populations. And such a call cannot be distinguished from one to defend the countryside. If I have stressed the spatial orientation of this post-apocalyptic politics, it is not to privilege a "correct" way to live together. That's another question, one of the implementation of post-apocalyptic content. Our question here has been to discern the shifting forms and increasing fever pitch of a battle for the prospects of collective life amidst the atomistic chaos of capitalism's forthcoming slow eclipse. It's the question of opposing the totality of this historical twilight with whatever collectivity we can become. If we began with considering "the city" as a form of thought that micrologically describes the world order as such, we reverse it here in the excavated call, buried throughout these apocalyptic fantasies, to take over the cities we already share in order to become sticking points in that order.[86] The city, our battlefield of third nature, is the common site of singular antagonism. We stand against the common enemy, this atrocious world that holds us back from acting in common.

So let us become different wolves with different hunger. Let's fly a proud black banner of the end of days under which we gather and on which we make that stand, a raft in the futureless drift of the present. To make evident not just the hard work of antagonism but also of construction, out of and through the channels of a system that will never give us what we want. Only then can we can start to refuse its catastrophe. In this negation set on the grounds of those cities salvaged and never-quite-dead, we write the post-apocalypse we need.

Endnotes

1. By "late capitalism," I mean something related to but somewhat different in emphasis from what Mandel designates in the book of that title (i.e. capital from the '60s on), while still retaining the emphasis on financialization. My emphasis is primarily the periodstarting in the mid '70s that is very much marked by the dissolution of modes of profit in the '50s and '60s: the post-Fordist era, the collapse of the time of what Robert Brenner calls "the long downturn," the sequence whose end we very well may be approaching.

2. Bull, Malcom. *Seeing Things Hidden* (London: Verso, 1999) 79.

3. The "dream image" is the term Benjamin uses to specify that halted conjunction of utopia and the "dialectical image" – caught at a standstill, it is the freezing of the present in the language of the past.

4. See p. 189 in the final chapter for a longer discussion of sustainability and anti-capitalism.

5. We might think here of Machiavelli's point about "toothed" buildings that give a point of departure and support for the next construction yet which also demand of it a certain contact with the past: the teeth lock in, like a zipper, with the ruins left behind and also prepare themselves to become such ruins.

6. Although this is not the place for it, it's worth investigating what's behind this dry countryside/wet city, one that extends far beyond the *Mad Max* trilogy. More generally, dystopian urban sci-fi seems incapable of imagining cities as other than constantly drizzling with slick pavement, perhaps linked to the commercial appeal excuse for the sex appeal of wet leather and trench coats, as well as a plenty of noir nostalgia and the general sense of a world that will not cooperate, even while it provides you with appropriately tousled hair.

7. Let us not forget hair gel, as Kim Newman urges in *Nightmare Movies*: its pure chemical density allows it to survive with flying colors.

8. This question of calculated neo-primitivism (and its accompanying conceptions of nature) will be returned to at length in the third chapter.

9. Badiou, Alain. "One Divides Into Two," in *Lenin Reloaded* (Durham: Duke University Press, 2007), 15.

10. Yet ... this is a longer gesture to track, too far for here, but there is another set of objects that perhaps crystallizes and deploys this *barely* far better than those productions that self-declare as minimal shifts of difference. Namely, the anti-minimal production of serial genre production, the relentless rehashing of a form that cashed in once, the repetition that tries its damnedest to escape difference. I think here of my great horror film loves, *giallo* and Hammer, Euro exploitation and minor studio '30s production, then beyond horror, to directors who can't get it quite right, the full-blooded, bawdy, surreal ceaseless iterations, reading the tradition wrong through too much fidelity, too much studio pressure, a tectonic weight on what should be just another low-level production. Not diamonds in the rough but symptomatic coal, doubled back on itself and the very processes of production pressing down. Beyond film, this would include psychotic pulp (writers like Jim Thompson), Weird fiction, the insane linguistic frottage of Harlequin romance, all those books that know it has "already been done," yet are commanded to do it all again, reaching out past themselves, raiding the tombs of other traditions. The feeling we have in front of the screen, knowing full well the director was told to play it straight, to make *this* just like *that* because *that* ruled the box office. And in front of you, things are very off: the feathers drop, a shadow boils, words that should never go together, and we all think, how the hell did

this happen?

11. That said, we may be getting our economic crisis revenge on this front, with both iconic industrial areas and new zones of production nearly halted, seemingly frozen in a dusty moment.

12. Cited in: Wyss, Beat. "*Merzpicture Horse Grease*: Art in the Age of Mechanical Reproduction." In *Kur Schwitters: Merz – a Total Vision of the World* (Bern: Benteli Publishers, 2004) 78.

13. As noted in the introduction, this does not mean "Communist" thought: it intends a wider set of instances of attempts to establish a politics against and beyond capitalism, and only some of these instances fell beneath the banner of a Communist party per se.

14. I use "apocalypse" here in the looser/more conventional sense of the "end with revelation."

15. Combined with the general amnesia of the survivors when they attempt to recall exactly what happened, this furthers the sense of not knowing how long it's been.

16. See the related discussion in the zombie chapter of the bad faith of false necessity, p. 83

17. Badiou, "The Communist Hypothesis," *New Left Review* 49, Jan-Feb 2008.

18. A serious consideration of "birth crisis" and the end of reproductivity is not something ventured in this book, but this is not to dismiss its importance.

19. This sense of too many survivors should be read both in the individual zombie narratives and in the cultural sphere as a whole, where zombie repetitions flower moronically, endlessly one more bit of pop detritus dressed up with a bit of spatter and carefully torn skin.

20. My mode of analysis here (as in the section on *Return of the Living Dead* [1985]) is heavily indebted to Marshall Leicester.

21. As we'll consider in the next chapter, this can be thought through according to the model of capitalism's "production"

of nature, as opposed to a model of simple dominance or harnessing.

22. As China Miéville reminded me, consider the specificity of *Venus* here: the explosion of love and Eros, the '60s shattering into the cosmos and raining down a new era of Thanatos to rule the day.

23. There are echoes of Heidegger and the bees that interested him. He doubted that bees stopped sucking at a flower because it realizes the flower holds no more honey. (He doubted that bees understood absence.) Consequently, he describes an experiment in which a bee was placed in front of a bowl of honey that exceeded the amount it could consume at once. The bee would suck at the honey and, after drinking "its fill," fly off, leaving the remainder of the honey there. But if the bee's abdomen was cut away while it was sucking honey, it was found that the bee would continue "consuming" far more honey that it could possibly hold. For Heidegger, this was proof of mechanical/instinctive consumption. A preferred example of mine is the capuchin monkey, a greedy little creature who, if given a continual supply of marshmallows, will eat to the point of vomiting, vomit, and then continue eating, until the point of ... and so on. (Capuchins are also capable of understanding the money form and exchange value, casting a certain not-so-favorable light on our own tendency toward indulgence that knows only certain physiological boundaries.)

24. Not to mention the amazing moment when Bub, the semi-domesticated zombie of *Day of the Dead*, learns to wield a gun and looks very John Wayne, right down to his halting bowlegged shuffle gait: the zombie as honorable stoic old West hero, the undead last bastion of noble American masculinity.

25. Additionally, the situation isn't exactly "post-catastrophic": it isn't the slow wind-down of irreversible event, but rather

that event never coming to a stop. There is no *post*, so to speak.

26. A zombie apocalypse scenario set in a factory doesn't exist, to my knowledge. (*Junk* takes place in an "abandoned" factory, but it is a combination of jewel thieves and military testing, not of zombie factory workers.) But it really should: something like a Meyerhold gasworks drama meets Jean Rollin's *The Grapes of Death*.

27. "Universal" is used here in the sense not of what is common across individuals but of what is the universal principle beneath which and by which individuals of a historical period exist.

28. For a more full consideration of *drive* and its relationship to apocalypse, see the discussion of Godard's *Weekend* in the "Combined and uneven apocalypse" chapter.

29. This remains the case for the later films in the Romero sequence, such as *Land of the Dead*, in which, to take one example, a suicide by hanging comes back to zombie life. This is distinct from the Boyle/Snyder/Pegg tendency which is *explicitly* about "transmission," shifting the absent term to "reanimation" itself.

30. Interview with Mariana McConnell, *Cinema Blend*, January 14, 2008: http://www.cinemablend.com/new/Interview-George-A-Romero-On-Diary-Of-The-Dead-7818.html

31. I'm still waiting for the most cringe-worthy meta moment to arrive, when a film will show Halloween party-goers (or zombie flash mobbers) dressed as zombies turn into real zombies, already fake decayed before the fact sets in. There is a different tradition worth noting, of avoiding detection by "playing" zombie, from the incredible sequence in *Zombies on Broadway* in which the trained monkey mimics a zombie walk to the moment in *Shaun of the Dead* when they practice their zombie lurch before successfully "fooling" the horde. This points more broadly to a crucial question throughout

the genre: how exactly do the zombies know who to attack? What, exactly, separates the living from the undead?

32. Wood, "Introduction to the American Horror Film," in *Movies and Methods, Vol. II*, ed. Bill Nichols (Los Angeles: University of California Press, 1985), p. 213.

33. It is this notion of consuming wrongly and enjoying wrongly that we should guard from these popular accounts, even as they need to be taken to task for their deeper implications.

34. Who would rarely see her or himself as such but knows it nevertheless, although there is the increasing tendency, barring the fleeting massification of false hope with the Obama campaign, to wear one's cynicism like a badge.

35. In no small part, because the very idea of "false consciousness" is a politically dangerous one, that tends to excuse behavior and forestall action on the grounds that people "don't know better."

36. Lacan, Jacques. *Le séminaire, Livre X: L'angoisse* [The seminar, Book 10: Anxiety] [1962-3], Miller JA, ed. Paris: Seuil, 2004.

37. As Isaac Kalish wrote me regarding this, a zombie needs a human like a fish needs a bicycle.

38. It's hard to imagine a zombie film in which zombies felt ashamed for consuming wrongly, although I'd love to see a version in which the zombies collectively shame one of their own for hoarding flesh, rather than sharing with the collective hunt, for consuming wrongly "wrongly."

39. There are, of course, exceptions, and the 2006 film *Fido*, to which we return, raises the question of zombie labor again. However, it is telling that in that film, it is an issue of *capitalizing* on the already zombified, fitting them with control collars, in the arch-entrepreneurial move, making money out from something that nobody wanted.

40. More on this shortly, in our consideration of the punk, the homeless, and the lumpen.

41. The insistence on "not giving" satisfaction shows itself

clearly here, in Sir James' further response: "I have not come all this way to interfere with local customs and antagonize the people just to satisfy your sensitivity about the welfare of wild animals." Perhaps, but he shows little hesitation in that interference and antagonism when it's on his terms.

42. To echo the intersecting modes (and time cycles) of production and how they "zombify" laborers, consider this striking passage from Isaac Deutscher's *The Prophet Armed: Trotsky 1879-1921*: "Another scene he was to remember was that of a group of labourers coming from the fields, in the twilight, with uncertain steps and with their hands stretched out in front of them - they had all been struck by night-blindness from undernourishment."

43. *Desire* here is not the act of wanting what you really want but rather the structure that allows for the simultaneous approach to and endless deferral of reaching those objects of desire. Desire self-reproduces.

44. Tronti, Mario. *Operai e capitale*. Torino: Einaudi, 1966.

45. O'Bannon's other film work, particularly his pivotal work with John Carpenter on *Dark Star* (1974) and as screenwriter of *Alien* (1979), should be a clue to the critical intelligence behind this seemingly lightweight zombie movie.

46. It is perhaps in this spirit that the film's distributors in West Germany re-titled it, *Verdammt, die Zombies kommen* [Damn it, The Zombies are Coming].

47. This leads to one of my favorite moments in the film, in which the owner of the morgue is told that what is in the twitching, rustling garbage bags (full of the sawed apart body parts of the meathook zombie) is, in fact, a shipment of "rabid weasels."

48. See here pretty much every H.P Lovecraft story.

49. And let us not ignore the corollary rise of vampires once more, now on the bedroom walls not just of self-declared Goths but all those who moved from *Harry Potter* (2001-

present) to *Twilight* (2008-present).

50. For full accounts of the history of the zombie film, which this chapter certainly is not, see Jamie Russell's *Book of the Dead: A Complete History of Zombie Cinema* (2005).

51. I write this with the awareness that although this will likely not produce many dollar signs, I am, a little bit perversely, perhaps contributing to the very thing I attack. This is perhaps unavoidable: a take-down job, particularly when the object in question is of enormous importance to you, means getting close.

52. The" *nomos* of the earth" is a concept raised by Carl Schmitt in a book of that title. *Nomos* might be translated as "law," but it should be conceived of as a sort of fundamental ordering, a functional system of organization and ideology around which relations of power crystallize.

53. Trotsky, Leon. *The History of the Russian Revolution. Vol. One: The Overthrow of Tzarism.* Available at: http://www. marxists.org/ archive/trotsky/1930/hrr/ch01.htm

54. See my discussion of crisis, catastrophe, and apocalypse in the introduction.

55. A related argument, from Massimo Cacciari, grasps the metropolis in particular as negation itself, as a manifested assemblage of "negative thought."

56. This also links to the opposition raised earlier (n. 6, p. 240) between the wet and the dry, visible in the Mad Max films and hitting its real stride in a film to be discussed shortly, Lars Von Trier's *Element of Crime*, in which a decaying Europe on the skids is everywhere flooded.

57. This is to be stressed as aesthetic and affect, not as setting. It is commonly remembered as one of the central images of apocalyptic cinema, but a broader survey brings in fewer films than we might recall. To be particularly, mentioned, are: *Doomsday, Twelve Monkeys,* Roger Corman's *Gas! Or, It Became Necessary to Destroy the World in Order to Save It, The*

Happening, The Time Machine, Terminator Salvation, and *Omega Man.*

58. In addition, we might note the future-oriented echoes between the conditions of *Stalker* and the very real conditions, and consequent decay-aesthetic, that came to be in Chernobyl.

59. We return to this issue in our discussion of VHEMT (Voluntary Human Extinction Movement).

60. As for whether farce is the correct alternative remains to be seen, though I doubt I'm not alone in my suspicions.

61. These might be thought of as related to "cosy catastrophe" fiction or films, in which a band of the few survivors begins to recreate/repopulate the world after its catastrophic destruction. Moreover, the post-catastrophic dystopian realist films are, in a way, the abortive attempt to produce a cosy catastrophe: their bleak vision confirms that if there is a likely repopulation or recreation, it will not be human.

62. To be clear, my interest here – as elsewhere – is not primarily in a labeling/accusation of the particular political undercurrents of the films. For example, my point is not that Haneke is an ahistorical and anti-materialist director or that *Time of the Wolf* "believes" in that ideological schematic. The point, instead, is that the film works through, and perhaps against, a way of thinking about "human nature" that underpins much of contemporary dominant political-social discourse.

63. I can't help but be struck by a forward echo to the end of *Escape from New York* and the nuclear consequences of a cassette of "Bandstand Boogie."

64. Given the fierce and situated misanthropy of Haneke's other films, it's a fair guess that this decency didn't particular exist before the Fall.

65. These are questions deserving a far longer account not offered here, although ones central to my next book on misanthropic anthropology, nihilism, and anti-abstraction.

66. Dantec, Maurice. *Cosmos Inc,* trans. Tina Kover (New York:Del Rey, 2008) 21.

67. The echoes of the object-world of salvagepunk is intentional: *Life After People* unintentionally lays the groundwork for a serious reinsertion of the human into that landscape of idiosyncratic destruction and crumbling, even as it restricts itself to imagining armadillos roaming a shopping mall or rats storming Vegas.

68. For a far-reaching and nuanced account of and call for the lost legacy of "militant modernist" architecture and its persistent communist tendency, against its detractors who say that modernists just forced Brutalist agendas onto the working class, see Owen Hatherley, *Militant Modernism* (Zero Books, 2009).

69. Comics, about which I can claim very little knowledge, are particularly slippery and remarkable in their narrative overdetermination. And while this is not the place nor I the writer to do so, it would be worth exploring their peculiar capacity to draw forth a sense of combined and uneven worlds, with the sense of events that are both mutually existent and mutually exclusive. This results largely from the structure of comic book publishing and the creation of publishing house "universes" (i.e. the DC universe, the Marvel universe), in which all the different story-lines and microworlds of individual series bleed over into one another, with characters from one appearing in others. Events happen that are not registered fully in other parts of the universe, massive internal contradictions emerge. However, unlike capitalism, comic books negotiate these crises of legitimacy with far more sophistication: reloading universes, creating parallel histories, rewriting the past, raising the dead. Or, we should specify, they do the same things capitalism does. They just admit it more openly.

70. Unless you are committed to a full primitivist position, in

which case, enjoy your non-symbolic language grunting in the dark corners of the forest as fiber-optic cables and robotic chainsaws creep ever nearer.

71. We return to this shortly, in terms of the crypto-Fascist blood and soil ending of *Wall-E*.

72. In a rather different cultural register, the paintings of Ed Ruscha – from the starkly flat burning gas stations and museums to the an overblown reproduction of celluloid reading "The End" – perfectly nail this pull-back to the position of abstraction.

73. Bordiga, Amadeo. "Murder of the Dead," 1951. Available at: http://www.marxists.org/archive/bordiga/works/1951/murd er.htm

74. Not me, despite any rhetorical tendency evidence to the contrary.

75. The shows, with all their "planned hookups" and putting into shared orbit its various bleach groomed and ab-hardened doll humans, consistently lack the real courage to expose themselves for what they are: the multiple orifice assemblage visions of Hans Bellmer put into constant motion, a sniveling frenzy of sheen and holes. Which, I should add, I would definitely watch in half-hour install-ments, proving perhaps that all we need to make tolerable the nadir of civilization is the honesty to reveal itself for what it's been all along.

76. My account here is focusing on the problems of the pastoralist and primitivist impulses, and as such, I don't fully consider another strand of green thought especially trumpeted by "ethical" corporations, who fold together a sense of the high-tech beyond the capacity of any individual communities – *you surely can't nano-bond carbon fiber to ethanol atoms, can you?* – with the promise of a "better tomorrow," a promise whose sheer repetition and deferral should leave us suspicious, to say the least.

77. We might ask, more broadly, what an inhuman aesthetic of the full nihilistic-apocalyptic green tendency would look like? Perhaps an alternate version of Werner Herzog's *Fitzcarraldo* in which Kinski is eaten by Amazonian insects in the first two minutes, leaving 156 minutes of teeming jungle nature while Herzog narrates about the fecundity of death? More likely, and more unsettlingly for the earth-tones and animal woodcut aesthetic lying behind much of the ecological movement, the closest form articulated in the 20th century may be in "purer" currents of suprematist design and minimalist sculpture, with their attempts to leave behind the human hand and eye to approach something beyond the field of the authentic individual and post-Romantic expression.

78. Given the failure of the Wall-E robots left on the earth, we can only doubt the technological prowess of those left to run things and the capacity of this inherited technology to continue saving them indefinitely.

79. I should note that tonally, the films have little in common: *Harmonies* is elegiac, mournful, and gut-punch staggering; *Jubilee* is queerly sneering and art-punkish in its powerful pathetic undercurrent; the *Europa* trilogy veers all over the map, even within the individual films.

80. It is also, as will become evident, arguably my favorite film ever made.

81. This is far and away the most psychoanalytically inflected section, brought out not to be adopted in a general framework or as a ready-made anti-capitalist optic but because it can help break down some of the more static inherited models of how we think about fantasy as something more than wish-fulfillment or utopian illusion.

82. Henderson, Brian. "Toward a Non-Bourgeois Camera Style." In *Movies and Methods*, ed. Bill Nichols (Berkeley: University of California Press, 1976) 422-438

83. Or "reactionary dictum," depending entirely on the context in which it is used (i.e. the justification of Stalinist state violence).

84. This second question might also be asked of Death Line's thematic heirs, the documentary *Dark Days* (2000) and the cannibalistic homeless horror fim *C.H.U.D.* (1984).

85. Like *Wolfen*, *Escape* is a film whose content mirrors its production history: the cityscape we see is from east St. Louis, the place found when the film crew went looking for the "worst city in America." It is a collapsed industrial hell, and it didn't take a whole lot of effort to turn it into the anarchic prison colony. Perhaps all that was required was adding some better lighting and entertainment options.

86. This relates in part to the Invisible Committee's description of the "Metropolis" in *The Coming Insurrection*: the Metropolis is not the massive city, but the diffuse spatial logic of capitalism spread over the landscape as a whole, the new complete apparatus of horizontal management and suburbanization of the whole, swallowing city and country alike.

Contemporary culture has eliminated both the concept of the public and the figure of the intellectual. Former public spaces – both physical and cultural – are now either derelict or colonized by advertising. A cretinous anti-intellectualism presides, cheerled by expensively educated hacks in the pay of multinational corporations who reassure their bored readers that there is no need to rouse themselves from their interpassive stupor. The informal censorship internalized and propagated by the cultural workers of late capitalism generates a banal conformity that the propaganda chiefs of Stalinism could only ever have dreamt of imposing. Zer0 Books knows that another kind of discourse – intellectual without being academic, popular without being populist – is not only possible: it is already flourishing, in the regions beyond the striplit malls of so-called mass media and the neurotically bureaucratic halls of the academy. Zer0 is committed to the idea of publishing as a making public of the intellectual. It is convinced that in the unthinking, blandly consensual culture in which we live, critical and engaged theoretical reflection is more important than ever before.